Step-by-step guidelines for designing classroom instructional areas such as Learning Stations, Interest Centers, Little Theatres, Media Corners, Game Tables, and Reading and Research Areas.

Descriptions and examples of small-group instructional techniques for peer-oriented students such as team learning, circles of knowledge, brainstorming, and case studies.

Detailed explanations for designing programmed learning sequences, contract activity packages, multisensory instructional packages, and tactual and kinesthetic games, with samples of each at every level.

Descriptions of current instructional programs: traditional, open classroom, alternative, and individualized, and illustrations of the learning style characteristics to which they respond.

Sample case studies that permit readers to test their developing ability to diagnose and prescribe for individuals with varied learning styles.

TEACHING STUDENTS THROUGH THEIR INDIVIDUAL LEARNING STYLES: A PRACTICAL APPROACH is packed with techniques, all based on valid and reliable research, that any teacher, administrator, college instructor, or parent can use immediately. These innovative teaching methods will build an instructional process that responds directly to the individual learning styles of each student.

Teaching Students Through
Their Individual Learning Styles:
A Practical Approach

Teaching Students
Through Their Individual Learning Styles:
A Practical Approach

Dr. Rita Dunn
Dr. Kenneth Dunn

Reston Publishing Company, Inc.
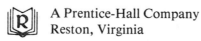
A Prentice-Hall Company
Reston, Virginia

Library of Congress Cataloging in Publication Data

Dunn, Rita Stafford
  Teaching students through their individual
learning styles.

  Includes bibliographical references.
  1. Individualized instruction. 2. Study,
Method of. I. Dunn, Kenneth J., joint author.
II. Title.
LB1031.D82   371.39′4   78-5527
ISBN 0-87909-808-2

Except where otherwise indicated, all photographs by Kenneth Dunn

© 1978 by
Reston Publishing Company, Inc.
A Prentice-Hall Company
Reston, Virginia

10   9   8   7   6   5   4

Printed in the United States of America

With special thanks
to
Isobel Cameron

Acknowledgments

To the very special people who have encouraged and inspired us in our professional careers:

Ethel J. Alpenfels Professor Emerita, Recipient of the Great Teacher Award, New York University, New York

A. Raymond Barretto Former Chairman, Department of Curriculum and Teaching, St. John's University, New York

Norton Beach Former Dean, College of Education, University of North Carolina

Paul F. Brandwein Vice Chairman, Harcourt Brace, Jovanovich, Inc. New York

Peter Clifford F.S.C., President, St. Mary's College, Winona, Minnesota

Raymond L. Collins Former Superintendent, Manhasset Public Schools, New York

Phil Donahue WGN-TV, Chicago

Wayne W. Dyer Colleague, Author, *Your Erroneous Zones* (1976)

Stanley M. Elam Editor, Phi Delta *Kappan*, Bloomington, Indiana

Willard S. Elsbree Professor Emeritus, Teachers College, Columbia University, New York

Mary Sarah Fasenmyer Dean, School of Education and Human Services, St. John's University, New York

Henrietta Fleck Professor Emerita, Recipient of the Great Teacher Award, New York University, New York

John A. Granito Dean School of General Studies and Continuing Education, State University at Binghamton, New York

Thomas F. Koerner Editor, The National Association of Secondary School Principals' *Bulletin*, Reston, Virginia

Leanna Landsmann Editor-in-Chief, *Instructor* Magazine, Dansville, New York

Richard Laster Executive Vice President, General Foods Corporation

Zaven Mahdesian Professor, St. John's University, New York

Morton Malkofsky Editor, *Learning: The Magazine for Creative Teaching*, Palo Alto, California

Paul Miwa Chancellor, University of Hawaii at Hilo

John H. Moehle Former Superintendent, Carle Place Public Schools, New York

George E. Parker Editor, Parker Publishing Company, West Nyack, New York

Bryce Perkins Chairman, Department of Curriculum and Teaching, St. John's University, New York

E. Edmund Reutter, Jr. Professor, Teachers College, Columbia University, New York

Nelson A. Rockefeller in his capacity as Governor, New York State

Robert Stewart Editor, Trade Division, Prentice-Hall Publishers, Englewood Cliffs, New Jersey

Howard M. Squadron Squadron, Ellenoff, Plesent and Lehrer, Fifth Avenue, New York

Ellis F. White Dean Emeritus, University of Northern Florida, Jacksonville, Florida

Contents

Preface

A Word from The Authors

Despite a wealth of well-conducted research, schools continue to function in the "dark ages" in terms of the teaching-learning process. Extensive data verify the existence of individual differences among youngsters—differences so extreme that identical methods, resources, or grouping procedures can prevent or block learning for the majority of our students.

This book, therefore, is designed to assist teachers, college instructors, administrators, and parents to discover the learning style of each student, and then suggests practical approaches that respond most effectively to specific learner characteristics.

Each chapter presents practical, tried and tested ideas and techniques that can be used as quickly as the teachers, administrators, and parents in a given school can absorb them and put them into practice. The ideas and techniques include all of the following:

- a thorough analysis of each of the 18 elements of learning style and an instrument and observational methods for recognizing them;
- detailed blueprints for redesigning classrooms to accommodate a wide variety of learning style differences;
- step by step guidelines for designing classroom instructional areas

such as Learning Stations, Interest Centers, Little Theatres, Media Corners, Game Tables, Reading and Research Areas;

- descriptions and examples of small-group instructional techniques for peer-oriented students such as team learning, Circles of Knowledge, brainstorming, and case studies;

- detailed explanations for designing programmed learning sequences, Contract Activity Packages, multisensory instructional packages, and tactual and kinesthetic games—with samples of each at every level;

- descriptions of current instructional programs: traditional, open classroom, alternative, and individualized, and illustrations of the learning style characteristics to which they respond;

- sample case studies that permit readers to test their developing ability to diagnose and prescribe for individuals with varied learning styles.

In a practical sense, therefore, these tried and tested techniques, all based on valid and reliable research, may be used by all those concerned with the teaching and learning process.

Teachers can use the text as a how-to guide to reach the learning style needs of individual students. Administrators can use the descriptions of methods and techniques as supervisory tools in assessing and aiding teachers to meet the learning needs of all their students. Central Office personnel can use the separate chapters as a basis for in-service courses and workshops that build teaching skills. Colleges can use the text as a basis for courses in theory and methods that will prepare or retrain teachers in diagnosing and prescribing for varied learning styles. Parent groups can use this book to understand, monitor, and support improved instructional programs. School districts can protect themselves against the increasing number of educational ''malpractice'' suits by accurate identification of student learning differences and provision of instructional prescriptions based on accurate data.

This book, then, was written to translate accepted research theory into practical techniques that any teacher, administrator, college instructor, or parent can use and try immediately. The acquisition of new skills, the re-design of classroom areas, and the provision of varied resources and methods will, in a relatively short period of time, build an instructional process that will respond directly to the individual learning styles of each of your students.

1

Understanding Learning Style and the Need for Individual Diagnosis and Prescription

Change in Public Attitude toward Education

In the not-too-distant past, schools and their teachers were protected by the fairly widespread belief that students who had not learned had not paid attention. In the first half of this century, crowded homes, hunger, family chores, illness, national origin, and religious backgrounds were also suggested as explanations for lack of academic progress, but those were the days before educators had learned to use IQ, socioeconomic status, or insufficient environmental stimulation as reasons for the failures of many pupils. Indeed, in those times, being poor was so common that poverty in itself was considered adequate motivation toward achievement. Later, in the 1950s and 1960s, rapid growth, extensive mobility, and belligerent student attitudes were widely accepted reasons for inadequate academic achievement.

During the past decade, however, the public has gradually undergone a complete reversal, and today, low achievement is blamed directly on the schools, their teachers, and the instructional programs or methods being used.

Increasing attention is being focused on the many functional illiterates who are awarded high school diplomas and then are pushed out into the job market, only to be condemned to unemployment, marginal employment, or welfare. Public concern has moved from voter unhappiness at school board meetings to taxpayer suits charging educational malpractice. An antieducation attitude has been voiced by legislators who have submitted bills that would reduce funds for education while strengthening accountability laws that would link better school performance to fiscal support. In a series of court actions, each burrowing successively deeper into school systems' vulnerability, primary focus has been on an individual's right to expect results from education and on a demand for accountability from educational personnel.[1]

Need for Individual Diagnosis and Related Prescriptions

Teaching methods in the 1980s should be very different from the approaches used in yesterday's classrooms. We are attempting to educate more children with varying levels of intelligence and diversified cultural backgrounds. These students have had varied emotional and psychological experiences, ranging from overindulgence to child abuse. These disparate youngsters have been exposed to highly stimulating technology and an exciting world in which survival is uppermost in the minds of many of their contemporaries. To bring them into a confining environment and to group them in a way that makes educational sense is virtually impossible unless we examine each of these complex individuals to identify exactly how he or she is likely to learn most effectively.

The task is not impossible, it is not even difficult, and it is exactly what the courts and the legislatures are demanding. Examine, at the federal level, Public Law 94–142, which requires diagnosis, the development of related prescriptions (contracts, programmed learning, instructional packages, assignments), individualized instruction, and a tightly monitored process that includes parental involvement for all handicapped children. Consider, too, that individualization techniques are now essential to improved instruction for the gifted and talented youngsters, as well as for the handicapped.

In accordance with several state and federal laws, teachers will need to begin to diagnose each of their students. What tools can be used to diagnose students? Achievement scores reveal only where the child is academically. IQ tests merely suggest a child's potential, not why he or she has not progressed further or more quickly. Personality instruments serve to explain the youngster's behavior, but they provide little insight into how to help him or her to achieve. It is possible however, for teachers to help each child learn more effectively by diagnosing the individual's learning style.

Learning Style Identification

We first became involved with the phenomenon called "learning style" as an outgrowth of trying to help slow learners narrow the gap between their ability to read and the grade level expectations held for them. In 1967, the New York State Education Department asked Rita to direct The Teacher Reserve, a graduate program designed to develop teachers who were capable of helping educationally disadvantaged students to learn. Mature persons who had earned a baccalaureate degree in liberal arts areas and who, therefore, had not been exposed to traditional classroom methodology were recruited into a master's degree program to develop innovative instructional strategies during daytime hours and essentially in public school classrooms.

Over a three-year period, approximately six hundred teachers-in-training, eight college professors, more than twenty classroom teachers, and at least five public school administrators worked together to facilitate learning for children who had not responded well to traditional teaching. Individualization was in its early stages at that time, and various kinds of learning activity packages, programmed learning, and games were used and evaluated.

It became apparent that selected methods often were highly effective with some youngsters, but produced only minor gains in others. For example, when we used small-group techniques, certain children thrived while others avoided all peer-oriented studies. When using programmed learning, some youngsters tired easily and could not sit still, while others would continue using the materials for hours on end, evidencing neither boredom nor fatigue. Games also were intriguing to many and boring to others. Some learned rapidly with one technique; others despised that method and refused to be enticed into using it after initial experiences. It rapidly became evident that if we were to help students to become academically successful, we would have to develop different methods and then, in some way, determine which might appeal to and be effective with selected learners.

At that time the profession was focusing on "relevance" and its relationship to academic achievement. In one school, we interviewed every student, at least one parent of each, and every teacher to identify (1) topics that might be interesting or relevant to students in that school, (2) topics that each student's parents believed their child would find interesting, and (3) topics that the students' teachers believed would be interesting to their classes based on expressed concerns, experiences, or talents. The findings revealed that of the three most relevant items indicated by the students, the teachers selected only one and the parents were incorrect on all three.

Using the three identified topics as the focus for our "relevant" studies (through which we planned to increase the students' reading levels), we designed Contract Activity Packages, short programmed learning sequences, stories, and games. Again, regardless of the curriculum, it appeared to be the methods that were attracting youngsters. Furthermore, although a few preferred alternative methods at different times or on different days, most students elected to use specific methods repeatedly once they had experienced success with them. The variety of responses to different methods caused us to examine the learner more closely.

We then investigated educational and industrial research concerned with how children and adults learn. We were amazed to find an abundance of literature that had been accumulated over an eighty-year period repeatedly verifying that each student learns in ways that are different from his or her peers.[2] Research data yield at least eighteen categories that, when classified, suggest that learners are affected by their: (1) *immediate environment* (sound, light, temperature, and design); (2) *own emotionality* (motivation, persistence, responsibility, and need for structure or flexibility); (3) *sociological needs* (self, pair, peers, team, adult, or varied); and (4) *physical needs* (perceptual strengths, intake, time and mobility).[3] (See Exhibit 1–1.)

Exhibit 1-1

DIAGNOSING LEARNING STYLE

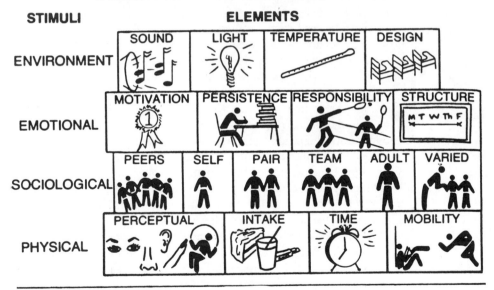

Designed by Dr. Rita S. Dunn
Dr. Kenneth J. Dunn

In 1968–69 we developed and experimented with the first series of questions designed to elicit student preferences for learning style elements from youngsters themselves. Several research studies have demonstrated that (1) students can identify their own learning styles; (2) when exposed to a teaching style consonant with the ways they believe they learn, students score higher on tests, fact knowledge, attitude, and efficiency than do those taught in a manner dissonant with their style, and (3) it is advantageous to teach and test students in their preferred modalities.[4]

During the next five years we continuously tested and revised the developing instrument, often with the help of graduate students at St. John's University in Queens, New York; seven school districts in Nassau County, New York; and the Board of Cooperative Educational Services (BOCES) in that county. By 1974 reliability and consensual validity had been established and much empirical data had been accumulated.

In 1974 Gary E. Price, then a colleague at St. John's University, became interested in the instrument. He conducted a content analysis of each of the questionnaire items and isolated those that achieved 90 percent consistency or better. A shortened form, the Learning Style Inventory (LSI) was then developed, and reliability and face and construct validity were achieved. During the past few years continuing research with children in many school districts verifies the individuality of how youngsters tend to function and learn.[5]

Analyzing the Basic Elements of Learning Style

Before you can diagnose your students to identify how each learns, you need to understand the definitions and implications of each of the elements that may affect them.

Environmental Elements

Sound [6]

Some proponents of open education programs suggest that children can work easily with noise, that they can block out sound or ignore it. Not so. Some children can block out sound, and so can some grown-ups. Some students only need a relatively quiet environment, while others require complete silence before they can concentrate.

Another group of youngsters cannot learn in silence. Whenever total silence is imposed on these students, they become aware of all the sounds they "never heard before." This is analagous to the times when you are alone in a house at 3:00 A.M. and hear many different kinds of strange noises. Youngsters in this group tend to reach out and turn on music whenever they begin to study; the melodies (rock or other) block out the extraneous sounds that might otherwise interrupt their train of thought. Even television is used by some youngsters as a combination security blanket and sound screen.

Analyze yourself. When you are concentrating on a term paper for a graudate course, a report that will be scrutinized, or something that requires your total attention, under what conditions do you work best? Do people's conversations distract you, or can you ignore them? Do you require a relatively quiet area? Or do you need absolute silence? Or are you in the group that automatically turns on the stereo or the radio?

Whatever your response, do not think that everyone else reacts as you do. In any group of thirty or more persons, some always insist that they can function well despite noise; others can tolerate certain kinds of sound; others must have total silence; and some will specify the type of sound that they need.

This is true of students of all ages. Some can function in one way, others in the opposite way. Knowing this, you can understand how necessary it is to design an instructional environment that includes areas and sections where students that need to may talk, interact, and share and areas where others may work alone in quiet; both types of youngsters may be found in any randomly selected group. Remember, too, that sound (or its absence) is not a factor for some students.

Light[7]

Light is a factor that appears to affect fewer people than does sound. Although some students are light sensitive and can tolerate only subdued lighting and others are light needy and require extremely bright lights before they can engage in reading or writing activities comfortably, most seem to be relatively unaffected by normal variations of light.

However, when pilot-testing our original learning style questionnaire, we found one or two youngsters in almost every group who intensely disliked camera bulb flashes and sitting near brightly lit windows or on beaches because of the glare. It was true, too, that many students appeared to be oblivious to light unless the environment changed and became dark to them, at which point they missed the light that they were unaware of previously.

Youngsters who tend to prefer subdued light often recount their parents' repeated cautions against reading in the dark, and yet they rarely remember to turn on additional lights to obtain the amount of lighting that the adults think necessary. The likely reason that such youngsters "forget" about adding the extra lights is that they feel comfortable without them. Such learners report that they grow tense when the lighting becomes excessive (for them).

People who require a brightly lit environment describe the reverse reaction. If the lighting is inadequate, they often become apathetic and find it difficult to remain alert. For them, bright light serves as an energizer.

Despite the fact that comparatively fewer people are affected by light differences than they are by many of the other seventeen elements, if you are one who either needs a great deal of light to concentrate or, conversely, if you cannot tolerate a well-lit room, you know how difficult it is for you to function effectively under what actually are adverse conditions—for you!

Temperature[8]

Many of us have had the experience of being in either a room or a car feeling cold and requesting that the air conditioning be lowered, only to be derided because others felt warm. If not, we have had the reverse occur—feeling uncomfortably hot while other persons in the identical environment complained of being cool. Can you also recall when, as a child, you were admonished to wear a sweater or other garment when going outdoors and felt put upon because you were warm and did not feel that you needed the additional clothing? Or, do you recall your own children complaining because you insisted that they wear warmer clothing than they wanted?

One of the more humorous incidents that occurred when we were testing students centered around a class discussion of definitions. When asked to explain the word sweater, one bright boy answered, "A sweater is something my mother makes me wear when she is cold!"

Individual reactions to temperature are unique. Some people can concentrate better when the environment is cool (or cold); when it becomes warm they feel drowsy and cannot function well. Others cannot concentrate when they are cool; anything other than warmth (and what is warm to one is not to another) can cause physical or emotional discomfort and can decrease productivity.

Since tolerance to temperature varies, how can we determine what might be the best thermometer setting for each classroom? Obviously we can't, for there is no "best" setting. We need to be aware of which sections of each room provide the most and the least warmth at various times of the year and then permit students whose learning style requirements are fostered by being either near or away from those sections to choose where they will work and learn.

If you are beginning to question how one small classroom that seems crowded now can incorporate enough varied areas to accommodate students who need (1) verbal interaction, (2) silence, (3) soft music to block out sound, (4) intense light, (5) subdued light, (6) coolness, and (7) warmth, do not be concerned. When people say, "It can't be done!" they merely are articulating that they don't know how to do it. Chapter 2 suggests low cost ways of redesigning ordinary classrooms to provide for students with varied learning styles.

Design[9]

When you read or write something that requires effort, do you find that you invariably migrate toward an easy chair, a lounge, a bed, or carpeting? If that is your usual way of concentrating on a task, you may be one of the people who require an informal design—one that is relaxed and casual.

Conversely, you may not be able to study in informal facilities; these may prevent you from producing or may make you drowsy and unable to achieve. Some people must actually sit on a hard chair at a table or desk in order to concentrate. For others, highly formal physical surroundings suppress motivation and creativity. For some people, of course, design is no problem or design needs vary with the type of motivation they feel toward the task. What type are you?

Let's translate a need for either a formal or an informal study design to the classroom. Youngsters who think best when relaxed, who often do their homework on the floor or in an easy chair, may find it difficult to be seated (particularly for long periods of time) at a desk. Often, students are bigger than the uniform seats provided and, after a short interval, begin to squirm and move about in discomfort. Teachers who notice the wiggling may not understand that young, growing bodies that are used to continual activity find it difficult to be passive for long periods of time in a formal situation that requires conformity. Such lack of understanding may lead to friction between the teacher and the youngster, but it could easily be reduced or eliminated if the student were permitted to work quietly on a patch of carpeting on the floor. It really shouldn't matter where the youngster learns, as long as he does learn. Classrooms should include sections where students may casually sprawl when involved in learning tasks and include other areas that provide desks and chairs for students who function effectively in a more formal design.

Emotional Elements

Motivation[10]

Most of us acknowledge that we should not teach motivated and unmotivated students in the same way, but often we do exactly that—with the predictable consequences of erupting discipline problems and student and teacher dissatisfaction. Motivated youngsters are eager to learn; they should be told exactly what they are required to do, what resources are available to them, how to get help if they should need it, and how they will be expected to demonstrate that they have learned what they have been assigned.

Unmotivated students should be given very short assignments. They must be given resources that complement their perceptual strengths. For example, if they learn more easily by hearing than by reading, they should be given the book they will need to use and a cassette tape recording of someone reading that section of the book containing the assignment. A capable student or parent can read small sections of a required text onto a tape or cassette for repeated use by poor readers. Such an aid facilitates the students' ability to complete their tasks and enables them to behave positively by making them capable of doing what they have been assigned.

Furthermore, since many unmotivated students are unenthusiastic about learning because they find it difficult to achieve, the use of either programmed learning (see Chapter 5) or multisensory instructional packages (see Chapter 6) as a substitute for class lectures or discussions also should aid in helping such youngsters to learn and in promoting more positive self-image, motivation, and behavior through personal success.

Finally, it is important to remember that a student who is not motivated to learn in a fairly conventional setting may become extremely interested in achieving in an individualized program. Such youngsters may become able to function responsibly when given opportunities to (1) make choices, (2) learn in accordance with their learning style preferences, (3) participate in paired or teamed peer group studies, and (4) self- or peer-test and evaluate themselves.

Persistence[11]

When given a task to complete, some youngsters will work at it until it has been completed. If they develop a problem with the assignment, they will find a classmate or a resource reference that will explain how to overcome the difficulty. As a last resort, if no other help is available, these students will seek the teacher's assistance and will then return to their work.

Other students, often those who we say have short attention spans, cannot continue their work for any length of time. The moment these youngsters experience any difficulty they lose interest, become irritated, begin to daydream, or become involved in social activities rather than complete their tasks. Just as students in a given group should be assigned different objectives based partially on their ability levels and interests, so should the length and type of assignment for individuals be varied based on your observations of their ability to complete or stay with a task. Students who find it difficult to sustain attention to a given task for twenty or thirty minutes will bear a double burden—that of learning and of learning within a time span that taxes their emotions and ability to function without becoming disruptive. This is one example where self-pacing should be considered and introduced. Permitting some students more or less time to complete given tasks is reasonable when we recognize that individuals vary greatly in terms of their abilities, interests, and learning styles.

Students should be given their objectives and a time interval in which to complete them with a clear understanding that although they need not continue learning without pause, they do need to complete the learning tasks. Students who need frequent relaxation periods and who are not made to feel delinquent or guilty about taking them (as long as they return to the task and complete it) may be emotionally able to acquire the prescribed or selected knowledges and skills, but in their own way, in a flexible time period, and in accordance with their total learning style.

This is an area in which the teacher will need to experiment. Some students will require a few simple tasks of relatively short duration to function adequately on an independent basis; others will be able to cope with longer tasks of varied complexity. An observation period in which the students begin with a few objectives and proceed toward tasks of increasing complexity, difficulty, and duration may be the most effective way of assessing a student's persistence quotient. It is suggested, therefore, that any first prescription or assignment (a mini Contract Activity Package, a short programmed learning sequence, a multisensory instructional package, or perhaps merely a few objectives and some corresponding resources) be a short one in order to develop student security through success with a new way of learning while also providing teacher opportunities to observe how well the youngster begins to function independently.

Responsibility[12]

Every teacher recognizes and appreciates responsible students. Invariably, such students follow through on a given task, complete it to the best of their ability, and often do so without direct or frequent supervision. Such youngsters require only (1) a clearly stated assignment that can be understood and completed, (2) resources that teach the information on a level with which they can cope, (3) a suggested time interval during which the task should be completed, (4) an indication of where assistance may be obtained if the task becomes difficult, (5) suggestions for testing themselves to note their progress and the aspects that require further study, and (6) alternative ways in which their achievement of the objectives may be demonstrated.

Unfortunately, many students are not responsible. When a task becomes difficult for them, rather than seek help, they permit their attention to be diverted. Sometimes they begin to annoy their classmates for want of action. At other times they become troublesome and cause a general disturbance. For these young people it is necessary to use methods that are different from those suggested for responsible youngsters.

When students cannot learn easily, they are likely to become discouraged or irritated. To help students avoid experiencing such self-defeating reactions, it is necessary to test them in order to identify the ways in which they are most likely to achieve. Then the methods that respond most closely to their learning style characteristics should be introduced.

For example, slow learners who do not read well should be given short assignments, written materials that are read to them on a supplementary tape, frequent encouragement and supervision, and much praise as each objective is completed. For youngsters who do not understand what they are reading, either an accompanying tape should explain the written content or tactual and kinesthetic games that further teach the concept or skill should be available. When students cannot learn alone, use small-group techniques such as circle of knowledge, team learning, brainstorming, or group analysis.[13] For youngsters who need structure and cannot work with peers, use programmed learning.[14] For youngsters who are slow learners, use multisensory instructional packages.[15]

As students begin to achieve and to feel increased confidence, their assignments may be lengthened or made slightly more demanding. Expect that individuals will behave responsibly when they are able to do what they are required to do without the fear of either embarrassment or failure. Continue to provide encouragement, frequent supervision, and deserved praise. Do not demand more than the student can achieve, for many become irresponsible when they realize that their serious efforts cannot produce success.

Structure[16]

Structure is the establishment of specific rules for working on and completing an assignment. It implies that certain things should be completed in a specific way within a definite time span. Structure limits the number of options that are available to a student and requires an imposed mode of either learning, responding, or demonstrating achievement.

Although creative youngsters squirm under mandated guidelines and find learning that way frustrating and unstimulating, others find it equally difficult to achieve without an imposed structure. It is necessary, therefore, to identify which learners are creative and would thrive when offered many opportunities to organize their own studying situations. It is equally important to recognize those who are unable to function comfortably unless well-defined directions and procedures are given to them.

Consider, for example, the situation in which a teacher asks an entire class to write a composition about "something that interests you." The creative, experienced, or alert student may consider many possible themes—and may not be able to choose one from among the many that come to mind, since decision making is a skill that is unrelated to expressing ideas in writing. Less creative students and those with learning disabilities may be unable to isolate a single idea to describe. In both cases, some structure is needed. For the youngsters who think of many ideas, a limit of subject, time, or seasonal alternatives might be appropriate. For those who cannot think of a single idea, the teacher might suggest several possibilities and ask that those individuals select one. A few others may need counseling and direction toward a single topic.

Structure, then, should vary in the amount and kind that is provided for each student, depending on the individual's learning style and ability to make responsible decisions. Motivated, persistent, responsible students usually require little structure and supervision, certainly far less than do the unmotivated—those who are not persistent or responsible. The creative youngster who can make decisions usually requires little structure. As you observe students in a learning situation, you will begin to recognize which need more or less well-defined guidelines and which respond better to options and choices while learning.

Sociological Elements[17]

For years teachers taught their students whatever had to be learned rather directly. When youngsters had difficulty in acquiring knowledge, teachers believed that their charges had not paid attention. Few realized that despite the quality of the teaching, some students are incapable of learning from an adult. These young people are uncomfortable when under pressure to concentrate under either teacher-dominated or other authority-dominated direction. They are fearful of failing, embarrassed to show inability, and as a result often become too tense to concentrate. For such students, either learning alone or with peers is a better alternative than working directly in either an individual or group situation with their teachers.[18]

Conversely, despite the recently coined generalization that "children learn better from other children than they do from their teachers," some students are unable to study or concentrate when involved with their peers. Rather than learn, they begin to socialize. In other instances, certain youngsters are ashamed to let their friends or classmates see that they cannot learn easily, and rather than admit their discomfort, they pretend to scorn their studies. In either case, this type of student may need an adult teacher in order to achieve.[19] Those students who cannot learn from peers often resent being required to do so and, of course, some learners have little desire to teach others.

Contrary to widespread belief, there is no single way in which to group students for maximum learning. Students learn in a variety of sociological patterns that include working alone,[20] with one or two friends,[21] with a small group or as part of a team,[22] with adults,[23] or, for some, in any variation thereof. It is important to identify how each student learns and to then assign to that individual the correct grouping, methods, and resources.[24]

How a student learns sociologically is easily recognized when youngsters are permitted to select the ways they will complete their assignments. Of course some learners who elect to work with friends will instead of studying together, socialize and in a sense prevent each other from achieving. In such cases you will need to speak with each one separately and clearly indicate that unless the pair (group, team) approaches its tasks soberly and can evidence achievement, members will be reassigned and prevented from working together. When such a warning fails, and the students do not demonstrate sufficient growth toward completion of their objectives, the grouping should be dispersed.

Physical Elements

Perceptual Strengths

Ask almost any educator whether people learn through different senses and the response is bound to be "yes!" That knowledge, however, is rarely translated into classroom practice. It has been estimated that 90 percent of all instruction occurs through the lecture and the question and answer methods, and yet, only between two and four students in each group of ten learn best by listening.

Years ago the research data tended to be confusing because studies frequently were undertaken to determine whether students learned better by listening or by seeing. Since a choice between the two senses was the only choice, findings tended to verify that either one or the other was superior.[25] Prior to the 1960s, researchers did not examine individual youngsters to identify whether each learned better or less well through methods and materials that taught them either through their auditory or visual perceptions. Nor were investigators aware that some people learn by touching (tactual) and that others require experiential or whole body (kinesthetic) experiences in order to learn and to retain what was learned. Further, some youngsters learn best through a combination of two or more senses.

Most schools operate as if all students are able to learn to read through any method—whichever system the teacher is familiar with is the one that is used to try to teach the children in that class. That fallacious reasoning is based on a lack of understanding of individual differences.[26]

- Youngsters who learn through their *auditory* sense can differentiate among sounds and can reproduce symbols, letters, or words by hearing them. Such students should be taught to read through a *phonics* approach.

- Youngsters who learn through their *visual* sense can associate shapes and words and conjure up the image of a form by seeing it in their mind's eye. Such students can learn through a *word-recognition* approach.

- Youngsters who learn through their *tactual* sense cannot begin to associate word formations and meanings without involving a sense of touch. These students should be given many experiences: (1) tracing words in sand, salt, or on clay; (2) writing the words on a chalkboard with water or chalk and on paper with pencil, crayons, and a pen; (3) molding the words with long sections of softened clay, forming the words in chocolate pudding (which may be eaten after the words are recognized correctly); and (4) piecing together the words with (a) alphabet macaroni; (b) sandpaper letters (picked up without looking—just by feeling—from among many such alphabetical forms in a shoebox or other container); or (c) pasting material such as felt, nylon, or burlap, onto letter forms.

- Youngsters who learn through their *kinesthetic* sense need to have real-life experiences in order to learn to recognize words and their meanings. Examples of activities that provide for the whole-body involvement of these students would include the teaching of new words by: (1) baking or cooking and focusing on the words in the recipe; (2) including the words in directions for building something; (3) having the children actually form the letters of the alphabet with their bodies, photographing the body-letter formations individually, and then combining the photographs to form new words; or (4) taking a trip and using the new vocabulary as part of the planning, the implementation, and the review.

- Youngsters who require a *combination* of senses should be taught through multisensory resources. For example, the text of a book should be read onto a cassette, and students who do not read well should be encouraged to follow the print as the tape "speaks." Learners who are not auditory may need a combination of visual and tactual or tactual and kinesthetic resources. For these students it is wise to attach either a tactual or kinesthetic game (depending upon the student's stronger perceptual sense) to the reading materials. Plastic step-on games can be used effectively for these youngsters as can fishing with magnets and other large manipulative materials.

- Youngsters with learning disabilities or those who do not learn easily should also be provided with multisensory materials through which to learn to read. Instructional packages that combine auditory, visual, tactual, and kinesthetic activities to teach a single concept or skill would be the most effective way to introduce reading to these students.

Some youngsters who read well are unable to extract much meaning from the printed words unless they hear the text being read. To illustrate, one day we found our daughter, Rana reading aloud on the lawn in front of our home. When asked what she was doing she replied, "I can only remember what I read when I hear the words." Since she had no one to read to, and because she had heard that flowers might grow better when spoken to, she had decided to read to the flowers in order to have a reason for reading aloud.

Rana was correct about how she retains information. Although she reads well, she does not remember details that she sees in print unless she can also hear them. If she uses a tape recorder to learn information, she learns easily; when she must rely on books, either she or someone else must read the text aloud.

One day, when she was in the eighth grade, one of her teachers directed the class to read a passage in a book and then to explain it in writing. As she read, Rana moved her lips and spoke the words. Her teacher told her to read silently. She explained that she had difficulty understanding what she was reading unless she heard the words, and asked if she might sit outside the room in the hall to read the information before she began to write the answers. The teacher responded in a derogatory manner, suggesting that if Rana could not understand a book without reading it aloud, she ought to obtain remedial assistance. He did not understand that many youngsters are auditory rather than visual learners and that many are the reverse. Despite the teacher's unintentional disparagement, Rana's understanding and acceptance of her own learning style has helped her to study and to learn through ways in which she can be successful. Had she not been aware, she might have had many more problems as a student.[27]

Intake

Observe children as they study or grown-ups as they focus on a task that requires continued concentration. Many take periodic breaks and make a beeline for the refrigerator. Some nibble, others drink. Some may smoke or chew gum. This need for intake, although affecting only a part of the population, is nevertheless evidenced by many learners.

Physicians suggest that food is often sought to replace the energy being expended; another cause is that intake relaxes the tension that some people experience when concentrating. Whatever the reason, we have found that when some youngsters are permitted to eat while they are learning, their grades and their attitudes improve.

If you are willing to try an experiment to convince yourself of the importance of intake for some youngsters, do the following:

1.   Test all the students in one class for learning style.

2.   Make a list of those who need intake and those who do not need intake.

3.   Tell the children that you are going to permit them to study one subject for part of each session in any way they choose, as long as each works quietly and disturbs no one else.

4.   Select one subject, such as spelling or math, with which you are willing to experiment for approximately one month. Set aside a part of each day or week when you will permit students to learn in the way they choose (alone; with a classmate or two; with you; on the floor; at their desks; near or away from light, heat, or sound; through tapes, books, or games; in the room, or in a resource center or library).

5. During each period when the students may study the selected subject in their own style, have available small, thin sections of raw carrots, green pepper, cauliflower, celery, or cucumbers. Establish rules for taking, discarding what is not wanted, and sharing. Those individuals who do not follow the rules may not participate in the experiment.

6. Many students will enjoy the raw vegetables at the beginning because of the novelty. After approximately eight sessions, most will stop taking samples. Watch the ones who do continue; they should be the youngsters who tested as being in need of intake when studying.

7. Compare the pretest and posttest scores of the students who were identified on the Learning Style Inventory (LSI) as requiring intake. The scores they earned in the same subject during the period before the experiment began should be lower than the ones they achieve while they are permitted to eat when studying. Examine the scores of the students who did not test as being in need of intake. Did their scores improve too? If that happened, can you explain why it did?

Keep an eye out for the student who, when concentrating, bites on fingernails, pencils, or other objects. A longing for intake may be prompting that behavior.

Time[28]

The proverbial night owls and eager beavers are diametrically opposite in their learning styles; one comes alive late at night and the other functions at maximum capacity early in the morning. This is true of students of all ages, too. Some people can perform well at one time of day, and others achieve most effectively at the extreme opposite time. Which are you? Or do you fall into the group that functions best neither early in the morning nor late at night? Are you a midmorning bright star? Is it after lunch that your head appears to be most clear? Or is it late in the afternoon that things of concern become clearest to you?

Years ago, education professors told their students, "Teach reading and math early in the morning, for that's when students are most alert." Nonsense! Some youngsters perform at maximum capacity very early in the morning while others really do not seem to awaken until late morning or noon; their most efficient functioning may vary greatly from early morning to late at night. Can the instructional environment be arranged to permit such a wide diversity of time functioning? Absolutely, particularly with middle and high school students where an open campus approach may be introduced[29] or with elementary youngsters where a program or instructional package may be taken home and studied in the evening.

Mobility[30]

Frequently those youngsters who receive the most discipline are the ones who are the least capable of reacting positively to it. Teachers assume that restless students require regimentation. They do not realize that some students need a great deal of mobility in the learning environment and cannot function well unless permitted to vary their posture and location often. Other youngsters are able to complete a task while in one physical position for a comparatively long period of time. The desire for mobility is a conglomerate function of one's physical, emotional, and environmental reactions, but most students cannot easily control their need to move while learning.

Students who require extensive mobility should be assigned to an informal setting where their frequent changes of position will not interfere with either the way the teacher is teaching or other learners' need to learn. Programs that tend to respond to the mobility needs of youngsters are either individualized or open. The differences between these two will be clarified in Chapter 8. In any event, it is important to schedule mobility for those who require it. Short assignments at different locations will aid students who need mobility to learn more effectively.

Using the Learning Style Profile

Before continuing with this chapter, we suggest that you try to analyze at least one student you know fairly well, using the Learning Style Profile (see Exhibit 1–2) to record your judgments. Review each of the eighteen elements just described and determine the learning style factors that are characteristic of that individual. Next, observe that same student carefully over a one week period. Consider the eighteen elements again, and should you change your opinion concerning the student's learning style, make the appropriate changes on the Profile. If you want to learn how accurate your assessment is, administer the Learning Style Inventory located in the Research Supplement after Chapter 8, have the student's answer sheet scored, and then compare your observations with the computer printout that will be sent to you.

Obtaining and Using the Learning Style Inventory

The Learning Style Inventory (LSI) diagnoses an individual student's learning style, and an accompanying manual suggests prescriptions for maximum learning and academic progress.

The LSI is based on factor analysis and is the first comprehensive approach to the diagnosis of an individual's learning style. This instrument, a useful tool in analyzing the conditions under which students prefer to learn,

Exhibit 1-2.

LEARNING STYLE PROFILE

Name_____Teacher_____School_____

Grade_____Counselor_____Date_____

Comments based on highest ratios noted on LSI or teacher observation:

I. Environmental   Sound_____

Light_____

Temperature_____

Design_____

II. Emotional   Motivation_____

Persistence_____

Responsibility_____

Structure_____

III. Sociological   Appears to work best: (alone, with one friend, small team, peers, adult, or varied).

1._____

2._____

3._____

IV. Physical   Perceptual Preferences_____

Intake_____

Time_____

Mobility_____

Checked by_____

assesses individual preferences in the following areas: (1) immediate environment (sound, light, temperature, and design); (2) emotionality (motivation, persistence, responsibility, and structure); (3) sociological needs (self-oriented, peer-oriented, adult-oriented, or combined ways); and (4) physical needs (perceptual preferences, food intake, time of day, and mobility).

The Learning Style Inventory will:

- Permit students to identify how they prefer to learn and will also indicate the degree to which their responses are consistent.
- Provide a computerized summary of each student's preferred learning style.
- Provide a basis for teacher-student interaction in the ways that each student learns best.
- Provide suggested strategies for instructional and environmental alternatives to complement the student's revealed learning style.
- Provide for appropriate student involvement in their unique learning prescriptions.
- Provide a computerized class summary so that teachers can group students with similar learning style elements.

The LSI can be completed by students in grades three through twelve in approximately thirty minutes.

These questions are sample items from the LSI:

- I study best when it is quiet.
- I concentrate best when I feel cool.
- I have to be reminded often to do something.
- I really like to mold things with my hands.
- It's hard for me to sit in one place for a long time.
- I do better if I know my work is going to be checked.
- Nobody really cares if I do well in school.
- I study best at a table or desk.
- The things I remember best are the things I read.
- I try to finish what I start.
- I hardly ever finish all my work.
- I can ignore most sound when I study.
- I like to study by myself.
- The things I remember best are the things I hear.
- I really like to draw, color, or trace things.
- When I can, I do my homework in the afternoon.

Option 1: Individual Summary

The individual summary (see Exhibit 1–3 for an example) for the LSI includes: the student's name or number, sex, date inventory was administered, school, teacher, grade, and class number; a consistency score, which indicates how accurate the responses are for that student; and the learning style profile for the student based on the way he or she responded to the series of questions for each subscale. The teacher is referred to the appropriate page in the LSI manual for suggestions in designing the learning environment for that particular student.

Exhibit 1–3.
A sample individual summary for the LSI.

Jane Doe	Sex F	Date
School Name	Teacher Name	Grade 11 Class 1

Consistency Score .90   Number of answers omitted or answered incorrectly 1

Learning style:	Reference:
1. Needs quiet	See manual page 6
3. Requires bright light	See manual page 6
6. Needs warm environment	See manual page 6
9. Self-motivated	See manual page 6
10. Adult-motivated	See manual page 6
11. Teacher-motivated	See manual page 6
15. Responsible	See manual page 7
17. Needs structure	See manual page 7
19. Prefers learning alone	See manual page 8
20. Peer-oriented	See manual page 8
25. Tactual and kinesthetic preferences	See manual page 9
30. Functions best in afternoon	See manual page 9

Option 2: Class Summary

The LSI sample class summary (see Exhibit 1–4 for an example) is a single page breakdown for all the students in the class. It includes each student's name or student number, preferred learning styles, and consistency score. The teacher uses this summary to individualize instruction and form groups of students with similar preferred learning styles. For instance, all the students with an x under subscale 1 indicate they need quiet and all the students with an x under subscale 17 indicate they study best when structure is provided. Detailed suggestions for arranging the learning environment to meet a student's learning style are in the LSI manual. The class printout summarizes all the information for each student on each subscale.

Exhibit 1-4
A sample class summary for the LSI.

School Name	Teacher Name	Grade 11 Class 1	Date
Student Name	Subscale number		Consistency Score

Student Name	1	2	3	4	5	6	7	8	9	10	11	12	13	14	15	16	17	18	19	20	Consistency Score
Gary Collins	x		x			x		x	x	x					x	x			x		0.85
Elyce Davis	x		x		x		x		x			x			x		x		x		0.85
John Evans	x			x	x			x		x		x			x	x					1.00
Susan Goldberg		x	x		x			x		x			x		x				x	x	1.00
Tom Huffington	x		x					x			x						x	x	x		0.46
Regina Miller		x		x				x			x				x		x	x	x		0.85
Margaret Peters	x		x			x		x		x						x			x		0.92
Jose Santiago		x		x		x		x		x	x					x	x		x		0.85
Maria Torres		x		x				x			x	x			x		x		x	x	0.92
Alice Weaver		x		x	x			x			x				x			x		x	1.00

Option 3: Subscale Summary

The LSI subscale summary (see Exhibit 1-5 for an example) indicates the number and percent of the total group that identified each factor as important to their learning style. For instance, twelve students—48 percent of the group—indicated that they needed little structure (subscale number 18). Using the LSI manual and supplementary references, the teacher can design the program and learning environment to complement each group of students' needs.

Relationship between Learning Style and Instructional Resources

During the years in which we worked to identify the scope of individual differences, we also experimented with a variety of resources to determine whether any relationship could be observed between specific learning style elements and materials through which students learn. Continuing study is necessary, but we have found that, for the most part, students with certain characteristics do tend to respond to selected resources. Exhibit 1-6 enumerates some of the more popular methods and materials being used in our schools and the learning style elements to which they (1) appear to respond, (2) apparently do not respond well, and (3) can be accommodated.

Exhibit 1-5.
A sample subscale summary for the LSI.

| School Name | Grade 11 Class 1 | |
Teacher Name	Date	
Subscale	Responses	Percentage
1	10	0.40
2	14	0.56
3	11	0.44
4	12	0.48
5	10	0.40
6	6	0.24
7	7	0.28
8	13	0.52
9	17	0.68
10	25	1.00
11	20	0.80
12	0	0.
13	17	0.68
14	0	0.
15	18	0.72
16	2	0.08
17	2	0.08
18	12	0.48
19	23	0.92
20	20	0.80
21	4	0.16
22	4	0.16
23	2	0.08
24	1	0.04
25	11	0.44
26	10	0.40
27	10	0.40
28	13	0.52

| | Total students | 25 | Total responses | 359 |

The information cited in Exhibit 1-6 has been verified through extensive observation and study, but exceptions do occur where specific topics tend to motivate students into active learning or during the first three or four times that youngsters use resources new to them.

The education profession may be on the threshold of an instructional revolution that promises positive and successful educational experiences for many youngsters who have not been able to achieve well in traditional schools.

Exhibit 1-6.

Method or Resource	Learning Style Characteristics to Which It Responds	Learning Style Characteristics to Which It Does Not Respond	Learning Style Characteristics to Which It Can Be Accommodated
1. Programmed Learning	Motivation, persistence, responsibility, and a need for structure; a need to work alone, a visually oriented student.	A lack of motivation, persistence, or responsibility; a need for flexibility or creativity; a need to work with peers or adults; auditory, tactual, or kinesthetic perceptual strengths.	Sound, light, temperature, and design; a need for intake, appropriate time of day, and a need for mobility.
	Note: Where programmed learning sequences are accompanied by tapes, they will appeal to auditory learners; when they include films or filmstrips, they will reinforce the visually oriented student; when teachers design small-group techniques such as team learning, circle of knowledge, or brainstorming, peer-oriented students may develop an ability to use programs more effectively than if they use them exclusively as individual learners.		
2. Contract Activity Packages	A need for sound and an informal design; motivation, persistence, and responsibility; a need to work either alone, with a friend or two, or with an adult, all perceptual strengths and weaknesses and the need for mobility.	None	Sound, light, temperature, and design; motivation, persistence, responsibility; sociological needs; perceptual strengths, intake, time of day, and the need for mobility.
	Note: Contract Activity Packages respond to all learning style characteristics provided that (1) they are used correctly and (2) multisensory resources are developed as part of them.		
3. Instructional Packages	A need for sound or structure; a need to work alone; all perceptual strengths.	A lack of responsibility; a need for peer or adult interactions.	Light, temperature, and design; motivation, persistence; intake, time of day, and mobility.
	Note: Because of their multisensory activities, instructional packages are very effective with slow learners. Unless the curriculum is extremely challenging, they may be boring to high achievers.		
4. Task Cards and Learning Circles	Motivation, persistence, responsibility, and the need for structure; visual or tactual strengths.	A lack of motivation, persistence, responsibility, or a need for structure; auditory or kinesthetic strengths; a need for mobility.	Sound, light, temperature, and design; the need to work alone, with peers, or an adult; intake and time of day.
5. Tapes, Audio Cassettes	A need for sound; motivation, persistence, responsibility, and a need for structure; a need to work alone; auditory strengths.	A need for silence; a need to work with peers or an adult; visual, tactual or kinesthetic strengths, and a need for mobility.	Light, temperature, and design; intake and time of day.

This does not suggest that the schools should become havens of permissiveness or "do your own thing" approaches. It does imply that you should become aware of students' learning styles and prescribe those methods and resources that respond to their environmental, social, emotional, and physical needs. You will be delighted with the positive attitudes and improved achievement of your youngsters, and you will find that you have increased your own pleasure in teaching.

2

Redesigning the Educational Environment

Building an Instructional Taj Mahal without Cost

The secret of building your own instructional Taj Mahal without cost (or very little) involves using in new patterns what you already have. The desks, chairs, tables, bookcases, file cabinets, and other furniture are moved to take maximum advantage of the space available and the individual learning styles of students.

Begin slowly, be flexible and receptive to new ideas and approaches, plan carefully, and continually evaluate how well the new design meets your objectives for each of the students in the class.

Room Redesign Based on Individual Learning Styles

Many teachers alter the seating assignments in their classrooms in response to discipline problems. Changing an individual to another seat without changing his or her total learning environment is a little like playing Russian roulette—one never knows what will happen.

For example, a student who likes to work with one or two peers might be moved away from friends because their voices disturb others. That youngster may become very unhappy, and, as a result, may not be able to con-

centrate on his or her studies. How much better it would be to establish
ground rules for when, how, and under what circumstances students may
teach each other and discuss what they are learning, so that peer-oriented
students may have time to learn together.

To begin redesigning your classroom to provide for varied learning
styles, you first must identify each of your student's learning styles—either
with the Learning Style Inventory (LSI) (see Chapter 1) or through your
own observations. Then, using the checklist below, begin to identify the
parts of the room that might lend themselves to each of the following:

- Places where several students may meet to discuss what they are learning
- Well-lit reading areas

- Warmer areas
- Desks or tables and chairs
- Sections that permit responsible students to work without direct supervision
- Sections that permit students to work alone, with a friend or two, in a small group, with an adult, or in any combination thereof, provided they show academic progress

- Essentially quiet and screened study areas for individuals or pairs
- Darker sections for media-viewing, photography, or dramatizations
- Cooler areas
- Carpeted and lounge sections
- Sections that permit close supervision of less responsible students
- An area where snacking may be available (preferably raw vegetables and fruits, nuts, and other nutritious foods)

Changing the Classroom Box into a Multi-faceted Learning Environment

Some teachers can visualize an entire room redesign by closing their
eyes. Others must move one seat or section at a time. Still others must try
several alternatives before deciding on a relatively permanent arrangement.[1]

Planning Step 1: Locating Dividers

The first planning step is to identify and locate as many things as possible that can be placed perpendicular to walls, unused chalkboards, and
spaces between windows. Such items include file cabinets, desks, bookcases, tables, shelves, material displays, screens, charts that can stand un-
supported, and cardboard cartons or boxes that may be attractively painted
or decorated. Even your desk can be used effectively this way. Do not overlook bookcases that may be partially fixed to a wall or those, such as library
stacks, that may seem too unstable to stand out into the room.

The custodians will enjoy the experience and novelty of assisting you
in this venture. They are your "design engineer assistants" and will be proud
of having helped you. To enlist their support, tell them why you are changing
your room and that your room will be easier to move around in and to clean—

because it will be. The custodians will also respond positively to the need to build supports and add backings to rickety bookcases. They may have good suggestions and, once involved, might be able to obtain that extra table, too.

Step 1 is the key to providing different types of areas and more space than you realized was possible.

Planning Step 2: Clearing the Floor Area

Look at your room. Walk around. There are likely to be boxes of science equipment, art supplies, reading materials, and other assorted items stacked on the floor (as well as crushed crayons, broken pencils, and such). Temporarily place this material outside the room or in a closet or corner. Later you will place these resources on top of the perpendicular units to provide additional screening and separation of the instructional areas such as the Learning Station, Interest Center, Magic Carpet (reading) Area, Media Corner, and Little Theater.

When moving the furniture and developing the physical environment, it is usually wise to do it with the students. They should be aware of what is going to be created and why, and that it will take a while to become ac- climated to the change. Their involvement in the development of the design invariably creates a positive attitude of acceptance for the revision and, of greater importance, the youngsters' suggestions and reactions help to correctly place students with specific learning styles.

Planning Step 3: Involving the Students

Should you elect to involve all your students, you might begin your conversation by explaining that, as in their apartments or homes, the way the furniture is arranged in an area should make sense for the people who live there; that some of the boys and girls who ''live'' in their classroom (and it is living for four or five hours each school day!) may enjoy the ar- rangement just as it is, but that others might feel uncomfortable because people are different from each other and some need certain things that others do not.

For example (and here begin to personalize with them), everyone in the present arrangement is seated, in a sense, out in the open, even if there are separations between groups. With many students at close range it must be difficult for some of them to concentrate as they see and hear the door opening, chairs and people moving, materials being used and replaced. Some need a quiet, cozy place to concentrate on their studies; for those people you would like to create small offices, dens, or alcove areas where they can be by themselves, or with a friend or two, to complete their work.

At this point you are certain to have their undivided attention; they will be curious, stimulated, intrigued, and individually motivated to redesign their classroom. You might ask how many students would like to serve as assistant interior decorators to aid you in rearranging the room to create spaces in which they will enjoy doing their school work.

One of the first things you will suggest is the establishment of some areas where small groups of students may literally turn their backs on what is happening in the room and become absorbed in their work. This can be done by facing their chairs toward any available wall space. You may add, "If I told you that you were going to face a wall, you might think, 'who wants to look at a bare space? *You* might, if I then said that each person facing a wall will be able to create his or her own bulletin board. You could display your work on it—the things you draw, write, paint, or sew; the models that you build; the photographs of your pets—wouldn't you like that?'' Most elementary and middle school students enjoy having a bulletin board in their seating area and making it attractive with a personalized decorating scheme.

To promote bulletin board motivation, use sheets of colored construction or drawing paper to form a rectangular wall area as wide as the desk adjacent to it. Scallop a border to complement the paper and vary the colors so that bulletin boards that are next to each other reflect individual decorative preferences. Frequently, there is not enough wall space in the room for each student to have a bulletin board, and some may not want the responsibility for keeping one attractive and current. Establish rules for what may or may not be displayed but, within the confines of good taste, permit wide variation based on student choice.

You can increase bulletin board space by using the backs of file cabinets, bookcases, closet doors (that can be left closed) and rarely used chalkboard sections. Plywood, cardboard, wallboard, and other building materials can be added to one side of bookcases that are open in both directions or to the side of a file cabinet.

Describe how you plan to clear one section of the room at a time; explain the kind of den or office it will be (number of students it can hold, light or shady, warm or cool, open or partitioned); and tell the students that if individuals would like to try locating in that area (either alone or with a friend or two, or occasionally three), they should so indicate by any method you suggest (raised hands, quietly spoken words). Preface any decisions by clearly explaining that students who shout for recognition, call out "Oooooh!", or in any way behave disruptively will slow down the process and will have to wait longer for their turn. (Do not confuse excitement with disruptiveness; be prepared to be flexible.)

It is also necessary to explain that they really have to understand themselves, that some of them work best alone. These students should not volunteer to sit with their friends, for if they do not complete their work, their seats will have to be changed; it's better to diagnose themselves correctly in the beginning. Conversely, if youngsters promise they will work well with a friend (even if they previously played more than they worked and therefore made little academic progress), give them an opportunity of trying to do so. Warn them, however, that if they do not show achievement, their seating arrangements will be altered. Students frequently become highly motivated when allowed to share a secluded section of the room with a friend or two, and they will often gradually conform to higher standards of behavior and effort than previously shown.

Mention to your students in this pre-redesign discussion that, just as they are used to the placement of the furniture in their homes, they are currently at home with the placement of the various items in their classroom. Explain that it takes time for people to adjust to new things, but that the more flexible they are, the faster they adjust. (This will encourage many of the pupils to experience positive reactions to the emerging redesign. In turn, they will then assist others to become acclimated to the new arrangement.)

Finally, assure the students that if they do not like the redesigned room, you will help them return to the present arrangement. Ask them, however, to agree to live with the new placement for at least one week before deciding whether to keep it or to revert to the way the room was arranged before the proposed change.

Once the students indicate a willingness to experiment with the classroom furniture and to remain with the change for at least a one-week trial period, you are ready to actually redesign.

Redesign: Preliminary Considerations

The major objective of changing the placement of furniture in the classroom is to provide different types of areas to permit students to function through patterns that appear to be natural for them and for their learning styles. Some students, however, may not know how they work best or where they prefer to sit; they can only try new placements and determine whether the arrangement is good or appropriate for them on the basis of how they react after the change. Therefore, rather than asking students where they would like to sit, begin by establishing the areas. Then, one by one, explain the advantages and disadvantages of each, describing the responsibilities of those who elect to sit in that den, alcove, office, corner, or section. Next, request volunteers. Students need only try the area for a one-week period; if they are dissatisfied, or unable to work there, changes can be made on a flexible basis with your approval.

Step-by-step to Partial or Total Redesign[2]

A simple way to begin is to clear a section of the room other than a window wall. Then identify all the movable objects in the room that can be used as perpendicular extensions to break up the linear effect and to provide small areas. If there are few movable items such as bookcases, file cabinets, tables, or chests available, low-cost dividers can easily be constructed with cardboard.

The movable objects may be used in a variety of ways in different sections of the room. For example, bookcases of varying lengths and widths may separate pairs of desks to provide privacy and to permit quiet areas (see Exhibit 2–1). Small groups of desks (three to five) may be isolated in a charming little den or alcove that encourages small-group teamwork (see Exhibit 2–2). The movable objects may also set apart resource instructional areas such as learning stations or media corners so that students may conduct their work out of the mainstream of activity (see Exhibit 2–3). In addition, dividers may be used to separate the motivated, persistent students from those who do not follow through on their prescriptions and who require constant supervision (see Exhibit 2–4).

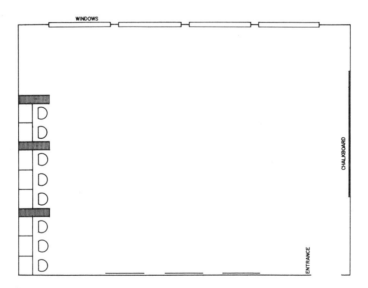

Exhibit 2-1.   Bookcases, file cabinets, extra tables, and other movable items may separate desks that have been arranged to face the wall so that students have their backs to the center of the room and can thus turn away from the hub of activity to concentrate on their work. The wall space directly in front of the desk is used for a personal bulletin board. The divider provides privacy for occupants on both sides of it.

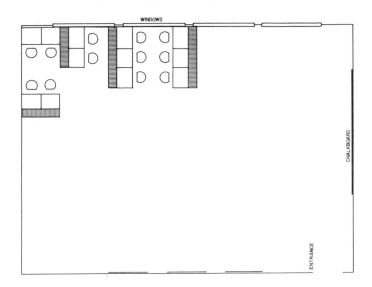

Exhibit 2-2.   To create small den areas for two or more pairs of students (selected by student preferences), separate the desks from adjacent groups by placing the movable objects perpendicular to the walls. Face each pair or small groups of desks toward the divider so that the paired students have their backs to other pairs. This arrangement is conducive to the development of close peer relationships between the members of each paired group, but not necessarily among the members of the two groups.

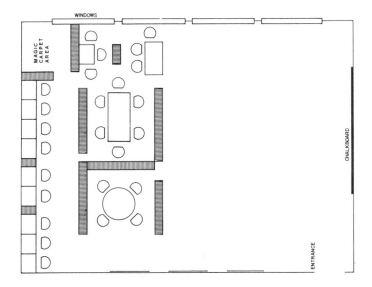

Exhibit 2-3.   Cleverly used dividers can separate the active area of the classroom (which frequently centers around interest centers and learning stations) from the magic carpet corners and other study-reading areas. Such an arrangement provides students with the options of working either in the center with others or studying alone, or with a friend at one's desk or den area.

31

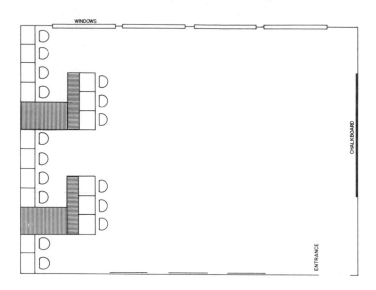

Exhibit 2-4.   Dividers may also be used to separate those students who are capable of working independently from those who need constant supervision. The former are provided den or alcove areas on the periphery while the latter are seated toward the center of the room where the teacher is closer and may work with them more directly.

When you have cleared the first section of the room, you may begin by saying, "Here is an area that is far from the windows. The lighting will probably be soft and the temperature may be a little cooler in the summer and in the winter (if that is true). If you think you'd like to work where the lighting is less bright and it's a little less warm than in other areas of the room, you may sit here with one or two friends—if you are certain that you'll work quietly with those friends and learn, too. This area, because it is next to the wall, will have a bulletin board space. Remember, if you accept the responsibility of the bulletin board, you'll have to keep it looking attractive, neat, and interesting. Is there anyone who would like to sit here with a friend or two?"

If one youngster volunteers, ask him with whom he would like to sit. If he names one or two friends, ask them if they would like to sit together with the person who nominated them. If so, ask them to each bring their seats and desks to the area (see Exhibit 2-2).

Show the students the wall section that will hold their bulletin boards and ask them again if they are willing to assume the responsibility for keeping their bulletin boards attractive, up-to-date, and interesting. If they respond affirmatively, give them an opportunity to try with your approval. They may immediately obtain the construction paper and masking tape (it does not pull off paint when removed) and begin mounting their boards. Move the first object that will be used as a divider and place it perpendicular to the wall at the end of the grouped desks to form the first private section in the room (see Exhibit 2–5).

If the divider that you have used to mark off the first den area is long enough to place two side-by-side desks on the other side, you can begin the second den area by describing that arrangement to the class. This would be an area that would tend to be a little lighter than the first, a little warmer, and would, again, offer a relatively secluded space to its occupants. This section also would contain space for individual bulletin boards. Again, request volunteers and, depending on your and their preferences, place their desks either directly against the wall as in Exhibit 2–5 or in back-to-back pairs (see Exhibit 2–6). Combinations of the two designs provide increased interior interest, but some people prefer either one or the other pattern. Exact placement is not of prime importance; what is necessary is that small groups of youngsters each have a place of their own in which to escape the activity and accompanying classroom distraction so that they may work effectively alone or with a friend or two.

Some dividers, such as a single file cabinet, aid in isolating an individual youngster who prefers to work alone. Explain that this is an area that permits a person to work quietly and independently, and encourage the students to know themselves and to select a placement that will enhance their learning style.

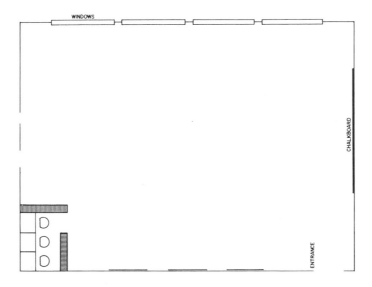

Exhibit 2–5. The first step in classroom redesign is to divide available wall space into small dens or alcoves to provide privacy and relative quiet for those students who need these elements to function effectively.

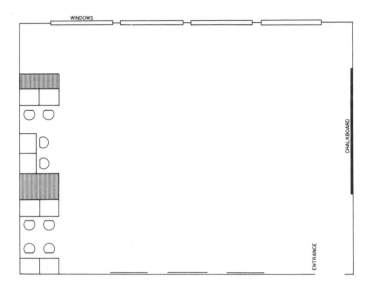

Exhibit 2-6.   This is an alternative beginning plan where two pairs of students share the same den area.

Establishing Instructional Areas

The Magic Carpet

After the second or third den area has been situated, identify two long dividers that can set off a magic carpet (a quiet, casual reading-meditating) corner of the room where absolutely no discussion is permitted. This should be close to the windows where students may go to relax, to read in silence, or to rest if they feel the need.

The term "magic carpet" is derived from the notion that the students within the area can "magically" withdraw temporarily from the noise and activities of the class, thus transforming this corner into the quietest area of the room. It is usually carpeted or pillowed. It holds no chairs, desks, or hardware—only many interesting books to be read. There are other places in the room (shelves, bookcases, display cases) that also house interesting books on every subject, but those are easily accessible to all students. The magic carpet books are only accessible to the students who are in the area for as long as they choose to remain. The teacher may be flexible, of course, and permit students to take books out of the area to be read elsewhere (perhaps by a pair), but the object of maintaining a current display there is to prevent other students, who may want to browse through or take a book away from the magic carpet area, from intruding on the privacy of the youngsters who are actually in that corner at any given time. The authors therefore suggest that a special group of nonmovable books (that may be duplicated in other sections of the room) be kept in this special area.

To establish the magic carpet area, use two bookcases (or cardboard open-shelf dividers) at right angles to each other in the corner of the room at the other end of the wall on which you began to establish the den areas. This should be a corner near or at a windowed section (to provide light for the readers). Place the two dividers so that each is perpendicular to one of the corner walls (as in Exhibit 2-7), but not touching each other. Leave room for a small entranceway that should be the only means of access to the magic carpet area. When established, spread a piece of Mystic tape on the floor stretching from the near entrance end of one bookcase to the near entrance end of the second. This suggests the line beyond which shoes are not permitted (to enhance its special nature and to prevent the carpeting from becoming soiled and undesirable to sit or lie on).

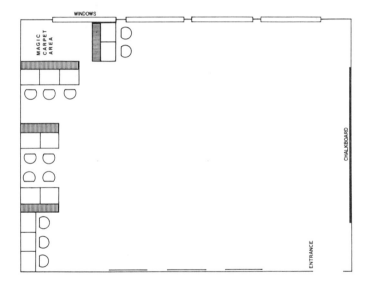

Exhibit 2-7.   The formation of a magic carpet area, a casual, carpeted area where students may read or meditate in silence.

Merchants who sell carpeting frequently will donate samples and remnants. These squares and rectangles then may be placed end to end inside the area to provide a clean, soft, inviting, and quiet place.

It is wise to establish rules to limit the number of students who may "ride" the magic carpet at one time. The number will vary in accordance with the size of the area, but should rarely be more than six. Explain that the area provides privacy and that the students who are using it should not be disturbed or intruded upon. Tell the youngsters that if they want to use the magic carpet area there is a good way to determine how many students are currently using it without looking directly into the area. First ask them how they might know this. If they cannot identify a method, remind them that only five or six students may use the area at one time. If there is no response, ask them about the rule concerning shoes. When they understand that they can count the number of shoes on the outside of the Mystic tape entrance line to compute the number of youngsters on the inside, give them a few examples to help them decide whether an individual may enter the area.

You might pose the question, "If I wanted to go inside the magic carpet area and counted (make believe you are really counting with primary and elementary pupils) one, two, three, four, five, six shoes, may I go in?" When they respond, ask, "Why?" Explain, if they do not, that six shoes indicate that three children are already using the area and that since as many as six children may use it at one time, three more may still enter.

After one or two additional examples, ask them, "If I counted one, two, three, four, five shoes, what might that mean?" They will offer various solutions, for example, someone is inside with one shoe on or someone lost a shoe. Respond that it could mean that someone did not place his shoes together, side-by-side, in the Mystic tape area and that another person accidentally kicked one shoe away from the taped line. Ask them what they could do if that ever happened and add that it would be kind to look for the missing shoe, locate it, and replace it next to the other half of the pair.

If you make this preparation for working in the magic carpet area gamelike, the students are likely to remember what they have discussed with you. The area (and the classroom) will then function with fewer crises than might otherwise be anticipated.

Expanding the Den Area Concept

Once the magic carpet area has been established, you will be able to determine how many desks may be placed against each of the two dividers that were used to mark off its boundaries. Show the students that you plan to place desks snugly up against each of the dividers to begin the formation of additional dens.

If the back of the divider is solid, place this solid part so that it faces the front (or the inside) of the room. When a desk is pushed up against that surface, the back of the divider (if high enough) becomes a bulletin board for each youngster who faces it. If the divider has only one open side (such as a one-sided bookcase), use the book shelf part on the inside of the magic carpet area and the closed shelf part on the outside to form a bulletin board surface. If both sides of the divider are open, place the books in the divider so that the bindings are easily accessible to the students inside the magic carpet area.

Explain the attributes of each of the two newly created den areas to the students, for example, "This section is near the windows. It is likely that the light will be brighter than elsewhere in the room. It is also near the heater. If you volunteer for this space, be certain that you like warmth. You'll also be near the magic carpet area, so you'll have to be able to avoid socializing with students as they enter and leave that section. Can you work quietly with only the friend you elect, and can you ignore the traffic going in and out of the area? If so, this may be a good location for you. You'll be responsible for keeping the top of the divider attractive and covered with new books, the bulletin board interesting and current, and so forth. If you would like to sit here with a friend or two, raise your hand."

After each of the two sections behind the two dividers that border the magic carpet area have been occupied by their new tenants, survey the entire wall area with which you have been working. Do you have room for an additional pair, a single youngster who wants to work alone, another divider to provide even more privacy? Add whatever appeals to you aesthetically and makes sense educationally. Your first wall should be near completion and may look something like the model in Exhibit 2–8 or 2–9. If not, do not be concerned. As long as the students are positive about their seating arrange-

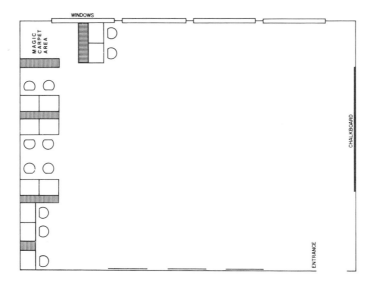

Exhibit 2-8.   This is one plan for the development of small den or alcove areas where two to four students may share their efforts toward completing their individual or group prescriptions. On the right, near the window corner, is the magic carpet area.

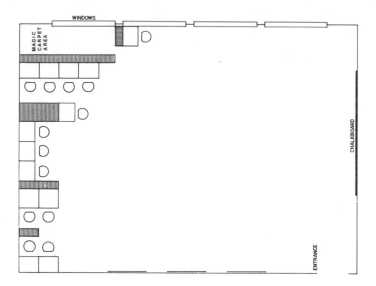

Exhibit 2-9.   This is an alternative plan for redesigning a far wall in a traditional classroom. This arrangement also features the magic carpet near the windows (to provide light) and on the far, rear wall (to provide quiet).

ments and you are willing to try the design, further adjustments may be made as the need for them becomes evident.

Once the far wall has been designed to your initial satisfaction, the front wall direcly opposite the one you have just completed should be redesigned. Begin with the section of the front wall that is directly opposite the magic carpet area. Establish a den by using two dividers to enclose the corner. Determine if you wish to place two pairs of youngsters, two groups of three students, or some other number. The width and depth of the den will depend on the number of desks and chairs you place there.

Once each of the dividers has been located perpendicular to one of the two right-angled corner walls, the students' desks may be placed so that they either face the interior wall (as in Exhibit 2-10) or face the back side of either one or both of the dividers (as in Exhibit 2-11). The latter placement is directly opposite from the way we used the dividers in the magic carpet area where students inside needed to be able to reach whatever occupied the shelves or drawers of the dividers used to form the area; here it will be the students who do not share this area who will need to be able to get to the materials housed in the dividers without intruding on the youngsters inside.

If a bookcase or cabinet is used as a divider on the outside of the corner den, two or three additional students may be placed at right angles to it on the outside of the corner area. These new desks could face the front wall and begin to form the next area. If the divider on the front wall of the

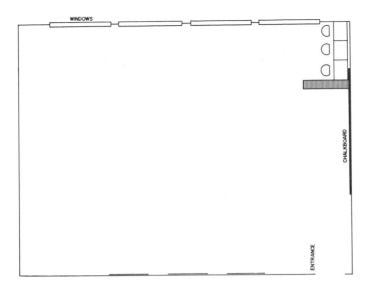

Exhibit 2-10. Students in this corner den have placed their desks so that they face against the interior wall, which provides bulletin board space for its occupants.

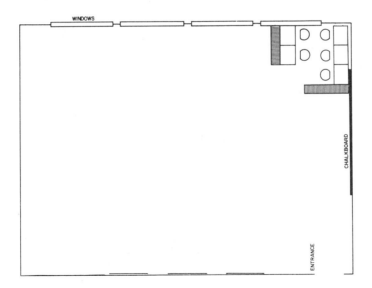

Exhibit 2-11. In this corner den some of the students' desks face against the back of one of the dividers and others face the interior wall.

corner area has neither side shelf nor side drawer space (such as a file cabinet where the drawers face the center of the room), desks may be placed up against the divider itself. A table may be used as a material resource center and may be flanked on both sides by dividers. This arrangement would permit an additional area where students who do not share a den area may meet to work together during a small-group instructional activity such as a circle of knowledge, simulation, or case study (see Exhibit 2–12).

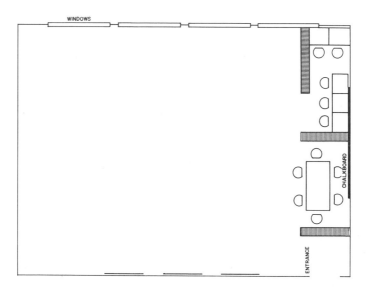

Exhibit 2–12.   A table has been designated as a material resource center (for example, a place where mathematics or reading materials may be available) and placed between two dividers to facilitate easy access to the materials and privacy when using them. This area can also be used as a small-group center where students who do not share a den may meet to work together.

Any of the techniques for grouping two to five students may be used to continue the pattern of establishing small den or alcove areas. The section nearest the door lends itself well to being a material resource section. Dividers may be placed at right angles to the walls near the entrance to provide an open passageway where books and manipulative materials (games, **reading and math equipment, and so forth) may be** selected easily without intruding on others (see Exhibit 2–13).

Behind the bookcases on the side wall near the door, two or three students' desks may be placed to form another den. When a wall includes a clothing closet, it may be feasible to establish only one den area behind the entranceway bookcase. The remaining section must be free for access to the closet. In older, traditional buildings, closets frequently have some stationary doors. These may be used for individual youngsters who prefer to work

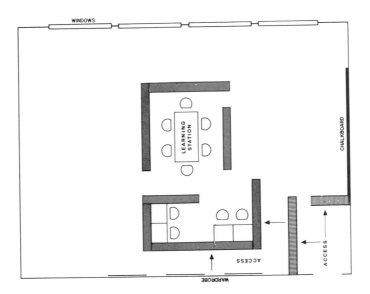

Exhibit 2-13. The entrance to a room serves effectively as a resource center, providing easy access to learning materials without intrusion on working students. Built-in wardrobes or bookcase walls may be made more functional by placing dividers three to four feet in front of them with access to the materials they house from the side away from the middle of the room. Student desks may then be placed against the dividers on the inside of the room to create new den areas.

alone. Their desks may be placed against the nonmovable doors that may then be used as bulletin boards (see Exhibit 2-14).

Where large, old-fashioned heating units are exposed to view it is possible to cover the surface with a protective, fire-proof material and to use the units themselves as areas against which one or two desks may be placed, using the portion of the unit above the desk heights as a bulletin board.

When sections of the room appear to be unusable for desk placement (such as long sections of wardrobe walls, built-in bookcase walls, or sink and other wet areas), it is attractive to leave an aisle between these sections and a series of horizontally placed dividers. This arrangement creates an attractive resource aisle on the periphery of the room and permits small dens to be established toward the inner part. Access to the materials placed in the dividers does not interfere with students engrossed in their studies outside the area (see Exhibit 2-13).

The various patterns of separating the rear and front walls of the classroom into small den areas to accommodate between two and five students should be extended all around the outer area of the room with the exception of closets or sinks. If sufficient space is available, it may be possible to establish one or more material resource centers or small-group meeting areas

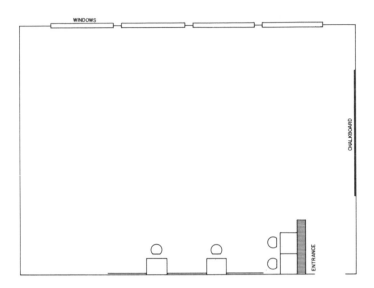

Exhibit 2-14.   Behind the entranceway bookcase is the first side wall den area. If this is a clothing closet wall and the closets include some nonmovable doors, individual youngsters may occupy the spaces directly in front of the stationary doors and may use the doors as bulletin boards. An alternative would be to establish a resource aisle directly in front of the wardrobe area by placing dividers approximately four feet away from the closets and permitting access to materials from the closet side (see Exhibit 2-13).

within the total design. The outer sections of the room should be maintained as quiet work areas for independent, paired, or small-group work. The teacher should move from youngster to youngster and from small group to small group to check each student's progress, to respond to questions, to guide youngsters in need of assistance, and to evaluate the quality of what has been completed.

Initially, redesign efforts should be restricted to the outer perimeter of the room. The center should be reserved for areas where students may work together in more gregarious or mobile activities. The den areas that foster privacy and small-group work, will aid in keeping the noise level down and student concentration high. Youngsters may work alone, in pairs, or in small teams in their dens or in the small-group instructional areas that have been established on the outer edge of the room. For more interactive activities, they may work in the center of the room. With this method, youngsters involved in their independent prescriptions can literally turn their backs on the activity in the center and remain with their tasks. Should it be appropriate to join those involved in the center of the room, at a holiday interest center for example, they need merely move to the larger area. Basic rules and procedures for moving from one area to another should be established to promote positive learning activities for all.

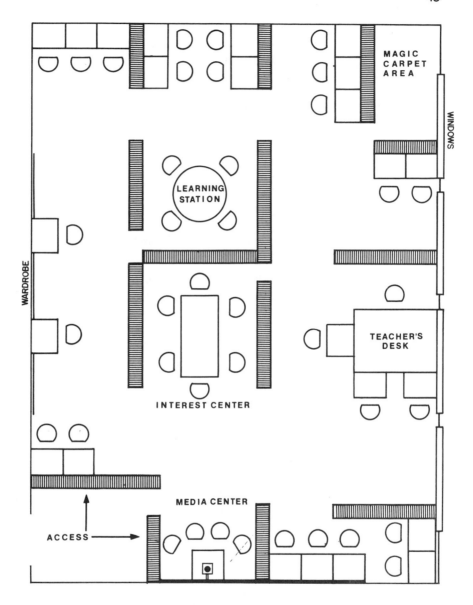

Exhibit 2-15.   This depicts a completely redesigned model classroom that provides for different learning styles.

The center area might include a learning station or two, an interest center, or a game table. If the teacher and class prefer, one of the corner den areas may be used as a little theater or a media corner. The room arrangement may be as creative as the teacher, but much of the practicality of this kind of redesign will not become apparent until experienced by the group for a week or more. The room should be revised, especially in the early stages, to meet needs as they emerge.

As you reconstruct your classroom, it is important to teach the students to use it effectively. This necessitates the ability to cooperate with peers; to choose from among appropriate alternatives; to complete assignments or tasks; to locate, use, share, repair, and return resources; and to function independently in an environment that requires increased decision making and student responsibility.

Exhibit 2-15 depicts a completely redesigned model classroom that provides for different learning styles.

Adding Creative Dividers and Designer Touches

Now that the basic room redesign is complete, you may wish to supplement furniture dividers, such as bookcases and file cabinets, with decorative floor-to-ceiling, see-through partitions to further the illusion of separation and to add interest and color. These inexpensive dividers may also be used to display student work or to post rules and objectives for instructional areas.

Colored Yarn

Obtain colored yarn from local merchants as a donation or from parents as a contribution. Stretch floor-to-ceiling lengths between two areas in straight, triangular, or other patterns (see Exhibit 2-16). This wall of yarn is most attractive and can be used to display student work or to post directions. Thumbtacks, staples, masking tape, or loops around metal ceiling supports can be used as anchors at the top and bottom. Have custodians aid in designing and tieing the yarn down. They will know what will work with minimum damage.

Plastic Beverage Tops, Paper Rings

Have the students save the plastic (nonmetal) rings from six-pack beverage containers. These may be attached to each other with colored string or wire to form see-through wall dividers similar to the colored yarn partitions. When these are weighted at the bottom, they need not be anchored to the floor, but you will find that they hold their shape better when they are. Colored chains consisting of construction paper rings, such as those usually made for holiday seasons, may also be used, although they are not as permanent as the plastic rings. These should be anchored and repaired as soon as they break (see Exhibit 2-17).

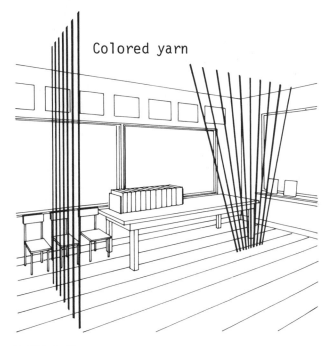

Exhibit 2-16.

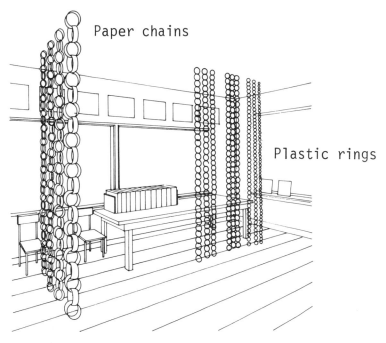

Exhibit 2-17.

Aluminum Foil, Construction Paper, and Paint

Leftover holiday wrappings, colored construction paper, unused paint, clear food wrappings, or aluminum foil can be used effectively to decorate walls, bulletin boards, cardboard dividers, and the backs and sides of file cabinets. Remnant wallpaper, shelf liner, and sections of carpeting, burlap, or cut-up old jeans can be used to create montages and attractive backs for dividers, walls, shelves, and mounted objectives. In addition to creating an attractive learning environment, you will promote interest and enthusiasm if you let the students and, occasionally, their parents help in the interior decorating process.

Other Instructional Areas

Math Tubs

Locate an old, discarded bathtub. Have the students scour and decorate it. Place it in the Math Learning Station and seek donated pillows or make some with the class. They should be large, colorful, and comfortable. Fill the tub with the pillows and establish a schedule for "swimming in math."

The students should be told that once in the tub they will be totally immersed in mathematics. They may think only of the mathematics they are reading, learning, or doing once inside this hideaway. The "magical waters" of the Math Tub will help them to learn, and you can chart their progress across an "ocean of objectives" that can be attached to the insides and outsides of this innovative instructional area.

Reading Houses

Salvage old lumber, bolts, nails, sandpaper, packing cases, and other materials that will allow you to design a reading tree house right in your classroom. Involve the custodians, local fire marshall, skillful or willing parents, and anyone else who can assist. Design it first, and carefully measure where it will go. Construct steady and safe ladders, platforms, and spaces for three or four children. Elementary school youngsters will love to read or study quietly away from the rest of the class, and older students will enjoy the privacy and quiet of such an area.

Office Buildings

Large sheets of cardboard or the sides of discarded delivery boxes can be used to construct separate compartments or "offices" for individual students. Those students that need to be alone to study or concentrate can crawl or climb into these spaces and screen out the rest of the class or even their neighbors in adjacent offices. The cardboard offices may be built in layers (two stories or levels) or into a maze to separate students. The office building can be painted with windows or with solid colored walls.

Secondary School Areas

Many of the previous suggestions are more appropriate for the elementary classroom, but the learning styles of secondary school students also require varied physical accommodations. For example, a number of junior and senior high students concentrate best while reading on either carpeting or in a lounge chair. They often seek an overhead cover and settle themselves below a shelf or a table. Some like open spaces while studying or conversing. Still others achieve quickly and well while listening to music.

Although groups of students change classrooms as do the teachers, it is possible to establish a few learning areas that vary the usual rows or circles in secondary classrooms. If several teachers who use a room can agree on leaving one, two, or even three instructional areas in place day after day, they will discover that media corners, research centers, or learning stations are useful in meeting the instructional and learning style needs of their students to the point where the inconvenience of making administrative arrangements is far outweighed by increased student interest and involvement.

Understanding and Using Alternative Instructional Areas[3]

Once the room has been totally redesigned, rules should be established for the use of varied instructional areas. Those students who demonstrate that they can learn effectively together by using any three or four small-group techniques without supervision should begin to use instructional areas such as Learning Stations, Interest Centers, Game Tables, Magic Carpets, Media Corners, and Little Theaters. In this way, youngsters may continue to work independently or with partners at defined learning spaces while the teacher focuses attention on the ones who cannot achieve without adult direction. Each instructional area serves specific purposes and thus attracts students with different learning styles, interests, and goals at varying times.

Separating the learning environment into multiinstructional areas encourages students to consider where they will find it most appropriate to do their work; where they will find the resources through which they may achieve their objectives; and whether they prefer working alone, with a friend or two, in a small group of peers, or directly with the teacher.

The instructional areas that may be established have characteristics in common. These include:

1. Clearly stated objectives (see Chapter 4), usually with some choice permitted such as, "Complete three (3) of the following five (5) objectives";

2.   Small-group techniques with which the students are familiar, such as circle of knowledge, team learning, brainstorming, case study, group analysis, role-playing, or simulations;

3.   Introductory, reinforcement, and evaluative activities related to the important objectives;

4.   Alternative activities on different levels of difficulty: task cards, activity cards, learning circles, and games;

5.   Self-correcting activities: task cards, activity cards, learning circles, and games;

6.   Multiple options so that the student is required to make some choices as he progresses;

7.   Multisensory resources;

8.   Opportunities for creative and imaginative projects;

9.   Attractive signs and decorations, and

10.   A self-contained space to provide privacy and a feeling of personal involvement.

Each area should be designed so that a given number of students may use it at one time. Depending upon the size of the area, the number may vary from four to six. See Exhibit 2–15 for the placement and design of various instructional areas.

Decide whether you will use a table, desk, carpeting, or selected furniture inside the area. If shelves are available, materials may be placed on them for usage. If shelves are not available, a table or other such item may be necessary for the display and usage of related task cards, books, activity sheets, packages, and other similar materials. Use attractive and lively colors to decorate the dividers, the inner walls, and the materials. Clear Con-tact is a useful covering, for it lasts a long time and prevents deterioration of much-used resources.

Identify the major theme or topic that a first center will be devoted to for the present. Develop clearly stated behavioral objectives that indicate to the students what they will need to learn about the current topic. Print some of the objectives on colored signs or banners and mount them on the inner walls. Have others duplicated for distribution to the youngsters working in this area. List the resources that are available for students for mastering the objectives you designed. Organize the resources for easy use through either shape or color codes, either to indicate various levels of difficulty or as suggestions for student selection based on ability.

Tape-record the difficult parts of the books when it is necessary that students use specific pages in them. If you do not have the time to read all the paragraphs onto a tape, get a parent or older student to do so. As you teach group lessons, tape-record whatever you say, the students' interruptions, your responses, their questions, and peer suggestions. Use these tapes as an auditory resource for students who were absent, who need reinforcement, or who wish to relisten to the content.

Develop additional resources as you move more deeply into instructional area teaching, and have students develop others. There should be a number of multisensory materials available to provide appropriate learning aids that match the perceptual learning style strengths of each youngster.

Learning Stations

A learning station is an instructional area that houses multilevel resources that relate to a specific curriculum such as social studies, art, language arts, science, or mathematics. The station should have introductory resources for youngsters who are just beginning to learn about a special topic; reinforcement materials for youngsters who are experiencing some difficulty in mastering elements of the topic; advanced resources for the very bright or very interested students; and small-group techniques, such as circle of knowledge, team learning, brainstorming, or case study, for youngsters who learn better when studying with one or two (or more) classmates.

Code the materials with color, shapes, or numbers to indicate to students those that are appropriate for their level of reading and comprehension ability. The station should be well-organized, attractive, and nicely maintained so that youngsters can find what they require easily and with a minimum of frustration. Students should be cautioned to return resources to their correct place and category of difficulty when they no longer are using them.

A learning station may consist of a table and shelves with accumulated materials where students select items or activities and take them to their own desks (or another area); it may also include a table, a desk, files for materials, and a few chairs or cushions for students who choose to work in the area or a carpeted corner or section where youngsters may work.

The materials at several levels of the topic being focused on at the station should be interesting, varied, and self-corrective (to facilitate student independence), and might include books, magazines, task cards, cassettes, dittos, instructional packages, contracts, programmed sequences, workbooks, learning circles, tapes, filmstrips, films, photographs, cartridges, loops, electroboards, study prints, assignments, slides, and games related to the selected topic. Directions for the use of resources should be attached to all items.

Access to the station should be open. Students should be able to visit, take items to another section of the larger room or area, or remain at the station to work or to discuss their activities with others. Regulations governing acceptable behavior in the area should be established so that students clearly understand exactly the ways in which they may function while at the station, including the sound level at which they may speak and work with others.

As students begin to use the instructional area, they will need to be taught how to:

- Locate, use, share, repair, and replace the available resources;
- Recognize materials that are appropriate to their individual reading and comprehension levels;
- Make selections from among approved alternatives;
- Evaluate their own and their peers' progress; and
- Maintain accurate records of those objectives and activities that they have completed successfully.

These skills are essential for functioning in any program that requires students to become increasingly independent. It is at this point that students are most likely to learn the study skills that are necessary for their continued academic growth—they are actually using materials and must begin to depend upon their own ability to assess their tasks correctly, to locate appropriate resources and information, to record what they need to remember, to select ways of demonstrating accomplished skills and tasks, and to evaluate their progress. Opportunities for creative experiences or performance demonstrations may be built into evaluation procedures. Use the first learning station as a beginning step toward establishing varied instructional areas. Motivated youngsters will move forward quickly, eager to become increasingly independent and to use varied materials with which they can function easily. The nonmotivated will progress more slowly, but they will begin to thrive as they become accustomed to imposed regulations and the selection of resources with which they can succeed.

Experiment, vary the resources and methods of providing access to them, and permit options so that students like working in (or out of) the area and feel comfortable without being under your direct supervision. Permit the youngsters time to identify their own learning styles and to experiment with related materials. If it takes too long (more than two weeks), suggest methods and materials for them and supervise their beginning involvement. If one technique does not work, try another after a given amount of time; two weeks seems to be a fairly good guideline for experimenting with a selected strategy. Keep introducing and testing new resources until each youngster is achieving to your satisfaction. If you suspect that a learner needs longer adjustment periods, proceed more slowly and extend some target dates. There is no foolproof formula to motivate every student, but your professional expertise will assist you in recognizing what is working and what has failed.

Interest Centers

A second instructional area where students may congregate to learn is called an interest center. This section of the learning environment should house interdisciplinary resources concerned with a selected theme (topic, unit, study) such as energy, pollution, transportation, racial conflict, or dinosaurs. Here, items related to many curriculum areas may be found, but they would be focused on one centralized sphere of interest.

In addition to the media resource materials related to the topic (objects, books, magazines, pictures, films, filmstrips, slides, cassettes, tapes, loops, cartridges, study prints), students might find: (1) assignment sheets (machine copies or workbook-type pages); (2) small-group assignments (circles of knowledge, team learning, brainstorming, case studies, simulations, role-playing, or group analyses);[4] and (3) games (crossword puzzles, fill-in-the-missing-letter assignments, task cards, and others) on which individuals or small groups might work. A program, contract, or instructional package on the topic could also be available.

Interest centers serve many purposes: (1) they are available as another option for students—an alternative way of obtaining information and concepts about a given theme; (2) they provide students with a means of gathering facts and concepts independently; and (3) they build small-group activities into the learning process to provide social interaction and group achievement. Interest centers, therefore, permit a teacher to begin to take advantage of individual learning styles by providing students with a choice of either working independently or with one or more other students. Although self-pacing is an important instructional goal, many youngsters prefer working with others and, for them, isolated studying and learning may not be desirable. Indeed, even those students who seem to think best while working on independent units often need to interact with others in order to test ideas and to grow.

Game Tables

Educational games are used extensively in schools today. Their major contributions to the learning process include: (1) introduction of a topic or concept; (2) application of information or concepts; (3) increased motivation and stimulation; (4) provision of an alternative teaching method or device; (5) opportunities for either individual or small-group focus on information through alternative media learning resources; (6) opportunities for independent concentration; (7) activities for small-group and interage shared experiences; (8) review or reinforcement of previously discussed or studied information; (9) remediation purposes; and (10) opportunities for relaxation as a break in the school day.

Games are available for all age levels (preschool through adulthood), in all curriculum areas, and as interdisciplinary approaches to study. A repertory of these instuctional devices provides alternative resources, methods, and activities for students and it increases their options for learning. At times you and the students may be able to invent new games or redesign existing ones to meet instructional goals or to take advantage of individual learning styles.

Game tables should be available to students in different sections of the classroom for use at appropriate times. When students have completed assignments, need or decide to use the games as media learning resources or activities, or wish to relax for a while, they should be able to go quietly to the table and select whatever is appropriate to their task or abilities. Games should be cataloged according to their level of difficulty or their relationship to the curriculum. The student will then know which games may be chosen so that options may be exercised as decisions are made.

Little Theaters

Another area guaranteed to provide an exciting, dynamic learning atmosphere is called the little theater—an imaginative title for a creative and stimulating center. Here, in a section of the room that may be darkened or partitioned when necessary, students are free to become involved in a series of projects that require application of the information they have learned through the use of media resource alternatives. Students are permitted to make slides, filmstrips, films, negatives, photographs, scenery props, costumes, backdrops for productions, rolled-paper "movies," multimedia presentations, transparencies, books and scrapbooks, and many other educational project materials related to drama, creativity, and production.

These projects are, of course, appropriately related to the curriculum, contracts, programs, or instructional packages; they provide application, review, reinforcement, and synthesis of ideas for the students. Students may write dialogue, scenes, plays, roles, or simply improvise, mime, or critically analyze what they see.

Media Corners or Centers

Most schools have limited equipment and must distribute their resources equitably among all classes in a given building. It is necessary, however, to provide each large group (twenty-five to thirty-five) of youngsters with enough hardware so that students may use the media equipment to obtain information, study concepts, and develop skills. At the same time, it is inefficient and unnecessary to carry heavy equipment from place to place.

Some school districts have established multimedia instructional resource centers to house their films; filmstrips; carousel, opaque, and over-head projectors; screens; cartridge viewers; duplicators; and other media equipment. In other schools this equipment is placed in various sections of the building, and students are permitted to leave their classrooms to use the equipment when appropriate.

Both methods of arranging media equipment have built-in drawbacks:

1.   If students are to be free to use the equipment when it appears necessary or appropriate to them, they must also be free to leave their room (area) and go to the equipment in another section of the building. Since many students may need to leave their room at the same time, a constant flow of incoming and outgoing students will exist. Unless the administration feels comfortable about an informal attendance procedure, it may be ex-tremely difficult to keep tabs on students' whereabouts. Of greater im-portance, the "right time" may slip by or be greatly wasted traveling to the media or waiting in lines.

2.   The student leaves his teacher and peers to go to another area. His teacher cannot supervise or assist him; his peers (unless they join him) do not share his learning experience.

In preference (or in addition) to either the totally centralized multi-media instructional resource center or the partially centralized learning center, teachers may establish a media corner in each room. This area can house one overhead projector, one or two single-viewer filmstrip machines, one super 8-mm cartridge viewer (optional), one sound projector (desirable but optional), three or four cassette tape recorders, and many blank tapes. Equipment may be exchanged among clusters of three or four classes joined together as "learning pods" or media instructional areas (MIAs) when needed. The larger, more affluent media centers could be used as a library resource to provide special materials.

Students should be free to take software (filmstrips, films, tapes, slides) from either the interest center or the learning station to the media corner and use it there as a learning resource. The software should be replaced carefully when the student no longer needs it. Cadres of students should form team task forces to assume the responsibility for demonstrating how to use, care for, repair, replace and organize the equipment and resources that complement the media center.

When one student begins to view materials, others are drawn into the procedure by interest, curiosity, or social awareness. Students should be permitted to join each other in viewing, discussing, studying, or analyzing the materials, provided each of the participants is receptive to the coopera-tive effort.

Gaining Parental Support

Now that you have redesigned your room to base your instructional program on individual learning styles, it is important to gain the support of your students' parents. Parents are interested in and often concerned about the concepts and strategies to which their children are being exposed, especially if they are new. Once the class has become adjusted to the redesigned room, invite parents in to visit and to discuss the rationale of the room or area redesign. Explain the advantages of capitalizing on each youngster's learning style and describe how the students participated in the developing arrangement. Once parents understand why the instructional environment has been altered, they usually are willing to support the effort until sufficient time has elapsed to yield both objective and subjective results, such as student responsiveness, teacher reactions, academic progress, and increased provision for individual differences and learning styles. Actually, the students themselves will presell the change with the enthusiasm they express at home about their new interior decoration.

As you read through subsequent chapters and follow the directions for creating Contract Activity Packages, programmed learning sequences, instructional packages, and multisensory resources, any or all of these may be placed in classroom instructional areas when appropriate.

3

Designing Small-Group
Instructional Techniques

Importance of Small-Group Techniques

Many students respond best to a learning situation that involves from two to five of their peers. Some of these youngsters may not be authority- or teacher-oriented for a variety of reasons. They may feel intimidated, anxious, or overly directed by adults or those in charge. Some may need the interaction of friends to stimulate them to learn; others are motivated by a team effort. Many relax when a group, rather than each of them individually, is responsible for a task, contract, or project. There also are students who gain persistence through group goals or who can deal more effectively with a short, specific portion of an assignment rather than with an entire task. Such youngsters often feel more responsibility to their peers than to either themselves or adults. For these reasons, or simple gregariousness, many youngsters' learning styles are best served if they are often permitted to work in groups.

First Concrete Step toward Individualization of Learning

Group work is a first step toward independence within the instructional setting, and working with others in school is early training toward that eventuality for most people in adult life.

Diagnose or observe the sociological elements of learning style for each of your students. Once you are convinced that a given youngster will learn best from and with peers, assign that student to a variety of small-group experiences.

Students who have been parent- or teacher-directed for most of their lives should first learn to make simple decisions and to assume the responsibility for completing simple tasks free of constant adult supervision. Use of selected techniques such as circle of knowledge, team learning, brainstorming, case study, and simulation provides a structure wherein learning occurs through cooperative small-group effort without the teacher serving as a constant guide or fountain of knowledge.

Small-group interactions also permit youngsters to solve problems in cooperation with other students so that they need not fear failure or embarrassment. Even if errors are made, sharing the responsibility with a group of peers sharply reduces the tension or trauma. Further, the small-group techniques help students to understand how other people reach decisions and work toward solutions. Finally, interaction with peers creates sounding boards on which to reflect ideas, build solutions, and suggest conclusions to the group and to the teacher.

Greater Learning Through Team Involvement

Over the years, a number of research studies have examined teams and groups as they strove toward achievement. Homans[1] postulated that groups are separate entities and cannot be viewed simply as the total of its members. Argyris,[2] Lorge et al.,[3] Hankins,[4] and many others in and out of education have demonstrated repeatedly that small teams often obtain better results than the individuals would have accomplished if working alone or with an adult. Poirier[5] studied students as partners and reported increased learning as did Bass[6], who pointed to group recognition, respect, and affection, as well as fun, as motivating factors toward higher achievement.

Learning Style Characteristics Responsive to Small-Group Techniques

Many learning style characteristics are responsive to small-group techniques that can be designed to accommodate multiple variations among students. They are especially appropriate for students who are peer-oriented, motivated, persistent, and responsible. They provide structure and auditory and visual experiences. Students who act as the recorder will gain additionally by writing (tactual) experiences.

Small-group techniques will accommodate the elements of light, temperature, design, time, intake, and mobility. Furthermore, motivation, persistence, and responsibility may be enhanced by the group process; members can exert positive peer pressure on those who are not strong in these areas.

Obviously, those who prefer to work alone or with adults and those who are creative and do not require structure are not as likely to benefit from small-group techniques.

Descriptions and Samples of Small-Group Techniques

Circle of Knowledge

The circle of knowledge technique is highly motivating and is an ideal technique for reinforcing skills in any subject area. It provides a framework for review in which everyone learns more or solidifies what he or she has already mastered.

This instructional approach permits students to:

- Review previously learned information in an interesting way;
- Focus thinking on one major concept at a time;
- Contribute to a group effort as part of a team;
- Serve as catalysts for additional responses;
- Develop ingenuity in helping team members to contribute; and
- Be exposed to and learn information without becoming bored.

Procedures

Several small circles of five to six chairs (no desks) are positioned evenly about the room. One student in each group should volunteer or be drafted, appointed, or elected as the recorder; members also may take turns. Only the recorder writes, although everyone participates and concentrates on thinking of many possible answers.

A single question or problem is posed, and whether written and re- produced or printed on a chalkboard, it must have many possible answers. Examples include naming all fifty states, identifying the possible causes of war, citing the products of a country, or listing synonyms for the word ''leader.''

Each circle of knowledge will respond to the same question simul- taneously (but quietly). A member in each group is designated as the first to begin, and the answers are then provided by one member at a time, clockwise or counterclockwise. No member may skip his turn, and no one may provide an answer until the person directly before him has delivered his; therefore, the answers stop while a member is thinking or groping for a possible response. No teammate may give an answer to another, but anyone in the group may act out or pantomime hints to help the person remember an item, an answer, or a possible response. Only the recorder may write, and he jots down (in a phrase or two only) the suggestions (answers, responses, thoughts) of each participant as the circle of knowledge continues.

At the end of a predetermined amount of time, the teacher calls a halt to the knowledge-sharing, and all recorders must stop writing the groups' answers. The number of responses produced by each group is noted, but credit is not given for quantity.

The teacher divides the chalkboard into columns and numbers them so that each represents one of the groups. In turn, a representative from each circle offers one of the answers suggested by that group. When an answer is provided, the teacher writes it in that group's column, and all the recorders in the room look at the list of answers developed by their group. If that answer is on the circle's list, the recorder crosses it off, thus gradually decreasing the length of the list until only the answers that have not yet been reported to the group and written on the board remain. This procedure continues until no circle has any remaining answers on its list.

The answers given by each circle of knowledge can be awarded points that are then recorded on the board to produce competition among the teams. The teacher might decide that each correct response will earn one point (or five or ten points) and that the circle achieving the most points will be the winner. Any time an answer is challenged by a rival circle, the teacher must decide whether it is right or wrong. If the answer is right and the challenger incorrect, the challenger's circle loses the number of points given for one correct answer. If the answer is incorrect and the challenger was right, the circle that sponsored the answer loses the points and the challenger's circle gains them.

The important thing to remember about circles of knowledge is that they may be used only to review something that already has been introduced and taught. Because the information required has been made available to the students previously, the time span permitted is usually a short one.

Examples

Primary   (Use a tape recorder to record each child's thoughts.)

- List as many things as you can remember that a policeman does to help us.
- Name all the vegetables that you can think of in two minutes.
- Name all the colors that you can in four minutes.
- List all the boys' names that you can think of that begin with the letter ''R.''
- Tell us all the things that you can do to make your mother happy on Mother's Day.

- Give all the words that you can that begin with the letter "B."
- Tell the names of as many baby animals as you can in three minutes.
- List all the words that you can think of that are kinds of furniture in a house.
- What are the rules that we should follow when our class takes a trip?

Elementary

- Name as many states in the United States as you can in two minutes.
- Name all the United States presidents that you can remember in three minutes.
- List the ways that a desert child's life is different from yours.
- What are some of the ways that we can show people that we really like them?
- List as many adverbs as you can.
- List as many products of (country) as you can recall in four minutes.
- Name all the songs that you can think of that have a girl's name in the title. (To avoid duplication, ask each circle to sing a line from the song it sponsors.)
- Make up as many examples as you can where two numbers added **together equal 9.**

  Model: _____ + _____ = 9

- Make up as many examples as you can where two numbers added together minus a third number equal 11.

  Model: _____ + _____ − _____ = 11

- How many examples can you create where two numbers, when added together and multiplied by a third number equal 100?

  Model: _____ + _____ × _____ = 100

Middle or Junior High School

- Name as many chemical elements as you can in three minutes.
- Give as many synonyms as you can for the adjective "small."
- List as many units of measurement and their metric equivalents as you can in five minutes.

- List the possible causes of war.
- Name as many American poets as you can.
- Name as many American plays as you can.
- Name as many books as you can that were written by Louisa May Alcott.
- List all the reasons that you can for people putting down other people.
- What are the things that you value most in life?
- Make up as many examples as you can where, when you use addition, subtraction, multiplication, and division (all four in one example) your answer equals 25.
- List as many rules as you can for writing a correct business letter.

High School

- What were the political implications of the caste system?
- Develop as many analogies as you can in four minutes.
- Name as many reasons as you can for changing the electoral college system.
- List as many ways as you can that pop art benefits our culture.
- Name as many eighteenth-century French painters as you can.
- List as many algebraic equations as you can using two unknowns and resulting in an answer of four.
- List as many causes of the Civil War as you can in three minutes.
- List all the natural forces that have changed the surface of our planet.

The format for presenting a circle of knowledge to students at any level is illustrated in Exhibit 3–1.

Exhibit 3-1
Sample format for circle of knowledge.

HIGH SCHOOL ENGLISH

CIRCLE OF KNOWLEDGE

Circle Members:

1. _____   4. _____

2. _____   5. _____

3. _____   6. _____

Recorder:_____

The Question:

List the titles of as many of Shakespeare's plays as you can.

1. _____	19. _____
2. _____	20. _____
3. _____	21. _____
4. _____	22. _____
5. _____	23. _____
6. _____	24. _____
7. _____	25. _____
8. _____	26. _____
9. _____	27. _____
10. _____	28. _____
11. _____	29. _____
12. _____	30. _____
13. _____	31. _____
14. _____	32. _____
15. _____	33. _____
16. _____	34. _____
17. _____	35. _____
18. _____	36. _____

37. _____

Circle of Knowledge Answers: (Used as a self-corrective guide *after* the circle of knowledge has been completed)

Shakespeare's Plays

All's Well That Ends Well	Macbeth
Antony and Cleopatra	Measure for Measure
As You Like It	The Merchant of Venice
The Comedy of Errors	The Merry Wives of Windsor
Coriolanus	A Midsummer Night's Dream
Cymbeline	Much Ado about Nothing
The Famous History of the Life of King Henry VIII	Othello, the Moor of Venice
	Pericles, Prince of Tyre
Hamlet	Romeo and Juliet
Julius Caesar	The Taming of the Shrew
King Henry IV, Part 1	The Tempest
King Henry IV, Part 2	Timon of Athens
King Henry VI, Part 1	Titus Andronicus
King Henry VI, Part 2	The Tragedy of King Richard II
King Henry VI, Part 3	The Tragedy of King Richard III
King Lear	Troilus and Cressida
The Life and Death of King John	Twelfth Night
The Life of King Henry V	Two Gentlemen of Verona
Love's Labor Lost	The Winter's Tale

Could you have done as well with his sonnets?

TEACHER'S SCORE CARD
For any circle of knowledge (on chalkboard or overhead projector)

	Circle 1	Circle 2	Circle 3	Circle 4	Circle 5
Round 1	1	1	1	1	1
Round 2	2	2	2	2	2

Round 3	3	3	3	3
Round 4	4	4	4	4
Round 5	5	5	5	5
Round 6	6	6	6	6
Round 7	7	7	7	7
Round 8	8	8	8	8
Round 9	9	9	9	9
Challenges	Challenges	Challenges	Challenges	Challenges
Won_____	Won_____	Won_____	Won_____	Won_____
Lost_____	Lost_____	Lost_____	Lost_____	Lost_____
Total _____	_____	_____	_____	_____

Team Learning

Team learning is an excellent technique for introducing new material. All the advantages of peer interaction and support described earlier are apparent in this approach. Enthusiasm, motivation, good spirits, positive results, division of labor, responsibility, persistence, self-image, and group recognition of individual efforts usually result.

Procedures

Begin by writing original material or by copying sections of commercial publications to form short paragraphs containing new information to be learned. Young students who are beginning readers may be able to absorb between three and six sentences collectively; advanced high school students should be able to understand and discuss entire articles, poems, or sets of diagrams with explanations. By developing team-learning exercises of varied difficulty you will not only be able to respond to different learning styles, you will also be able to establish groups to work on new materials according to the ability level and rate of learning in each small team.

At the end of the printed reading (or diagramatic) material, list a series of questions that should be answered by the group. Some of the questions should be related directly to the printed reading passages; others should be answered through inference and analysis by the group. In this way, students will develop two skills and will more likely retain the new information. By finding answers in the assigned material through rereading, underlining, or discussion, the individuals in the group will learn how to seek and to obtain specific information. The more difficult inference questions will promote reasoning and group decision making.

When the printed materials are ready, you may assign students into groups of four to six. (Six should be the maximum for most small-group techniques.) As students demonstrate responsibility, you might permit some degree of self-selection of groups. Groups should be allowed to sit on the floor or at clustered tables according to their preferences. Other variations include a round circle of chairs, hassocks, or a couch and chairs in a conversational grouping. The learning style elements of design, mobility, time, intake, and so on should be considered as part of the team-learning assignment.

When comfortable, the group should elect, assign, or accept a volunteer to serve as recorder. It is the recorder (and only the recorder) who needs to write the group's responses to the questions. Short, succinct answers are important to keep the discussion and learning process moving. Some of the other students may elect to write the answers, too, but only because they believe they'll remember the material through note-taking.

Any member may help other participants on the same team, but all the effort must be concentrated within the group. One way to promote quiet and order if teams are in competition on a specific team-learning exercise is to tell the class that other teams are free to use answers that are overheard from other groups working on the same exercise.

After one or two team-learning experiences, groups of students will develop team relationships and begin to question and analyze the material with enthusiasm and animated, but productive, conversation. You will need to walk around and assist with the process the first time or two, but you will discover newfound freedom to work with individuals or other groups very soon after the students gain initial experience with this teaching strategy.

Time limits may be imposed or left open, depending on the learning style and need for structure of the members of each group. An alternative to strict time limits would be to assign some team-learning prescriptions to a group as homework or as a free-time activity.

For the purposes of comparison, participation, and reinforcement, the recorders of teams working on the same assignment should be asked to share with the entire group those responses to the material that were developed and approved by their membership. This is done by numbering each group and then asking team 1 for a response to a question, asking team 2 for a second one, and so on, in rotation.

Write each recorder's responses on the chalkboard and instruct students to cross an answer off their lists if it duplicates theirs; they thus will be left with only answers that have not yet been called out. Other team members should respond on the second or third round. The recorders should pass their lists to the students who will be answering next. Eventually, you and the class will proceed through all the questions, permitting most of the team members to participate. In this way, errors and misinformation are not likely to be retained. Moreover, all questions will be answered, and everyone will have had a chance to participate actively.

As with the circles of knowledge, you and your class may elect to use a team competition approach with points based on the correct number of answers given by each team. Competition among teams is usually friendly and stimulating; often different teams win. Furthermore, the competition does not pit one individual against another where loss of self-image is a serious risk.

Team learning presents new material in a fashion that responds to such important learning style elements as structure, design, time, mobility, intake, learning with peers, motivation, persistence, responsibility, and visual and auditory perceptual strengths. (Kinesthetic and tactual resources could be added to team learning exercises for those who require them.) Sample team learnings are shown in Exhibit 3–2.

Exhibit 3-2
Sample format for team learning

ELEMENTARY

TEAM LEARNING

Team Members:

1. _____   4. _____

2. _____   5. _____

3. _____   6. _____

Recorder:_____

The History of Measurement[7]

Primitive people measured things by using parts of their own bodies— hands, feet, arms, legs, fingers. One of the most common ancient units of length was the cubit—the length of a forearm from the bend of the elbow to the tip of the outstretched middle finger. The length of a person's foot, the width of the palm, the length of a finger, the width of a thumb—these were all early units of measure.

1.   What are some of the different parts of the body used to measure things?

List at least three (3).

a.   _____

b.   _____

c.   _____

d.   _____

e.   _____

2.   How long was a cubit?

_____

3.   Which word tells you that measuring goes back a long way?

_____

4.   Do you think that using a person's own body is a good way to measure things? Why?

_____

5.   Early rulers used their own body measurements as the royal standards. If you were king, what would you do? Write an official document your decree.

_____

_____

_____

_____

_____

_____

6.   Have at least three (3) classmates follow your decree and measure one object agreed upon by all of you.

7.   Why is it important to know the history of measurement?

_____

_____

_____

_____

MIDDLE OR JUNIOR HIGH SCHOOL

TEAM LEARNING

Team Members:

1.   _____   4.   _____

2.   _____   5.   _____

3.   _____   6.   _____

Recorder:_____

Learning about the Eye[8]

Read the Following:

Light is reflected from an object. It passes through the cornea, a clear covering that protects your eye. Then it passes through some liquid called "aqueous humor" and then through the pupil—the "window of your eye." (The pupil looks like a black dot in the middle of your eye.) A muscle opens the pupil when there is not much light and makes the opening smaller if there is a lot of light. The muscle is called the "iris." The iris is the colored part of your eye. Behind the pupil is the lens, which is something like the lens in a camera. The lens turns the picture upside down and projects it onto the retina, which is like a screen on the rear wall of your eyeball. Millions of nerve endings in the retina send messages through your optic nerves to your brain. Your brain turns the picture right side up again.

Your eye has three protectors outside the eyeball. Shading your eyes are the eyelids, which protect them from lights that are too bright and from strong gases such as ammonia. You close your eyelids when you sleep, and you close them automatically when you blink. Blinking spreads tear fluid over the corneas and cleans them as windshield wipers clean the glass in an automobile. The eyelids and the eyelashes also protect your eyes from flying insects and bits of dirt. The eyelids close automatically when an object, such as a ball, comes toward your eyes. The eyebrows above the eyes are protectors, too. They act as cushions against blows from above and keep perspiration from dropping into your eyes.

Assignment:

1. What are some parts of the eye mentioned in this writing?

a. _____   d. _____

b. _____   e. _____

c. _____   f. _____

Can you name at least four (4) more?

_____   _____

_____   _____

2. What are the functions of at least seven (7) parts of the eye?

a. _____

b. _____

c. _____

d. _____

e. _____

f. _____

g. _____

3. Name the three protectors of the eye.

a. _____

b. _____

c. _____

4. How do each of the protectors do their work?

a. _____

b. _____

c. _____

5. Explain in your own words how the eye sees.

_____

_____

_____

_____

_____

_____

_____

6. Think of what a camera looks like and think about its parts. Are there any similarities or differences between a camera and the eye? If so, list them.

_____

_____

_____

_____

_____

_____

7. If you were unable to see, how would you find out what some things looked like?

_____

_____

_____

_____

8. Write a short poem explaining how the eye works.

_____

_____

_____

_____

_____

HIGH SCHOOL

TEAM LEARNING

Team Members:

1. _____   4. _____

2. _____   5. _____

3. _____   6. _____

Recorder:_____

Contemporary Music Lyrics[9]

Directions:

Listen to the record *Where Do The Children Play* by Cat Stevens, or read the lyrics. Then answer these questions.

1.   What type of "jumbo" plane is being discussed in our society?

_____

Can you name some examples? _____

_____

2.   List at least five (5) advances in our society that Cat Stevens refers to in his song.

a.   _____   d.   _____

b.   _____   e.   _____

c.   _____   f.   _____

_____

3.   Which line in the song refers to the gas and oil shortage?_____

_____

4.   Which elements of nature does Cat Stevens think are being destroyed by man's progress? Can you list more than four (4)?

_____

_____

_____

_____

Brainstorming

Brainstorming is an exciting group participation designed to develop multiple answers to a single question, alternate solutions to problems, and creative responses. It is an associative process that encourages students to call out—one of the few times this is permitted in our schools. Thus it responds to personal motivation and does not suppress natural spontaneity.

In addition to increasing motivation, the technique of brainstorming offers many practical advantages. Brainstorming is:

- *Stimulating.* It offers a unique, freewheeling, exciting, and rapid-fire method that builds enthusiasm in nearly all participants.

- *Positive.* Quiet and shy students usually become active participants because they are not put down; their contributions are masked by the group process. Conversely, those who usually dominate endless discussions are structured into offering succinct suggestions.

- *Focused.*   Diversions and distractions are eliminated. Stories and speeches irrelevant to the question or otherwise not pertinent are eliminated.

- *Spontaneous and creative.* Students serve as a sounding board that generates new ideas. Creativity is released during the momentum of the process.

- *Efficient and productive.* Dozens of suggestions, facts, ideas, or creative solutions are generated in a matter of minutes. Additional steps or plans of an activity can be brainstormed, as well as more specific answers for general responses (subset brainstorming).

- *Involving and Image-building.* Self-image is enhanced for students who see their ideas listed. Group pride and cohesiveness increase, too, as the members begin to feel a part of the unit that created the lists.

- *Ongoing and problem solving.* The results are recorded and may be modified and used in new situations.

Procedures

The brainstorming leader also acts as recorder. His or her functions include recording all responses, asking for clarification or repetition, synthesizing large phrases into short key ideas, and keeping the group focused on each single topic. The leader should not comment, editorialize, or contribute; his or her effort should be concentrated on producing an effective and productive session.

Setting

From five to ten students should form a fairly tight semi-circle of chairs facing the leader. (Larger groups can be effective at times.) Behind the leader is a wall containing three to five large sheets of lecture pad paper or newsprint double-folded to prevent strike-through marks on the wall (see Exhibit 3–3). These sheets, approximately twenty to twenty-four inches wide and thirty to thirty-six inches high, should be attached to the wall with masking tape and placed a few inches apart at a comfortable height for recording. The leader should use a broad-tipped felt marker for instant visability by the entire group. A timekeeper should be appointed for the two- or three-minute brainstorming segments, but he or she may participate. It is useful to have additional sheets available and an overhead projector to permit groups to analyze, plan, or do subset brainstorming for specific aspects of general answers.

Exhibit 3-3.   For optimum results, a brainstorming session consists of a tight semi-circle of five to ten participants.[10]

Rules for Participants

1. Concentrate on the topic—"storm your brain."
2. Fill the silence—call out what pops into your head.
3. Wait for an opening—don't step on someone's lines.
4. Record the thoughts in short form.
5. Record *everything*—no matter how far out.
6. Repeat your contribution until it is recorded.
7. Be positive—no put downs, body language, or editorial comment.
8. Stay in focus—no digressions.
9. Use short time spans—one to three minutes.
10. Analyze later—add, subtract, plan, implement.
11. Brainstorm from general to specific subsets.

Samples: Brainstorming

Elementary:
Call out all the synonyms you can think of for "leader."

Elementary:
Instead of using a cliche such as "Quiet as a_____,"
(mouse is usually given) let's brainstorm: "As quiet as a_____
_____ing."

You will soon have delighted groups calling out as quiet as a "snowflake falling," and "eyelid closing," a "mosquito landing," or a "mother worrying." You might do this for all of the usual cliches found in compositions, and praise those who use creative substitutions.

Junior High School:
List the desirable characteristics of good leaders.

Junior High School:
Provide synonyms for an entire sentence, one word at a time:

	(adjective)	(noun)	(verb)			(noun)
The	large	boy	ran	to	the	hill.

Take one minute (60 seconds) for each word. Then consider the limitless number of combinations to find the funniest sentence, most precise description, most creative arrangement, and so forth.

High School:
List all the solutions you can think of to car pollution.

High School:
Call out as many ways as are possible to prevent poverty.

High School:

Problem Solving: (Three-part brainstorming)

What would constitute an ideal energy program? (Three minutes)	What are the obstacles to this ideal program? (Three minutes)	What can we citizens do to overcome the obstacles and guarantee adequate energy? (Three minutes)

Case Study

A case study stimulates and helps to develop analytical skills. Four to six students can spend considerable time discussing and interpreting short, relevant stories that teach them something you believe they ought to learn.
Case studies provide:

- A strategy for developing material within the student's frame of reference. The characters, situations, and events can, if constructed properly, strike responsive and understanding chords.

- An approach that can be stimulating and meaningful if student identification is fostered and debate is structured to understand different points of view on recognized problems and situations.

- Safe, nonthreatening situations for students who can enter the analysis without direct personal effect.

- Training and development in problem solving, analytical skills, arriving at conclusions, and planning for new directions in learning situations and in real life.

Guidelines for the Development of Case Studies

Format   Case studies may be written as very short stories, audio or video-taped dramatizations, films, psychodramas, news events, or historical happenings—real or fictional. The use of chronological sequence aids students in following the flow of events and in analyzing key issues. Flashbacks and other complex approaches should be avoided except for the most advanced students.

Focus   The case should focus on a single event, incident, or situation. Ability to analyze is aided by a high degree of concentration on the reasons that precipitated the event, the attitudes prevailing during a given incident, or the sharply defined points of view of those dealing with a problem.

Relevance   Reality or "potential credibility" related to the frame of reference of the students is critical to the success of this small-group technique. The participants involved in analyzing the case must be able to recognize, understand, or even identify with the people in the situation because what they do or say seems authentic or possible. The style of writing should attempt to capture the flavor of familiar places, people, and their actions at a level that is at, or slightly above, the levels of understanding of the participants.

Increasing Motivation   After initial training in the analysis of case studies, involve students in the actual writing and acting out of roles in subsequent cases. Both relevance and motivation will increase as students become involved and begin to feel a sense of ownership of their new creation or variation of an older case.

Procedures

Elect, seek volunteers, or appoint a leader and a recorder from among the four to six participants. Have the group read the case at the beginning of the session. As the students become more familiar with this approach, you may wish to assign the materials as prior reading exercises to increase the amount of time devoted to group discussion.

The leader should not dominate the session but should keep the group on target for the allotted time. The recorder should participate and also concentrate on capturing the essence of the group's responses to various analytical questions. He or she must periodically verify all notes with the group to obtain consensus.

Key questions for the case study or short story must be developed in advance, although others may be suggested by the group as they delve deeply into the problem or situation. Questions may begin with factual checkpoints but then should move quickly into possible reasons, alternative motives, and the analysis of the subtleties and complexities of human experiences and interactions as well as values, standards, and other abstractions. Finally, students should be asked to reach conclusions and to apply developing insights to new situations.

Analyzing case studies should build student powers of interpretation, synthesis, description, observation, perception, abstraction, comparison, judgement, conclusion, determination, and prediction.

Sample Case Study: ELEMENTARY SCHOOL — VALUES

Purpose:

Understanding some of the reasons that cause others to behave the way they do, even when they want to be different.

The New Student

Ellen arrived with her family from out of state in the beginning of November. She felt out of place and uncomfortable. It had been difficult to make friends in her former school, and here it seemed impossible. She felt left out and behind in her work here in the sixth grade, even though she was told that she had been an excellent student when she was younger. Everyone seemed to belong to an in-group.

Ellen was quiet at first, but then began to try to work her way into one of the groups. She walked into a circle of girls before class started and said, "You know, the way girls dress in this school is really way out of it. No one here is really cool. At my last school all the girls wore French jeans. Here, you're still wearing ordinary slacks. Why, no one here has even started to wear overalls, and we dropped them last year."

One of the girls stared at Ellen and said to the others, "Let's go into the classroom. The hall's getting polluted." They all left, leaving Ellen behind. She became embarrassed and fought to control developing tears as she ran down the hall.

Analysis Questions:

- What is the key problem in this case study?
- Who is "right" — Ellen or the girls?
- What would you do immediately to help Ellen?
- What would you say to Ellen? To the group of girls?
- Pretend you are one of the other girls. What would you say about Ellen?
- What are three things you could do to help Ellen become part of the class and feel welcome?

(Scores of cases like this one and their analyses can be developed about a variety of situations dealing with values, attitudes, interactions, or preferences.)

Sample Case Study: MIDDLE OR JUNIOR HIGH SCHOOL — LIVING HISTORY

Purpose:

Understanding emotions and attitudes, coping with a difficult situation, developing alternative solutions.

The Unwanted Visitor

At the time of the Boston Massacre, British soldiers were feared, despised, and unwanted by many colonists who still considered themselves loyal British subjects under the rule of King George III. Nevertheless, the crude, red-uniformed soldiers were housed in homes in Boston where they ate the food, used the bedrooms, and sometimes engaged in mistreatment of the local citizens. Their red uniforms earned for them the derogatory term "lobster back."

For their part the British soldiers were not pleased to be far from home among hostile "barbarians." Some youngsters, perhaps of your age, undoubtedly found those red-coated lobster backs inviting targets for snowballs in the winter. This type of harassment, added to the irritable confrontations on the streets and commons of Boston, may very well have led to an accidental, or at least unnecessary, firing by the troops on the unarmed citizens of Boston.

Analysis Questions:

- If you had lived in Boston during the American Revolution, how would you have felt about British soldiers living in your home? Why?

- Why was "lobster back" a derogatory term? Why was this term used instead of some other one such as "red flannel-head"?
- How would you feel if you were one of the British soldiers?
- What would you have done to ease the tension in town to prevent the massacre and needless loss of life?
- Have there been similar situations in history since the Revolutionary War?

Sample Case Study: SENIOR HIGH SCHOOL—ENGLISH

A series of incidents or consecutive events may not be interesting in and of themselves.

For Example:

What Happens Next?

Mark stretched. The muscles rippled across his back. His mind came awake slowly, and he smiled as the memory of yesterday spread across his consciousness like warm waves at a tropical beach. He pulled himself out of the bed. The sunshine bathed his lean body; the future belonged to him!

Analysis Questions:

- How do you know Mark was feeling good?
- What might have happened yesterday?
- How does the passage support your position?
- Have you ever felt the way Mark did? Explain why.
- Describe what happened next in Mark's life.
- Use the selection to indicate why you believe the next series of events you created is plausible.

Alternate Case Study Assignments:

Select a favorite novel, short story, or narrative poem.

1. Write the next chapter.
2. Send a letter to one of the main characters describing what happens next.
3. Have the main character write a story or journal of succeeding events.
4. Report the next series of events to the newspapers.

5.   Write a soap opera scenario for television about the main characters just after the end of the novel or story.

A Final Word on Small-Group Techniques

These four small-group techniques and others you use or devise are essential to building independence and for responding to those youngsters whose learning style clearly indicates a need to work with peers.

- *Circle of knowledge* reviews and reinforces previously learned material.
- *Team learning* introduces new material and uses both factual and inference questions.
- *Brainstorming* releases creative energy and aids in planning and solving problems.
- *Case study* develops analytical skills and builds empathy and understanding of people as they work together to solve problems or cope with crises.

There are variations and other small-group techniques such as simulations, role-playing, group analysis, task forces and research committees.[11] Select or develop those that will respond to varied learning styles, and your instructional role will take less effort eventually and will be far more rewarding for you and for your individual students.

4

Designing Contract Activity Packages to Respond to Individual Learning Styles

Contract Activity Packages[1] (CAPs) are one of the three basic methods of individualizing instruction. In addition to responding to specific learning style differences among students, they are more effective than a large-group lecture or question and answer discussion for the following reasons:

Self-pacing

When we stand before a group of students and explain what we are trying to teach them, many youngsters can absorb the content only as quickly as we are able to relate it. Given different resources through which to learn, these students could achieve more rapidly. Others, of course, find that the flow of words is too rapid for them to fully understand. As teachers, we cover in one lesson what we believe the majority of students are capable of assimilating, but we proceed with the full knowledge that some students are capable of learning much more than they are being exposed to in a given time, while others are capable of learning only a fragment of what we are highlighting during that period. We understand that the lecture method is effective for only a percentage of students, but, for the most part, we have not replaced it with better techniques.

If we teach too much too quickly, we are bound to lose the less able student. If we keep a pace that is slow enough so that the less able student may keep abreast, we unwittingly irritate or bore the brighter youngster. If we try to vary the pace to provide interest, both groups may miss important learning elements during the presentation.

In contrast to a group lecture, Contract Activity Packages permit individual pacing so that students may learn as quickly or as slowly as they are able to master the material. In addition, youngsters are neither embarrassed because others grasp the content more quickly than they do nor bored because they must wait for selected classmates to catch up with them before the class is introduced to the next knowledge or skill area. Each learner works independently, but may, by choice, team up with classmates who can pace themselves similarly.

Varied Academic Levels

Whenever we address an entire class, instruction is, of necessity, geared to the academic level of the largest number of students present. We all know, however, that in every group some need to learn information in its simplest form while others are interested only when the concepts become complex and challenging. Selected students can hear something once and retain it, while others require extensive reinforcement before they are capable of either understanding or remembering. Those who learn easily in class are likely to be bored by the detailed repetition that others require; those who learn slowly may become frustrated by their inability to acquire the knowledge that some of their classmates do with ease. In contrast to a group lecture, Contract Activity Packages are designed so that students are able to function on the academic level most suitable to them and need not cope with concepts or facts that are otherwise inappropriate to their ability.

Independence

When we speak to a large group, students are dependent on us for their intellectual growth and stimulation. Further, each youngster is required to learn the same thing at the same time to the same extent and in the same way. Since learners differ from one another in ability, achievement, interests, and learning styles, their dependence on us as a primary source seriously limits the academic progress of some. Finally, despite our belief in ourselves as excellent teachers, it is important to recognize that some students learn better through a multimedia approach than they do from an articulate, knowledgeable adult, and that the large-group lecture does not meet their learning needs. Since nature endowed each person with unique sensory strengths and limitations, many students are able to learn more and learn it better through visual, tactual, or kinesthetic resources rather than through an auditory approach—which is what a lecture or discussion is.

Through the use of Contract Activity Packages, youngsters become personally responsible for learning what is required. They are given specific objectives and a choice of media resources through which they may learn. Although they are told exactly what they must learn, they are not told which resources contain the necessary answers. Because of their exposure to a variety of materials in their search for explicit information included in their objectives, students obtain much ancillary knowledge. Often the required concepts are included in several resources—thus providing multimedia repetition.

Moreover, since students may select the resources they use (from a list of approved ones), the self-selection factor improves their motivation[2] and permits them to work in ways in which they feel most comfortable. Self-pacing permits them to learn as quickly as they can, but well enough to retain what they have studied. As they become accustomed to exercising freedom of choice and assuming responsibility, they become increasingly independent of their teacher and learn to use resources to their advantage. They begin to recognize that they can learn easily and well by themselves, and gradually they develop sufficient confidence to move into new studies on their own. They eventually take pride in their ability to teach themselves, and, ultimately, they use the teacher as a guide and facilitator rather than as a "fountain of knowledge" from which to absorb information.

Teachers who believe that the greatest gift they can give to their students is a love of learning and the tools to teach themselves will adjust to their new roles gradually. Those who chose to teach for the self-gratification of having students serve as an admiring audience for their performances will need to identify the students who require an authority figure, who learn by listening, who are able to learn at the time of day when they are scheduled for classes, who can remain seated passively for the length of each class or subject period, and who are so motivated that they will learn merely because the teacher suggests or projects that it is important to do so.

Reduced Frustration and Anxiety

If education is important, as the compulsory education laws imply, everyone should become educated. If everyone should be educated, everyone should be encouraged to learn as well and as quickly as is possible—for that person. Since the majority of youngsters are neither gifted nor extremely "bright," imagine how discouraged they must feel every day of the week when they realize that they must use all their resources to live up to the teacher's expectations while a few of their classmates exert little effort and invariably appear to know all the answers.

Although some successfully hide their anxiety, many verbalize that they "don't like school" while others "drop out" even as they occupy their seats in the classroom. Despite the fact that both national and state commissions[3] have recommended the development of alternative programs that respond to "the great diversity of students and needs . . . within the schools,"[4] innovative or different approaches to learning are often suspect and are expected to continually produce higher academic achievement and more positive student attitudes than are evidenced in traditional educational settings.

Contract Activity Packages reduce student anxiety and frustration without requiring extensive change in the organization. They can be used in a self-contained classroom at any level and with most students. Youngsters are permitted to learn in ways that they find most amenable: by themselves, with a peer or two, in a small group, with the teacher, through resources of their choice, at their seats, or on the floor, and so on. It is important that rules be established that clearly indicate those behaviors that are acceptable and non-acceptable when students are permitted to learn through this method, and that these regulations are adhered to firmly. It is also important that students are trusted to proceed seriously and to accomplish their objectives. Youngsters who do not work effectively on their CAPs should be cautioned and advised that they will not be permitted to continue learning that way unless they achieve minimum grades on each examination related to their studies. Research has demonstrated that, in many cases, teachers are unable to identify the special needs of youngsters[5] but that when they do and teach the students the way they learn, student motivation and achievement increase significantly.[6] Obviously, when students want to achieve and when they do, their anxiety and frustration decrease.

Capitalizing on Individual Student Interests

All students must learn to read, to write, to express themselves well, and to compute. Beyond these "musts," there is no curriculum that every student everywhere should, of necessity, master. There is no need for every youngster to know of the rainfall in exotic places and to commit to memory foreign products, capital cities, rivers, and other such extraneous facts that comprise the required curriculum for many classes. It is equally ludicrous for every student to be required to study algebra, a foreign language, industrial arts, music appreciation, or many of the subjects in a standard curriculum. We understand that the intent of extensive exposure to a variety of different studies is to expand the horizons and interest of students—but the opposite often occurs. When youngsters have to take specific subjects without choice, they often become recalcitrant and negative.

Perhaps schools might experiment with a series of cluster subjects, such as those that are found in most curricula, and offer their students a choice of any four out of seven, or five out of eight. It is true that some students might never be exposed to social studies, or literature, or the arts, but we suggest that most would learn in depth the areas that they select to study. As Mager and McCann suggest, motivation increases with the amount of control that we exercise over what, when, and how we learn.[7]

If you believe that it is necessary for all students to learn the usual school curriculum, consider the things that we do not teach in school that touch their lives directly, such as divorce, pollution, racism, sex roles, poverty, the energy crisis, and inflation.[8] A Contract Activity Package can be used to introduce these and other topics of interest to those for whom they will have value. CAPs, therefore, will free you to direct your major energies toward (1) students who need direct interaction with you and (2) subjects that require mastery by all—reading, language and computational skills, and interpersonal values.

Learning Style Characteristics Responsive to Contract Activity Packages

Contract Activity Packages are responsive to most learning style characteristics, for they may be used flexibly with some students and with exacting structure for others, as described in the following examples:

1. If sound is needed, an earplug may be used to isolate radio or recorded music for those who benefit from it. If discussion is important, an instructional area (such as a learning station or interest center) can be established in a section of the room and blocked off by perpendicular items to provide an inner sanctum for its occupants and to protect their classmates from being distracted by movement or talk. Rules for discussion need to be set so that no one outside the instructional area should hear the words of anyone inside, but that is a management strategy that will be necessary whenever you begin to accommodate the classroom to individual learning styles. The youngster who requires silence can use another instructional area—the magic carpet—where no one may speak and where the adjacent dens or alcoves are used for essentially quiet activities.

2. When students are permitted to work on their CAP anywhere in the classroom as long as they work quietly, do not interrupt others, and respect the rules that have been established, they automatically adjust light, temperature, and design to their learning style characteristics.

3. The motivated, persistent, and responsible students should be given a series of objectives to complete, a listing of the resources that they may use to obtain information, suggestions for how and where to get help should they experience difficulty, and an explanation of how they will be expected to demonstrate their achievement of the objectives. They then should be permitted to begin working and to continue—with occasional spot-checking —until their task has been completed. The unmotivated, the less persistent, and those who tend to be irresponsible should be given only a few objectives,

the listing of resources that may be used, and suggestions for obtaining assistance when it is necessary. These youngsters, however, require frequent supervision and constant encouragement and praise for their progress. You will need to circulate among them, ask questions, check on their understanding of what they are doing, and comment favorably when you observe their effort. Were you to treat the motivated students in the same way, you would be interrupting their concentration and diverting them. But if you don't check on the unmotivated students when they have difficulty with an assignment, they become frustrated, involved in diversionary activities, or ''give up.''

4.   The CAP permits students to work either alone, with a friend or two, or as part of a team through the small-group activities that are included. Youngsters may also work directly with the teacher when difficult objectives require adult assistance.

5.   The resource alternatives section of the CAP includes auditory, visual, and tactual or kinesthetic resources, thus permitting students to learn through their strongest perceptual strength and to reinforce what they've learned through the next strongest sense. The CAP may be used anytime during the day or taken home for evening studies. Youngsters may snack on raw vegetables as they work if they feel they need to, and they also may take short breaks for relaxation—as long as they return to their objectives and continue working on them until they have been completed.

Case Studies Describing Students Whose Learning Styles Are Complemented by Contract Activity Packages

1.   Lisa, a fourteen-year-old junior high school student, is an outstanding artist. As soon as she completes her homework and required projects, she finds her way down to the art room to browse or continue with her newest creation. The art teacher does not have the time to teach Lisa when other classes are present, but she feels guilty because she knows that Lisa has free time, loves art, and remains in the area because she so enjoys working with the media. Miss Jones cannot, however, stop her teaching assignment to direct Lisa.

Students who are motivated and responsible may continue either academic or creative studies independently—through a Contract Activity Package.

2. Jimmy sat in bewilderment and anger. The teacher was dictating a series of Spanish words so quickly that there was no way that he could ever catch up. Had he been given more time to

think about each word as it was pronounced, he might have been able to recognize it and then write a synonym; but the pace at which Mr. Cimino was dictating was just too rapid for him.

Students who need to work more slowly than the members of their group will progress at their own pace and achieve successfully when using a Contract Activity Package.

3. Doug had no interest in anything other than the care and curing of animals. He wandered off his path to school whenever he spied a bird or insect and followed it with his eyes as far as possible. Wounded cats and stray dogs were his hobby, and the thought of an animal without a home brought tears to his eyes. Although Doug could read, his interest in the basal reader lasted for a sentence or two before his active mind drifted off into thoughts of where his pet hamster might escape to if it were freed from its cage or what might be happening to the sparrow that had raised its babies in his birdhouse last spring. He had little tolerance for any of the subjects that were taught in his class, and although he was not disruptive, he was gradually withdrawing into himself and becoming bored while his teacher became frustrated.

Students who cannot become interested in the required curriculum and who turn off while sitting in their seats, can master important skills and knowledge through topics that are interesting to them—through a Contract Activity Package.

4. Margaret was a straight A student who completed her assignments long before her classmates. She was not peer-oriented and did not enjoy tutoring slower youngsters. She was, however, an avid reader and was extremely interested in adventure stories that described interplanetary life. She had read every book on that subject in the school library and had, on occasion, rewritten the endings in creative plays or stories based on her understanding of conditions on other planets. Because of her interest in this area, she asked her teacher if she could learn more about the subject by attending a special exhibit on that theme at the planetarium.

Students who are academic achievers or who are interested in special areas of study may learn in-depth, advanced, extended, or creative aspects of that area either in school or at various other locations through a Contract Activity Package.

5. Every time Skip began to work by himself, he would begin to feel worried that he was not doing the correct assignment in the correct way and that he would not complete his work on time. His anxiety caused him to question his teacher repeatedly for directions, clarification, suggestions, or reactions.

Students who are unable to become sufficiently independent to work by themselves may use the small-group techniques in the Contract Activity Package to begin to achieve with selected classmates.

Basic Principles of Contract Activity Packages

A Contract Activity Package is an individualized educational plan that facilitates learning because it includes each of the following elements:

1. *Simply stated objectives that itemize exactly what the student is required to learn.*

Do you recall studying for a test in college and trying to determine the "important" items on which you might be tested? Much of the teaching at all levels is conducted in an atmosphere of mystery; we introduce many concepts, facts, and skills and then require students to intuit those items that, in our opinion, are worthy of commitment to memory and retention. This approach, though common, is not logical. If specific knowledge is worthwhile, we ought to indicate that to our students and then encourage them to learn those things so well that they retain them. Knowing what is expected is central to individual motivation.

Instead of continuing the pedagogical game of "I'll teach many things, and you try to guess which I'll include on the test!", we recognize that every student cannot learn everything that we teach—because of their individual ability, experience, interest, and learning style differences. We then diagnose each student to identify whether he or she is capable of learning many things or just a few things in one assignment (lesson, Contract Activity Package, program, or instructional package). Motivated, persistent, responsible students may be given a series of tasks to complete; their opposites should be given fewer tasks. Brighter students may be given a number of things to learn; slower achievers should be given shorter "prescriptions."

When we tell youngsters what they are expected to achieve, we have given them their objectives. When we also explain the ways in which they may demonstrate that they have mastered their objectives, we are giving them a statement that is called a "behavioral objective."

More information about how to write objectives for students will be included in the next section of this chapter.

When students are given simple statements that itemize those objectives for which they are responsible, they need not be concerned about everything and can focus on just the tasks that they must master. This freedom from unnecessary anxiety reduces their concern and tension and permits them to go ahead and learn the "important things"—that is, what is important to them.

2. *Multisensory resources that teach the information that the objectives indicate must be mastered.*

Students are given a list of available resources that they may use to learn the information required by their objectives. The resources should be multisensory: visual materials such as books, films, filmstrips, study prints, or transparencies; auditory materials such as tapes, records, cassettes, or movies; tactual materials such as task cards, learning circles, and games; and interesting kinesthetic learning experiences. The resources are suggested sources of information, but the students are free either to use them or to identify other materials through which they may learn. If students use resources that have not been listed in the Contract Activity Package, they must identify them by direct reference when demonstrating the knowledge they have gained. Because youngsters are free to select the materials through which they will learn, the choices are called "resource alternatives." It is important, of course, to help students to recognize their perceptual strengths so that they use materials that respond to their strongest sense to introduce information and materials that respond to their next strongest sense to reinforce what they've learned.

3. *A series of activities through which the information that has been mastered is used in a creative way.*

When we first became involved in individualizing instruction in 1967, we used Learning Activity Packages (LAPs) that included behavioral objectives, resources through which to learn (which were called "activities"), and a posttest by which to assess the student's progress. We found that students were able to examine their objectives, use the resources, acquire the necessary information, and pass the test at the end of the LAP. Three months later, however, their retention rate was approximately 58 percent.

When experimenting with alternatives to LAPs, we found that if we added two procedures to the existing system, we could increase student ability to remember information that had been learned by approximately 20 percent. The first was a series of activities in which students were required to use the information they had learned in a creative way. Based on Mager and McCann's studies completed in 1962,[9] we permitted students a choice (from among approved alternatives) of the activities they would complete. This section of the CAP is thus called "activity alternatives." The second section that tends to increase retention for peer-oriented students is called "reporting alternatives."

4. *A series of alternative ways in which creative activities developed by one student may be shared with one or more—but no more than six to eight—classmates.*

We found that when students engage in a creative activity they often want to share it with their peers. The sharing serves as either an introduction or a reinforcement of the material to the person who is being shown the activity, but it also provides the person who created it with reinforcement and a sense of accomplishment. This sharing—or reporting—increases retention of what has been learned, and, in addition, serves as a self-fulfilling experience for some.

5. *At least three small-group techniques.*

Individualization does not imply that children must work or learn in isolation. Rather, it suggests that each student's learning style be identified and that each learner be permitted to learn in ways that complement his or her style. Since many students prefer to work in small groups or in a pair,[10] and since others evidence this preference when their requirements become difficult, at least three small-group techniques (of the teacher's choice) are added to each Contract Activity Package so that sections of the CAP that are difficult may be attacked (and conquered) by a few students working together.

Although the small-group requirements are not mandated for every youngster, they do serve to act as an aid for students who find it difficult to complete intricate tasks or to learn difficult concepts by themselves.

6. *A pretest, a self-test, and a posttest.*

Each Contract Activity Package has a single test attached to it. This test may be used to assess the student's knowledge of the information required by the CAP's behavioral objectives before the CAP is assigned, so that students who have already mastered those concepts and skills need not be burdened with the same subject matter again.

The assessment device also may be used by the student to identify how much of the information required by the behavioral objectives he or she has already mastered and how much remains for the student to learn after he or she completes the CAP. Self-assesment builds "ownership" of the contract and its objectives.

Finally, you may use the same assessment device to test the student after the behavioral objectives have been mastered, the resources have been used, the activity alternatives have been completed and shared with selected classmates, the three small-group techniques have been done, and the self-test taken. You may, if you wish, develop three separate assessment devices, but since the test questions are directly related to the individual behavioral objectives, it is just as valuable to use the single test for all three situations. This approach establishes a pattern of revealing what is expected, removes the mystery, and builds motivation.

Step-by-step Guide to Designing a Contract Activity Package

The first Contract Activity Package that you design takes time because you must adopt several new techniques with which you may be relatively unfamiliar. The second CAP is not difficult to write at all, and by the time you embark on your third, you'll be assisting colleagues and administrators by explaining the process and the reasons for each stage.

Step 1   Begin by identifying a topic, concept, or skill that you want to teach.

There are two kinds of CAPs. The first, a curriculum CAP, covers a topic that you would like to teach all or most of the students in your class. The second, an individual CAP, deals with a topic in which only one (or a few) students might be interested. Because we are assuming that this is your first effort at CAP development, we suggest that you identify a topic that would be appropriate for most of your students. When you have completed this first CAP, you will have the skills to write as many as you wish—some for individuals, others for small groups—and the majority for use with an entire class.

Step 2   Write the name of the topic, concept, or skill that you have decided to teach as a title at the top of a blank sheet of paper.

Examples:

The First Thanksgiving

How Tall Are You In Metric Terms?

Colors: What They Do To and For Us

Ants

Step 3   List the things about this topic that you believe are so important that every student in your class should learn them. Then list the things about this topic that are important—but that slow achievers need not necessarily learn. Finally, consider the things about this topic that might appeal to special students, for example, the musically talented, the artistic, the traveler, the carpenter, the cook, and so on. List these special-interest items.

Examine your developing list of objectives. Be certain that the most important ones to be learned are placed first. These should be followed by items that are also of consequence but that everyone need not master. Finally, add the special items that you believe might be of interest to selected students.

All the most important items will become the required learnings for most of your students. Many of the secondary list of important items will be required of some, and some of the more difficult items will be required of a few advanced students. The way in which you assign the number of required objectives will help you to individualize the Contract Activity Package.

When the CAP is completed and ready for use, diagnose your students and assign the largest number of learning requirements to the high achievers. Remember that motivation is increased by options—always permit students some choice. For example, you might suggest that a very bright sixth grader master, ". . . any sixteen of the following nineteen objectives." A slower student in the same class might have a choice of ". . . the first seven and any additional five." Some teachers even try: "Complete any twelve of your choice." Another alternative would be, "Do any three in the first group, numbers 1–3 in the second group, and any two in the third group."

Step 4 Translate the important items into behavioral objectives.

When students are given a list of items that should be learned, these items are called objectives, and they become the students' short-term instructional goals. Since acquired information can be demonstrated in many ways, it is important that youngsters be given an idea of how they will be expected to demonstrate what they have learned. Recognizing individual differences, we acknowledge that people are capable of evidencing knowledge through different skills and talents. We therefore give students (1) a general indication of how they can verify mastery of their instructional objectives and (2) specific alternatives (a) to increase their motivation and (b) to capitalize on their strengths.

Years ago, Mager suggested that a behavioral objective include (1) an identification and name of the overall behavioral act, (2) the conditions under which the behavior was to occur, and (3) the criterion of acceptable performance.[11] After years of working with these objectives, we are convinced that when all three items are included, the objectives become too lengthy and complicated for most students to comprehend; are not individualized, and therefore do not respond to learning style, interest, ability levels, or talents; and are not used as efficiently or as humanistically as is possible.

Therefore, we suggest that behavioral objectives—which suggest the behaviors that may be used to demonstrate mastery of specific learning goals—be written in the following generalized way and that specific behaviors that may be used to demonstrate acquired knowledge or skills be optional through a series of activity alternatives.

Example:

Behavioral Objective
Explain why the Pilgrims came to the New World

This objective clearly indicates what must be learned (why the Pilgrims came to the New World), but it does not box learners into explaining in a specific way. Since why the Pilgrims came can be explained in many different ways, we give the students a choice of how they will show that they know the answer by listing a series of activity alternatives directly below the behavioral objective and permitting each individual to decide which of the activities he or she prefers.

Step 5   Design at least three or four activity alternatives for each behavioral objective (or for a group of related objectives) so that students may choose how they demonstrate that they have learned what their objectives require of them.

In effect, the activity alternatives permit students to select the conditions under which they will perform, or demonstrate their mastery.

Examples:

Behavioral Objective

Explain at least three (3) reasons why the Pilgrims came to the New World.[12]

Activity Alternatives

1.   With a group of your classmates dramatize (act out) at least three (3) reasons why the Pilgrims came to the New World.

2.   On a cassette, describe a character in a story about the Pilgrims that you read. State at least three (3) reasons that person had for coming to the New World.

3.   Write a story about the different things that happened to the Pilgrims before they were able to sail to the New World aboard the Mayflower. Explain why those things made the Pilgrims want to come to the New World.

Behavioral Objectives

1.   Describe at least three (3) new things the Pilgrims taught the Indians.

2.   Describe at least three (3) ways that the Indians taught the Pilgrims to survive.

3.   Describe at least three (3) new things the Indians taught the Pilgrims.

Activity Alternatives

1.   Write an original story describing how the Indians and the Pilgrims helped each other by teaching each other important new things.

2.   Keep a make-believe diary about your experiences as either an Indian or a Pilgrim living during the Pilgrims' first years in the New World. Explain at least three (3) things that each was able to teach the other.

3. Make an original filmstrip describing several ways in which the Indians and the Pilgrims helped each other by teaching each other.

Step 6 Create a reporting alternative for each of the activity alternatives that you have designed.

As indicated before, the activity alternative permits students a choice of how they will use the information they have learned so that it is reinforced. Once an activity has been completed, most students enjoy sharing their product with others. Sharing an activity achievement with others provides additional reinforcement for the person who developed it. In addition, it serves as either an introduction of new material or a repetition of previously studied material for the students who serve as the listeners, viewers, players, or participants. Furthermore, the sharing may be another way of demonstrating acquired knowledge or skill.

Example:

Behavioral Objective

State at least one (1) important thing about any eight (8) of the following people:

1. Myles Standish	7. Roger Williams
2. Squanto	8. John Alden
3. Massasoit	9. Priscilla Mullens Alden
4. John Carver	10. William Brewster
5. Samoset	11. Pocahontas
6. William Bradford	12. John Smith

If you can state one (1) thing about each of ten (10) of the above people, you are very, very special!

Activity Alternatives

1. Make a time line listing the dates and events in the lives of the eight (8) or ten (10) people that you choose.

2. Draw and then dress paper dolls as they would have been dressed had they been the people listed above.

3. Make up a poem or a song that tells at least one (1) important thing about the people you selected.

Reporting Alternatives

1. Mount the time line in our room and answer any questions your classmates or your teacher may ask.

2. Give a two-minute talk to three or four people telling them about the characters you drew.

3. Mount your poem or record your song. Ask a few of your classmates to write a reaction to it for your CAP folder.

4. Write an original story, play, or radio or television script that describes something about the people about whom you chose to learn.

5. If you can think of an activity that you would prefer to the ones listed above, write it on a piece of paper and show it to your teacher for possible approval.

4. Put on a radio or television show; play or rehearse the script with classmates and ask a few students to observe it and then comment in writing. Add their comments to your CAP folder.

5. If your original activity is approved, develop a reporting alternative that complements (matches) it.

What follows is a sample list of activity and reporting alternatives that may be used to develop options for all students. You will want to identify those activities that would be motivating for your students, adapt and rewrite them so that they are appropriate for the specific Contract Activity Package that you are designing, and use them as part of the choices you permit. They may also be used as activity cards (see Chapter 7) for placement at learning stations, interest centers, or other instructional areas.[13]

Activity Alternates

1. Make a miniature stage setting with pipe-cleaner figures to describe part of the information you learned about your topic.

2. Make a poster "advertising" the most interesting information you have learned.

3. Design costumes for people or characters you have learned about.

4. Prepare a travel lecture related to your topic.

5. Make a "movie" by drawing a series of pictures on a long sheet of paper fastened to two rollers. Write a script for it.

6. Describe in writing or on tape an interesting person or character that you learned about and dramatize something he or she did.

7. Write or tell a different ending to one of the events you read about.

Reporting Alternatives

1. Display the stage setting and figures and give a two-minute talk explaining what they represent and why you selected them.

2. Display the poster and give a two-minute talk explaining why you found the information interesting.

3. Describe to a group of classmates how you decided what the costumes should be, how you made them, and the people who would have worn them. You could also hold a fashion show with the help of friends.

4. Give the lecture before a small group of classmates. You may also tape-record it for others who are working on the same topic.

5. Show your movie to one or more small groups of classmates.

6. Ask a few classmates to tell you what they think of the person you portrayed.

7. After sharing your thoughts with a classmate or two, ask them to think of other ways the event could have ended.

8. Pantomine some information you found very interesting.

8. Let a few classmates try to guess what you are pantomiming.

9. Construct puppets and use them in a presentation that explains an interesting part of the information you learned. Have a friend photograph your presentation.

9. Display the pictures and the puppets.

10. Make a map or chart representing information you have gathered.

10. Display the map or chart and answer questions about it.

11. Broadcast a book review of your topic, as if you were a critic. Tape-record the review.

11. Permit others to listen and tell you if they would like to read the book, and why.

12. Make a clay, soap, or wood model to illustrate a phase of the information you learned.

12. Display the model and answer questions as a museum guide might.

13. Construct a diorama to illustrate an important piece of information.

13. Display the diorama and answer questions as an artist might.

14. Dress paper dolls as people or characters in your topic.

14. Give a two-minute talk about the doll characters.

15. Make a mural to illustrate the information you consider interesting.

15. Display the mural and answer questions that arise.

16. Build a sand-table setting to represent a part of your topic.

16. Explain the setting to other students. Ask them to evaluate your effort in a few short sentences.

17. Rewrite an important piece of information, simplifying the vocabulary for younger children.

17. Develop a project about the information with the children.

18. Make a time line, listing important dates and events in sequence.

18. Display the time line and be prepared to answer questions.

19. Write a song including information you learned.

19. Sing the song in person or on tape for a small group of students.

20. Make up a crossword puzzle.

20. Let other students try to complete it. Check and return their answers to them.

21. Make up a game using information from your topic.

21. Play the game with other members of your class.

22. Direct and participate in a play or choral speaking about your topic.

22. Present the dramatic or choral creation to a small group of classmates.

23. Write a script for a radio or television program; produce and participate in this program.

23. Present the program for a group of classmates.

24. Develop commentaries for a silent movie, filmstrip, or a slide showing on your topic. Use your own photographs or slides, if possible.

24. Present the program for a group of classmates.

25. With others, plan a debate or panel discussion on challenging aspects of your topic.

25. Hold the debate and participate in it.

26. Write a news story, an editorial, a special

26. Mount and display your writing. Ask

column, or an advertisement for the
school or class newspaper explaining
your views concerning any one aspect
of your topic.

three students to write "letters to the
editor" praising or chastising you as a
reporter.

27. Write an imaginary letter from one character to another. Tell about something
that might have happened had they
both lived at the time and place of your
topic.

27. Display the letter.

28. Make up tall tales about your topic.
Either write or tape-record at least two
of the tales you create. Illustrate them.

28. Permit others to react to them.

29. Keep a make-believe diary about your
memorable experiences as you lived
through the period concerned with your
topic.

29. Read a portion of your diary to some of
your classmates. See whether they can
identify the period concerned with the
topic. Add the diary to the resource
alternatives available for other people
who are studying the topic.

30. Try to find original manuscripts, old
page proofs, first editions of books, book
jackets, taped interviews with authors
or other interesting persons in the community, autographs of authors, or any
other documentation related to your
topic. If the material cannot be brought
to school, organize a small group trip
to visit the place where you found the
items.

30. Take the group trip or bring photographs and a description of the materials to class.

31. Document some original research you've
found on your topic using bibliographies,
footnotes, and quotations.

31. Submit the research to your teacher.

32. Search the library card catalog and
periodical index and list all the books
and articles concerned with your topic.

32. Add the list to the resource alternatives
for your topic.

Step 7 List all the resources that you can locate that students may use to
gain the information required by their behavioral objectives.

Try to find multisensory resources if they are available. Categorize
the materials under separate lists, for example, books, transparencies, tapes,
records, magazines, games, and, if you have them, programs, instructional
packages, task cards, or learning circles. Use these broad divisions as titles,
underline the title, and below it list the names of the resources that are available. Students may use additional materials if they wish, but they should
either show them to you or refer to them in their work. Because students
may select which resources they will use, these materials are called resource
alternatives. For examples, see the resource alternatives included in the
sample CAPs in this chapter.

Step 8   Add at least three small-group techniques to the developing Contract Activity Package.

Identify the most difficult objectives in your CAP. Develop a team learning to introduce those objectives that require in-depth knowledge, insight, or extensive explanation. Design a circle of knowledge to reinforce what you taught through team learning. Use any of the remaining strategies —such as brainstorming, group analysis, or case study to help peer-oriented youngsters to gain information. Circles of knowledge are simple to create; try a few. Team learnings require more time, but they are well worth the effort for they will enhance learning for many of your students and simultaneously free you to work directly with the ones who are authority-oriented and need your supervision and guidance. For examples, see the samples of small-group techniques included in Chapter 3 and in the CAPs in this chapter.

Step 9   Develop a test that is directly related to each of the behavioral objectives in your CAP.

An assessment instrument or exam that is directly related to stated objectives is called a "criterion referenced test." Questions for such a test are formed by either restating the objective or by phrasing it in a different way.

For example, if the behavioral objective was "List at least three (3) reasons why the Pilgrims left England," then the question on the examination should be "List at least three (3) reasons why the Pilgrims left England."

You may, of course, be creative in the way you test your students. For example, if the behavioral objective was "List the items that the Pilgrims were able to take aboard the Mayflower," you may phrase the test question in the same way or you could show an illustration of the Mayflower and several packages and provide some playful hints for your students—as Vivian Ricupero did in Exhibit 4-1.

Step 10   Design an illustrated cover for the Contract Activity Package. (For an example, see Exhibit 4-2.)

Step 11   Develop an informational top sheet.

On the page directly after the illustrated cover, provide information that you believe is important. Some items that may be included are:

- The name of the Contract Activity Package
- The student's name
- The student's class
- The objectives that have been assigned to or selected by that student
- The date that the CAP should be completed
- The date that selected parts of the CAP should be completed (for students in need of structure)

- A place for a pretest grade
- A place for a self-test grade
- A place for a final test grade
- The names of the classmates that may have worked on this CAP as a team
- Directions for working on or completing the CAP

Exhibit 4-1.   Sample Contract Activity Package Test.

List the items the Pilgrims were able to take aboard the Mayflower:

1. _____   6. _____

2. _____   7. _____

3. _____   8. _____

4. _____   9. _____

5. _____   10. _____

Step 12   Reread each of the parts of the Contract Activity Package to be certain that they are clearly stated, well-organized, in correct order, and grammatically written. Check your spelling and punctuation.

Exhibit 4-2.   Sample cover for a Contract Activity Package.

The First Thanksgiving

(You may color the illustration).

Step 13   Add illustrations to the pages so that the CAP is attractive and motivating.

Step 14   Duplicate the number of copies that you will need.

Step 15   Design a record-keeping form so that you know which students are using and have used the Contract Activity Package and how much of it they have completed successfully. (See Exhibits 4–3 and 4–4.)

Step 16   Try a CAP with those students who can work well with any three small-group techniques.

Be prepared to guide and assist the students through their first experience with a CAP. Establish a system whereby they can obtain assistance if they need your help. Placing an "I Need You" column on the chalkboard or on a chart and having youngsters sign up for help when they are stymied is usually effective. Direct them to place their names beneath the title and to return to their places until you are free to come to them. They should not interrupt you, but rather, they should busy themselves on other objectives or tasks—or get help from a classmate—until you can get to them.

Suggestions For Perfecting a Contract Activity Package

1.   Although it is not incorrect to repeatedly state: "You will be able to . . .", it does become repetitious and often provokes humor. It is suggested, therefore, that at the top of the behavioral objectives you write:

<u>Behavioral Objectives</u>

Example:

By the time you have finished this contract, you will be able to do each of the following things:

1.   Explain each of these words:
   (a)   dinosaur
   (b)   mammal
   (c)   archeology
2.   List at least five (5) man-eating animals that you have seen.
3.   Name three (3) prehistoric animals.

2.   Anytime that you use a number in the objectives, spell out the number, then, in parenthesis, write the numeral. This technique is used to accentuate the number for youngsters who may overlook that specific.

NAME: _____	CONTRACT: _____
	_____
	_____

OBJECTIVES	DATE COMPLETED	ACTIVITIES COMPLETED	GROUP TECHNIQUES COMPLETED
1.			
2.			
3.			
4.			
5.			
6.			
7.			
8.			
9.			
10.			
11.			
12.			
13.			
14.			
15.			
16.			

Exhibit 4-3. This form provides an overview of a middle school student's progress and is used with the contract system where students select their objectives from a list of enumerated options.[14]

```
┌─────────────────────────────────────────────────────────────┐
│                                                             │
│   CONTRACT                        DATE _____           │
│                                                             │
│                                                             │
│   My Tasks For The Day                                      │
│  ┌──────────────────────────────────────────────┬──────┐   │
│        1. Reading _____  ║        │
│        2. Math _____  ║        │
│        3. _____  ║        │
│        4. _____  ║        │
│        5. _____  ║        │
│                                                             │
│   My Choice For The Day                                     │
│                                                             │
│        1. _____  ║        │
│        2. _____  ║        │
│        3. _____  ║        │
│        4. _____  ║        │
│        5. _____  ║        │
│   I need help with: _____   │
│   I enjoyed: _____ because _____   │
│   _____   │
│                                                             │
│   SIGNED: _____   │
│                                                             │
│   Teacher's Comments: _____    │
│   _____   │
│   _____   │
│   _____   │
│   _____   │
│                                                             │
└─────────────────────────────────────────────────────────────┘
```

Exhibit 4-4.   One second grade teacher designed this self-scheduling form for use with the contract system she had adapted for her students. She was often amused at the reasons children stated for having enjoyed the various activities in which they had engaged. One youngster had enjoyed class because she had "beaten the boys." Another enjoyed math because he had "suddenly understood." A new child crossed out the section entitled "I enjoyed:" and wrote in "Nothing. This is an awful lot of work."[15]

Example:

"List at least three (3) tools that archeologists use in their work."

3.   Use complete and grammatically correct sentences. Do not capitalize words that should not be capitalized. Contracts should be excellent examples of good usage, spelling, and grammar for students. If you wish to emphasize a word, (for example, a word new to the student's vocabulary), underline the word.

4.   Use the phrase "at least" before any number of required responses to motivate selected students to achieve more than is required.

Example:

List at least five (5) words that are generally associated with the world during the time when dinosaurs lived. Can you think of a sixth (6th)?

5.   Be certain that the objective does not become an activity. The objectives state what the student should learn. The activity makes the student use the information that has been learned in a creative way.

Example:

Explain what a dinosaur looks like in any of the following ways:
a.   Draw a picture of a dinosaur.
b.   Make a clay model of a dinosaur.
c.   Write a short paragraph about how dinosaurs looked.
d.   Make up a poem describing what a dinosaur looked like.

6.   For each small-group technique, begin at the top of a new page. Name the technique and then number through six and place lines on which the students' names may be written. Do the same for the recorder.

Example:

TEAM LEARNING:

Why The Pilgrims Came to the New World

1. _____   4. _____

2. _____   5. _____

3. _____   6. _____

Recorder:_____

7. In the reporting alternatives, never ask a youngster to report to the entire class. Have an activity shared with one, two, or a few classmates, or the teacher. It is difficult for a student to hold the entire class's attention; and if one is given the opportunity, it must be offered to all. Instead, have the students report to a small group. If the activity is outstanding, ask the student to share it with a second small group. You either may assign students or ask for volunteers to listen to the report.

8. The title of each of the major parts of the CAP should be underlined, for example, Behavioral Objectives or Activity Alternatives.

Sample Contract Activity Packages

Following are several samples of Contract Activity Packages developed by teachers and used successfully at different levels with students whose learning styles matched the approach of this method.

Primary Level: Plants[16]

When Contract Activity Packages are used with young children who are not yet reading well, each section should be (1) typed on a primary (large print) typewriter, (2) printed on large oaktag or poster board, (3) displayed prominently in a section of the room or in an instructional area such as a learning station, and (4) read onto a cassette so that the youngsters can hear the CAP sections being read while they read the words (follow the tape and the text simultaneously).

For primary pupils it is important to add tactual games, such as an electroboard, a learning circle, or task cards to the resource alternative list (see Chapter 7). In the example that follows (Exhibit 4–5), cut-out parts of the plant that are labled, color-coded, and attractive would be particularly effective if boxed with directions and used as a reinforcement.

If this is your pupils' first experience with CAPS, assign only one or two objectives to slower youngsters. Give them a few opportunities to begin to feel secure with this method before deciding whether it is effective for each individual. When it stimulates certain children and provokes their thinking and knowledge skills, continue its use. When you find that selected students do not respond well to it (even if they are permitted to work with one or two classmates), set aside the CAP system *for those youngsters* and introduce instructional packages to them. The latter method is potent with students who require multisensory resources and structure, are self-oriented (rather than peer-oriented or teacher-oriented), and learn essentially through tactual or kinesthetic means.

The Contract Activity Package is most effective with youngsters who are creative, peer-oriented, in need of mobility and interaction, and who do not enjoy too much structure. You will note that it is an especially well-organized system, although it does permit flexible learning arrangements and options for students.

Exhibit 4-5.   Sample primary level Contract Activity Package: Plants

CONTRACT ACTIVITY PACKAGE
PLANTS

NAME:_____TIME:_____

OBJECTIVES:_____

PLANTS

By the time you complete this contract you will be able to do at least _____ of the following activities: (Listen to the tape on *Plants* as you read about the things you will learn and do.)

What you can Learn to Do*

A.   List the four (4) parts of a plant.

Activity Alternatives

(Do Activity 1 and three (3) others.)

1.   Take apart a small plant and see what grows above the dirt and what grows below the dirt. Then draw a plant and label the parts.

2.   Describe the parts of the plant on a cassette tape.

3.   Make a flower plant collage with material scraps and label each of the parts.

4.   Play a record that has pretty music, and pretend that you are a flower growing.

5.   Make tissue paper flowers. Ask _____ to show you how.

6.   Write or tape a haiku poem. (See task card.)

7.   Draw the four (4) parts of a plant in the sand.

Reporting Alternatives

(Do the matching Reporting Alternatives.)

1.   Mount the drawing on the bulletin board.

2.   Play the tape to three (3) other children.

3.   Mount the collage on the bulletin board.

5.   Ask two (2) friends if they can guess what you are doing.

5.   Show other children how to make the parts of a paper flower.

6.   Recite your poem to three (3) friends.

7.   Show two (2) friends how to draw flowers in the sand.

What You Can Learn to Do

B.   List four (4) things that are needed to help a plant grow.

C.   Show two (2) ways you can start a plant to grow.

D.   Name at least three (3) places where you might find plants in your neighborhood.

E.   Look at at least four (4) different kinds of fruit seeds and describe the kind of plant that would grow from each seed.

*In this CAP for primary youngsters the behavioral objectives are called, "What You Can Learn to Do."

Activity Alternatives

(Do Activities 1 and 2 and two (2) others)

1. Plant some lima bean seeds, radish seeds, or any type of seed you wish in two plastic cups filled with soil. Take care of one and put the other one into the closet. Wait two weeks.

2. Visit a park, a neighbor's garden, or the florist (with someone older) and talk to the people about how they take care of plants.

3. Make a picture-graph showing how many inches tall the plant grew in two weeks.

4. Take a piece of plant from the classroom shelf and place it into a glass of water. Look at it everyday.

5. Make a covered terrarium from small plant cuttings brought from home. Record a cassette tape about how you take care of the terrarium.

6. Put a stalk of celery into a cup of water that has food coloring in it. Describe what happens onto a cassette tape.

7. Carefully break or cut open fruit and take out the seeds. Put the different kinds of seeds into plastic bags and make a chart with them. Cut out pictures of fruit from magazines (or draw them) and place them next to the matching seed bags.

Reporting Alternatives

(Do the matching Reporting Alternatives)

1. Observe the two (2) soil cups with three (3) friends and compare what happened.

2. Try to get some other children interested in growing plants by talking about what the florist or gardener told you.

3. Show and explain the graph to three (3) friends. Display it on the bulletin board.

4. Show and explain to three (3) friends what happened and how this section becomes a new plant.

5. Play the tape to two (2) friends and one (1) parent.

6. Play the tape to two (2) friends and a sister or a brother.

7. Display the chart and ask some children if they know what kind of plant will grow from the different kinds of seeds.

What You Can Learn to Do

F. Tell what happens to the leaves on a tree during summer, fall, winter, and spring.

Activity Alternatives

(Do any two (2) Activity Alternatives)

1. Draw a picture of what a tree would look like in the summer, fall, winter, and spring.

2. Cut and paste magazine pictures that show how trees look in the four different seasons.

3. Dramatize how a tree feels in the summer, fall, winter, and spring.

Reporting Alternatives

(Do one (1) Reporting Alternative)

1. Mount the drawing on the bulletin board.

2. Mount your collage on the bulletin board.

3. In the little theater area, show three (3) classmates how a tree feels during the

different seasons. Can you get someone to take your picture as you are acting? If so, please show me your photographs after they have been developed.

Resource Alternatives

Films

1. Growth of Flowers, Coronet.
2. How Does a Garden Grow? Film Associates of California.
3. The Tree, Dimension Films.

Filmstrips

1. Children in Spring, E. B. F.
2. How Do Plants Get where They Grow? Filmstrip House.

Books

1. Bethers, Ray. *How Does It Grow?* New York: St. Martin's, 1963.
2. Collier, Ethel. *Who Goes There in My Garden?* New York: William R. Scott, 1963.
3. Eggleston, J.S. *About Things That Grow.* Chicago: Melment, 1965.
4. Krauss, Ruth. *The Growing Store.* New York: Harper, 1947.
5. Simon, Norma. *Tree for Me.* Philadelphia: Lippincott, 1956.
6. Tresselt, A.R. *Under the Trees and through the Grass.* New York: Lothrop, Lee & Shepard, 1962.
7. Udry, Janice May. *A Tree Is Nice.* New York: Harper & Row, 1956.
8. Walters, Marguerite. *See How It Grows.* New York: Grosset & Dunlap, 1954.
9. Watson, J.W. *Wonders of Nature.* New York: Golden Press, 1962.
10. Webber, I.E. *Up Above and Down Below.* New York: William R. Scott, 1963.
11. White, R. *Growing Plants.* New York: Primary Press, 1973.

When you choose a book, you may also take its matching tape to help you read all the words.

<u>Records</u>

1. *The Carrot Seed.*
2. *2001 Prelude.*

<u>Games</u>

1. Plant puzzle.
2. Name the missing part: (One child takes away a part of the plant game; the other child must guess which part is missing.)

<u>Small-group Activities</u>

TEAM LEARNING

Team members:

1. _____   4. _____

2. _____   5. _____

3. _____   6. _____

Recorder:_____

(You may use the tape recorder to record your names and answers.)

Read *The Carrot Seed* as you listen to *The Carrot Seed* record.

A. Name at least three (3) things that the boy had to do to make his carrot grow.

1. _____

2. _____

3. _____

How about one more!

4. _____

B. Why did his mother, father, and older brother say, "I'm afraid it won't come up!"?

_____

_____

_____

_____

ROLE-PLAYING

Go to the little theater area to put on a performance.

Three (3) children will be the actors. One child will play the role of a farmer, one child will play the role of a park garden maintenance worker, and one child will play the role of a florist.

1. Act out what the farmer and the gardener would do if there were no rain for a long time. Let each person explain why rain is important for plants.

2. Act out what the farmer and the gardner would do if there were no sun for a long time. Let each person explain why sun is important for plants.

3. Act out what the florist would have to do if he needed many new plants. He should explain how to start new plants.

CIRCLE OF KNOWLEDGE

Group Members:

1. _____   4. _____

2. _____   5. _____

3. _____   6. _____

Recorder:_____

(You may use the tape recorder to record your names and answers.) In three (3) minutes, say into the tape recorder any words that you can think of that have to do with growing plants. Set the timer for three (3) minutes and stop when the time is up.

What Have You Learned?

(Test directions and questions should be recorded on tape.)

1. Name four (4) parts of a plant.
2. What is the name of the part of a plant that grows under the soil?
3. Name three (3) things that help a plant to grow.
4. Name two (2) ways to help a new plant to begin to grow.
5. Name three (3) places where you can find plants in your neighborhood.
6. What happens to the leaves on the trees in the summer, fall, winter, and spring?
7. What kind of plant will you get from a radish seed?—a lemon seed?—and an apple seed?

Another way of using a Contract Activity Package with primary students was suggested by faculty members of the Westorchard School in Chappaqua, New York (see Exhibit 4–6). Youngsters call this CAP either the "man" or "clown"[17] because of its shape when filled in, colored, and joined together on a bulletin board or suspended from overhead with yarn. The finished product responds to all the sections of a CAP, but the headings are worded simply for younger children. When finished, a student signs his or her name and gains in self-image as he or she sees it displayed.

So that young readers can easily read the text on the clown, it is recommended that the clown be constructed with the following dimensions: head, 8″ × 5¾″; torso, 4½″ × 7″; hands, 4¼″ (at the widest point) × 3″; the area in which the legs are drawn, 4½ × 7″. When the parts of the clown are assembled, the overall dimensions will be about 20″ × 13½″.

Elementary Level: Ants[18]

Contract Activity Packages are used to teach both a standard curriculum and one that is interesting to only selected students. If you can get your colleagues to develop a "bank" of these educational plans, you (and they) will be able to borrow ones that appeal to a variety of youngsters. Adaptation of an existing CAP is easy and really pays off in terms of increased student motivation and achievement.

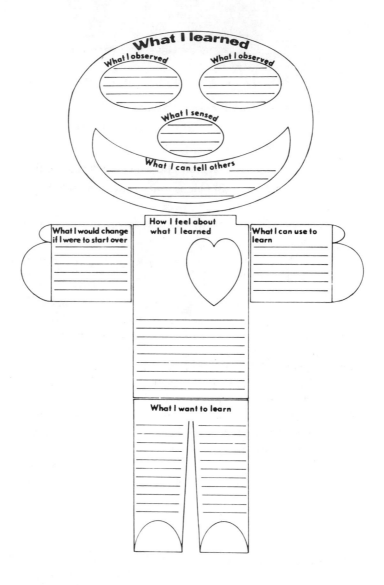

What I learned

What I observed

What I observed

What I sensed

What I can tell others

How I feel about
what I learned

What I would change
if I were to start over

What I can use to
learn

What I want to learn

Exhibit 4-6.   The Clown-man Contract
Activity Package.

This Contract Activity Package (Exhibit 4–7) was designed for children between the ages of eight and eleven. Most of the students would be assigned Objectives 1 through 6, with allowances made for those who usually experience difficulty with a new topic, method, or experience. The highly achieving children would also have a choice from among Objectives 7 through 11. A grade of 90 percent on the final examination would be expected of each learner—but each would be tested only on the objectives actually assigned or selected.

Despite its length, this CAP has been stimulating to many different kinds of students. Although shorter versions and mini-CAPs are easier to use with younger students or slow achievers, by selecting only those objectives and related resource and reporting alternatives that are appropriate to each student, you can, in effect, individualize the use of this educational plan.

Exhibit 4-7. Sample Elementary Level Contract Activity Package: Ants

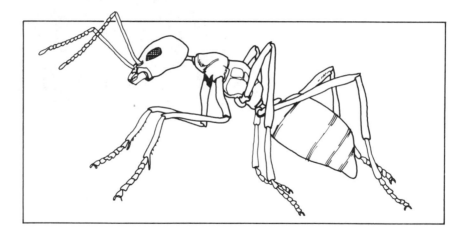

My Contract Activity Package on:

ANTS

Name:_____

Objectives Completed:_____

_____

_____

_____

Date received:_____

Date Completed:_____

Behavioral Objectives

Complete objectives_____through_____and any other_____.

Objective 1

Describe the different stages an ant goes through before it is an adult. Do at least one (1) of the following:

Activity Alternatives	Reporting Alternatives
1. Make a rolled paper movie about the stages of an ant's life.	1. Show your movie to a small group. Answer their questions.
2. Pretend you are an egg that was just hatched. Write a story of how you went through the various stages of development.	2. Read your story to several of your classmates.
3. Make a mobile of the stages of an ant's life.	3. Show your mobile to several of your classmates and then mount it in your room.

Objective 2

Given a drawing of an ant, you will be able to identify the following :

a. antenna
b. head
c. thorax
d. abdomen

e. compound eye
f. foreleg
g. middle leg
h. hind leg

Do at least one (1) of the following:

Activity Alternatives

1. Make up a crossword puzzle using the vocabulary words you have learned.

2. Make a picture dictionary using the vocabulary words. Add to your dictionary any new words you find.

3. Prepare an overhead transparency showing the body parts of an ant.

Reporting Alternatives

1. Make copies of the crossword puzzle and let other students try to complete it. Check and return their answers to them.

2. Share your picture dictionary with a friend, and see if your friend can tell what the terms are from looking at the pictures.

3. Show the transparency to a group of children and explain the body parts.

Objective 3

Name the three (3) types of ants that make up an ant colony. Be certain to describe the special job each does.

Do at least two (2) of the following:

Activity Alternatives

1. Make a drawing for a U.S. postage stamp honoring one (1) of the three (3) types of ants in an ant colony. Paste it to an envelope of suitable size that you've made.

2. Make a diorama showing the three (3) types of ants. Be certain to include their special jobs.

3. Make a two-minute tape recording describing the different types of ants and their special jobs.

Reporting Alternatives

1. Put your envelope and stamp on display. Explain to two (2) other classmates why you chose to honor this type of ant.

2. Show your diorama to several of your classmates. Place your diorama on display for others to see.

3. Ask two other students who are working on the same topic to listen to the tape.

Objective 4

Describe what life is like in an ant colony. Tell about some of the interesting things that happen there.

Do at least one (1) of the following:

Activity Alternatives	Reporting Alternatives
1. Make puppets and scenery for a puppet show about "A Day in the Life of an Ant."	1. Present your puppet show to a small group of your classmates.
2. Paint a mural showing some of the interesting things that happen in an ant colony.	2. Display and explain your mural to four (4) other students.
3. Make your own ant colony. Instructions are included in this contract. See Worksheet 1.	3. Explain how you made your ant colony. Answer any questions your small group may have. Display your ant colony for others to see.

Objective 5

Tell at least five (5) ways ants and people are similar. If you can name more, you will show your superior knowledge.

Do one (1) of the following:

Activity Alternatives	Reporting Alternatives
1. Plan a picture demonstration showing how ants are like people (live together, work together.)	1. Show the picture demonstration to two (2) children. Answer questions that may arise.
2. Write a poem comparing ants with people.	2. Share your poem with three (3) children.
3. Organize a group to pantomime the ways ants and people are alike.	3. Let a small group of three (3) to five (5) children try to guess what you are pantomiming.

Objective 6

Some ants have special talents enabling them to perform tasks like those of dairy farmers, warriors, harvesters, mushroom growers, or weavers. Choose at least three (3) of these ants and describe their special talents. Be certain to tell if they look different because of the kind of work they do.

Do at least two (2) of the following:

Activity Alternatives	Reporting Alternatives
1. Make a game, "Who Am I?" Write as many clues as you can for identifying the different kinds of worker ants without giving away the answers.	1. Have a small group play the game with you. Show another group how to make a similar game.
2. Prepare a bulletin board with pictures of worker ants and their special talents.	2. Explain your bulletin board to two (2) or three (3) others. Put your bulletin board on display.
3. Make a miniature stage setting with clay	3. Display the stage setting and ant figures

figures to describe worker ants and their talents.

and give a two-minute talk explaining them (what they do, why you selected them, and so forth).

Objective 7

List at least three (3) ways the formica rufa ant is useful to human beings. You're super if you can think of more!

Do at least one (1) of the following:

Activity Alternatives

1. Write a script for a radio program interviewing a formica rufa ant on how it is useful to human beings.

2. Design your own activity alternative. (Ask the teacher's approval).

3. Make a scrapbook showing how the formica rufa ant is useful to human beings.

Reporting Alternatives

1. Produce and present the radio program for a group of classmates and the teacher.

2. Demonstrate your new activity alternative to interested students (as well as to the teacher).

3. Display the scrapbook. Ask at least two (2) classmates to comment on it in writing.

Objective 8

You will be able to name the two (2) stomachs of an ant and describe how the ant uses each.

Do one (1) of the following:

Activity Alternatives

1. Prepare a tape with yourself as the guide and conduct a tour through the two stomachs of the ant. Be certain to tell us the name of each stomach, what happens there, and how the ant uses each.

2. Pretend that you are a scientist, and with the aid of a poster or transparency, prepare a lesson on "The Two Stomachs of an Ant."

3. Make a clay, soap, or wood model of the two stomachs of the ant.

Reporting Alternatives

1. Play the tape to several of your classmates. Be prepared to answer any questions they may have.

2. Present your lesson to several classmates. Ask them some questions and be prepared to answer any they may have.

3. Display the model and answer questions as a lecturer might.

Objective 9

Describe the compound eye of an ant, telling:

a.   what it looks like,

b.   how it works, and

c.   how well the ant can see.

Do at least one (1) of the following:

Activity Alternatives	Reporting Alternatives
1. Pretend you are an eye doctor and examine the eyes of several ants with a magnifying glass. Make a picture chart of what you see.	1. Share the results of your examination with several classmates. Mount your picture chart on the bulletin board.
2. Ants and other insects can see almost all the way around them. How far can you see? Try the experiment on Worksheet 2. Write the results.	2. Try this experiment with a small group of classmates. Be prepared to answer any questions they may have.

Objective 10

You will be able to tell the secret of the ant's "kiss."
Do at least one (1) of the following:

Activity Alternatives	Reporting Alternatives
1. Write a short newspaper article telling about the ant's "kiss" and how you discovered its secret.	1. Share your article with three (3) of your classmates.
2. Draw a picture of the ant's kiss on a piece of oaktag, twelve times eighteen (12 X 18).	2. Explain your picture to a small group and be able to answer any questions.
3. Write a two-minute talk about the secret of the ant's kiss.	3. Give your talk to four (4) others. See if they understand the secret of the kiss.

Objective 11

Tell at least five (5) reasons for the great number of ants that exist. You're an expert if you can name more.
Do at least one (1) of the following:

Activity Alternatives	Reporting Alternatives
1. Write a collection of poems explaining the reasons for the great number of ants that exist. Draw pictures for your poems. Put them into a booklet. Make a cover for the booklet and write an introduction.	1. Read two (2) of your poems to some of your classmates. Display your booklet.
2. Write a news story about an imaginary attack by driver ants of Africa. Make a large diagram of the attack.	2. Tell your story to a small group as if you were a TV newscaster. Refer to your diagram as you speak.
3. Write questions on the reasons for the great number of ants and what is being done to keep them under control. Organize a panel participation program.	3. Present the panel participation program to a small group in class.

Resource Alternatives

Books

1.	Bronson, W.	*The Wonderworld of Ants*
2.	Chauvin, Remy.	*The World of Ants*
3.	Cook, Thomas	*Ants of California*
4.	Costello, David	*The World of the Ants*
5.	Creighton, William	*The Ants of North America*
6.	Crompton, John	*Ways of the Ant*
7.	Doering, Harald	*An Ant is Born*
8.	Forel, Auguste	*Ants and Other Insects*
9.	George, Jean	*All Upon a Sidewalk*
10.	Goetsch, Wilhelm	*Ants*
11.	Goetsch, Wilhelm	*The Ants*
12.	Gregg, Robert	*Ants of Colorado*
13.	Harpster, Hilda	*The Insect World*
14.	Haskins, Caryl	*Of Ants and Men*
15.	Hope, Alice	*Biography of an Ant*
16.	Hutchins, Ross	*The Ant Realm*
17.	Hutchins, Ross	*Insect Builders and Craftsmen*
18.	Lavine, Sigmund	*Wonders of the Anthill*
19.	Mason, Herbert	*The Fantastic World of Ants*
20.	McCook, Honry	*The Ant Communities and How They are Governed*
21.	Michener, C. D.	*American Social Insects*
22.	Morley, Derek	*Ant World*
23.	Myrick, Mildred	*Ants Are Fun*
24.	Newman, Leonard	*Ants from Close Up*
25.	Norsgaard, Ernestine	*Insect Communities*
26.	Pallister, John	*The Insect World*
27.	Pickering, Peggy	*All about Ants*
28.	Pitt, Valerie	*A Closer Look at Ants*
29.	Schneirla, T.	*Army Ants*
30.	Schoenknecht, Charles A.	*Ants*
31.	Shuttlesworth, Dorothy E., and Su Zan N. Swain	*The Story of Ants*
32.	Simon, Hilda	*Exploring the World of Social Insects*

33. Smith, M. R.   *House-infesting Ants of the Eastern United States*

34. Wasman, Eric   *Psychology of Ants and Higher Animals*

35. Wheeler, William   *Ants: Their Structure, Development and Behavior*

Films

1. *Ant Colony through the Year*
2. *Ants—Backyard Science*
3. *Ants—A Social Insect*
4. *Insect Collecting*
5. *Insect Mounting and Preserving*

Games

1. *Cootie*   Schaper Mfg. Co., Minneapolis, Minn.
2. *Giant Ant Farm*   Childcraft Education Corp., Edison, N.J.

Teacher-made Resources

1. Worksheets
2. Task cards
3. Charts, pictures, and transparencies in the classroom, as well as in books and sources within the school and district libraries, may be used.

Small-group Activities

TEAM LEARNING

Team Members:

1. _____ 4. _____

2. _____ 5. _____

3. _____ 6. _____

Recorder:_____

"THE ANT AND THE CRICKET"

A silly young cricket, accustomed to sing
Through the warm, sunny months of gay summer and spring,
Began to complain, when he found that at home
His cupboard was empty and winter was come.
    Not a crumb to be found
    On the snow-covered ground;
    Not a flower could he see;
    Not a leaf on a tree;
"Oh, what will become," says the cricket, "of me?"
At last by starvation and famine made bold,
All dripping with wet and all trembling with cold,
Away he set off to a miserly ant,
To see if, to keep him alive, he would grant
    Him shelter from rain;
    A mouthful of grain
    He wished only to borrow,
    He'd repay it tomorrow;
If not, he must die of starvation and sorrow.
Says the ant to the cricket, "I'm your servant and friend,
But we ants never borrow, we ants never lend;
But tell me, dear sir, did you lay nothing by
When the weather was warm?" Said the cricket, "Not I.
    My heart was so light
    That I sang day and night,
    For all nature looked gay."
    "You sang, sir, you say?
Go then," said the ant, "and dance winter away."
Thus ending, he hastily lifted the wicket
And out of the door turned the poor little cricket.
Though this is a fable, the moral is good;
If you live without work, you must live without food.

                                         Unknown Author

Assignment

1. Why do you think this cricket is silly and young?

_____

_____

2. What are some of the phrases in the poem that tell you that the cricket is very hungry?

a. _____

b. _____

c. _____

d. _____

e. _____

3. What does the phrase ". . . famine made bold" mean?_____

_____

_____

4. After he heard that the cricket sang all spring and summer, what advice did the ant give the cricket for the winter?_____

_____

_____

5. What do you think the cricket should have done during spring and summer?_____

_____

_____

6. Do you think the ant had a right to be "miserly"? Explain your answer._____

_____

_____

7. Write a short group poem explaining what the cricket might do if he were given a second chance.

_____

_____

_____

_____

_____

_____

8.   This poem is a "fable." It is a story told in a roundabout way. The story is a mixture of wisdom and make-believe that teaches a lesson. What do you think is the lesson of this fable?_____

_____

_____

9.   If you would like to read more fables, you can get any of the following books:

Jacobs, John J., ed. *The Fables of Aesop.* New York: Macmillan, 1964.

Jones, Vernon, ed. *Aesop's Fables.* New York: Doubleday, 1912.

McKendry, Joseph, ed. *Aesop Five Centuries of Illustrated Fables.* New York: The Metropolitan Museum of Art, 1964.

Parker, Willis L., ed. *The Fables of Aesop.* New York: Little & Ives, 1931.

CIRCLE OF KNOWLEDGE

Circle Members:

1.   _____   4.   _____

2.   _____   5.   _____

3.   _____   6.   _____

Recorder:_____

In five (5) minutes, list the many ways that ants are harmful to people.

CIRCLE OF KNOWLEDGE

Circle Members:

1. _____   4. _____

2. _____   5. _____

3. _____   6. _____

Recorder:_____

In ten (10) minutes, list the many ways that ants are helpful to people.

ROLE-PLAYING

Environmentalist_____

Farmer_____

Council member_____

Member of the community_____

A town council meeting is in progress. Many members of the community are disturbed about the insecticides that are being used by the farmers to control the fire ants that are destroying crops. By role-playing, demonstrate how each of the above listed persons might explain and defend his or her position.

WORKSHEET 1

A Home for Ants

You will need a quart-size jar, a pan of water, some thin cloth, some black paper, some rubber bands, and some soil.

1. Fill the glass jar with loose soil to about two (2) inches from the top.

2. Place the glass jar in a pan of water to keep the ants from escaping. Have a thin piece of cloth ready to use as a cover.

3. Now dig up an ant colony from an anthill. Be certain to get a queen ant, which is larger than the other ants. You may have to dig down deep to get the queen. Try to get some eggs and a pupa, too.

4. Put the colony into the glass jar. Stretch the cloth across the top of the jar and fasten it in place with a rubber band.

5. Ants like to live in dark places, so wrap a piece of black paper around the jar; otherwise the ants will build their tunnels deep inside the jar where you can't see them. Keep the paper around the jar except when actually observing the ants.

6. Feed the ants a few grains of sugar each week. The sugar grains can be sprinkled over the soil at the top of the jar.

7. Keep the soil moist, but don't soak it.

8. Keep a record of what you see.

WORKSHEET 2

Experiment: How Far Around Can You See?

1. Look at something straight in front of you. Don't move your head or your eyes.

2. Stretch your right arm straight out in front of you.

3. Wiggle your fingers. Can you see them wiggle?

4. Now move your arm a little to the right. Keep moving your arm to the right. When do you stop seeing your fingers?

5. Do the same with your left arm.

6. Then move one arm up slowly, until you can't see it.

7. Then move it down lower and lower.

8. How far can you see up, down, and to each side?

9. Record what you have learned.

WORKSHEET 3

Find the Parts of an Ant

b	o	r	c	a	f	o	r	e	l	e	g	t
m	a	l	o	n	e	c	t	o	z	u	n	k
r	n	d	m	l	u	e	b	c	h	i	e	d
w	t	s	p	g	h	d	a	e	h	o	m	r
x	e	a	o	t	v	u	l	t	a	r	o	p
b	n	o	u	e	h	t	h	y	c	o	d	a
i	n	f	n	j	i	o	l	p	q	r	b	s
m	a	i	d	b	n	l	r	e	c	r	a	t
s	t	i	e	o	d	y	r	a	l	g	w	k
g	l	u	y	w	l	s	r	o	x	n	g	l
c	h	g	e	l	e	l	d	d	i	m	o	l
a	t	e	f	u	g	d	e	l	i	b	i	e

antenna
head
thorax
abdomen
compound eye
foreleg
middle leg
hind leg

WORKSHEET 3

Answer Key

b	o	r	c	a	f	o	r	e	l	e	g	t
m	a	l	o	n	e	c	t	o	z	u	n	k
r	n	d	m	l	u	e	b	c	h	i	e	d
w	t	s	p	g	h	d	a	e	h	o	m	r
x	e	a	o	t	v	u	l	t	a	r	o	p
b	n	o	u	e	h	t	h	y	c	o	d	a
i	n	f	n	j	i	o	l	p	q	r	b	s
m	a	i	d	b	n	l	r	e	c	r	a	t
s	t	i	e	o	d	y	r	a	l	g	w	k
g	l	u	y	w	l	s	r	o	x	n	g	l
c	h	g	e	l	e	l	d	d	i	m	o	l
a	t	e	f	u	g	d	e	l	i	b	i	e

WORKSHEET 4

Jumble

The letters of these crazy words are all mixed up. To play the game, put them back into the right order so that they make real words. Write the letters of each real word under each crazy word.

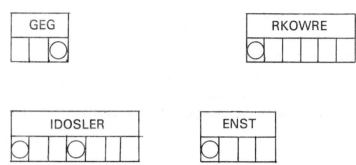

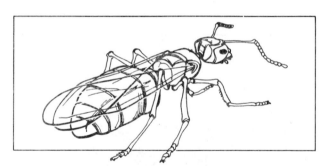

The queen ant must lose these, before she can start her colony.

You are now ready to solve the jumble. Study the picture for a hint. Then play with the letters in the circles. You'll find that you can put them into order so that they make your answer.

Print Your Answer Here:

Answer (hold up to mirror):

Answer: wings   nest   soldier   worker   egg

SELF-ASSESSMENT TEST

1.   Name the different stages an ant goes through before it is an adult. Write at least two (2) sentences describing each stage.

_____

_____

_____

_____

2.   Look at the drawing of the ant. Label the following parts:

a.   antenna   e.   compound eye

b.   head   f.   foreleg

c.   thorax   g.   middleleg

d.   abdomen   h.   hind leg

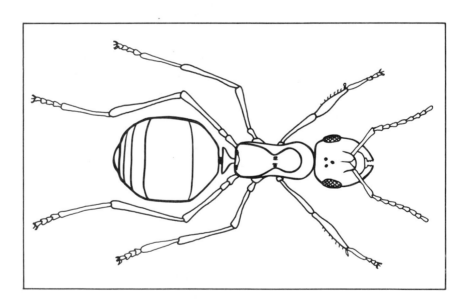

3.   Name the three (3) types of ants that make up an ant colony. Be certain to tell the special job each does.

_____

_____

_____

_____

4. Write a short paragraph describing what life is like in an ant colony. Include:

a. the different kinds of work the ants do,

b. what the ants eat, and

c. how the ants are cared for.

_____

_____

_____

_____

_____

_____

5. List at least five (5) ways ants and people are similar.

_____

_____

_____

_____

_____

6. _Matching:_ Write the letter of the word that goes best with each phrase.

a.   aphids   _____1.   These ants invade houses and manage to get into all kinds of food.

b.   harvester ants   _____2.   This kind of ant "sews" nests made of leaves.

c.   fungus-growing ants   _____3.   These ants are known as ant "cows," and their honey is sometimes called "milk".

d.   fire ants   _____4.   These ants are noted for their sting; they store seeds underground and manage stored crops.

e.   weaver ants   _____5.   These ants plant their own small gardens underground.

7.   List at least three (3) ways the formica rufa ant is useful to human beings.

_____

_____

_____

_____

_____

8.   Name the two (2) stomachs of the ant and describe how the ant uses each.

_____

_____

_____

9.   Describe the compound eye of an ant. Tell:
     a.   what it look like,
     b.   how it works, and
     c.   how well the insect can see.

_____

_____

_____

_____

_____

10. Tell the secret of the ant's kiss.

_____

_____

_____

_____

11. Tell at least five (5) reasons for the great number of ants.

_____

_____

_____

_____

Secondary Level: Shakespeare—The Plays[19]

The following CAP (Exhibit 4–8) is designed for ninth through twelfth grade students and should be completed in approximately two to three weeks. Objectives 1 and 2 are required of all; Objectives 3 through 8 are of varying difficulty, but tend to be suitable for "average" eleventh- and twelfth- grade students or advanced ninth- and tenth- graders.

Shakespeare: the Plays

Procedure

Select and read one (1) play from the following list. You may use texts provided by the school or bring your own from home.

Love's Labours Lost   *Much Ado about Nothing*
The Comedy of Errors   *As You Like It*

Two Gentlemen of Verona   Twelfth Night

Richard III   Julius Caeser

Romeo and Juliet   All's Well that Ends Well

A Midsummer Night's Dream   Measure for Measure

The Merchant of Venice   Hamlet

The Taming of the Shrew   Othello

The Merry Wives of Windsor   King Lear

Indicate play chosen:_____

Behavioral Objectives

By the time you have completed this contract, you will be able to do Objectives 1 and 2 and one additional Objective of your choice to be selected from among the remaining six.

Objective 1

Describe the plot, theme, and at least four (4) characters in the play you selected. (Required)

Activity Alternatives

1. Write a report that describes the plot, theme, and at least four (4) characters in the play you selected.

2. Rewrite your play as a short story suitable for small children but retaining the essence of the play.

3. Pretend you are a theater critic for a newspaper; write a review of the play.

4. Tape-record your analysis.

Reporting Alternatives

1. Share your report with a group of four to six (6) students, and then submit it to your teacher.

2. Give your short story to some small children to read; observe their reactions.

3. Post your review on the bulletin board.

4. Play your tape for a group of four to six students and your teacher.

Objective 2

Some quotations from Shakespeare have become so well known that they are now commonly-heard expressions. For example, "It's Greek to me" (from *Julius Caeser*) is now a common expression used to indicate a person's complete lack of knowledge of a subject, language, or such. And who can argue with Shakespeare's observation that "The course of true love never did run smooth," (*A Midsummer Night's Dream*)?

Select at least six (6) quotations from the play you selected that you've heard before, or find new and thought-provoking statements in it that are worthy of notice. (required)

Activity Alternatives

1. List the quotations and briefly, their significance.

2. Make a word search puzzle of these quotations.

3. Make decorative plaques (suitable for hanging) of these questions.

Reporting Alternatives

1. Post your list on the bulletin board.

2. Have some fellow students find the hidden quotations.

3. Display your plaques for your classmates.

Objective 3

Analyze how Shakespeare effects characterization of at least three (3) protagonists through the use of imagery. Consider his use of figurative language, such as metaphors, similies, and analogies.

Activity Alternatives

1. Draw portraits of the characters in the play as you visualize them from the descriptive passages in the play.

2. Make puppets of the characters as you see them from the verbal descriptions given in the text.

3. Decide which current actors or actresses would be perfect for the roles. Write them letters explaining why you consider them perfect for the parts.

Reporting Alternatives

1. Display your portraits and offer a brief commentary concerning why you see them this way.

2. Have your puppets "tell" some classmates and your teacher about themselves.

3. Read your letter to a group of four to seven and to your teacher.

Objective 4

Conflict is the basis of all drama. Identify the central conflict in your play. Remember, it could be *external* (a character against social forces) or *internal* (a character divided within himself as to a course of action) or *both.*

Activity Alternatives

1. Write letters to Ann Landers (or Dear Abby) explaining the conflict from the point of view of two (2) characters. (Use the first-person narrative style.)

2. Tape-record the conflict, as the two (2) characters perceive it—as though they were calling a "hotline" for help.

3. Write a newspaper feature story discussing the problems of the two (2) characters

Reporting Alternatives

1. Read your letters to some classmates; ask them how they would solve the problem. Post your letters on the bulletin board, leaving room for advice from your classmates.

2. Play the tape for a small group of your classmates and your teacher.

3. Pass the feature article among a few of your classmates. Ask for their opinion of

from an objective, third-person viewpoint.

conflict based on the way you have presented the material. Did you, for example, take sides unconsciously?

Objective 5

Based on the female characters in your play, analyze how Shakespeare generally views women. Isolate those features, whether physical, psychological, or both, that seem dated from those that persist even now.

Activity Alternatives

1. Write a report on your findings; be certain to include citations from the text to support your position.

2. Write a script for a television documentary dealing with the similarities and differences in attitudes toward women then and now.

Reporting Alternatives

1. Submit your report to the teacher or read your report to a small group of classmates. Ask if any attitudes are relevant to their plays.

2. Produce and present the program.

Objective 6

Determine at least three (3) biographical factors that influenced Shakespeare and, in turn, his play. Consider, for example, the manners and mores of Elizabethan society and how this influence is apparent in the formation of Shakespeare's attitudes as reflected in his characters and central themes.

Activity Alternatives

1. Pretend you've just received the news that Shakespeare died. Write a thorough obituary outlining his life and career for those unacquainted with either.

2. Tape a twenty (20) minute talk chronicling Shakespeare's life and literary achievement; use appropriate references to his play.

Reporting Alternatives

1. Post the obituary on the bulletin board or inform a small group of classmates and your teacher of his death, and read the obituary.

2. Play the tape for some classmates. Ask if any of the related incidents remind them of similar episodes in the play they've read.

Objective 7

Isolate, from the situations and actions occurring in your play, at least four (4) basic elements of Shakespearean comedy or tragedy.

Activity Alternatives

1. Make a collage depicting the various comic or tragic elements or events.

2. Sketch a series of cartoons and make each frame illustrative of a comic or tragic element. Caption each frame appropriately.

3. Prepare a twenty (20) minute lecture entitled "The Comic (or Tragic) Elements in Shakespeare's Plays."

Reporting Alternatives

1. Display the collage for your classmates and teacher.

2. Display the cartoons for your classmates and teacher.

3. Give the lecture to a small group of classmates. Ask them if they can recall similar situations in the plays they've read.

Objective 8

Choose at least three (3) minor characters from the play you've read and explain their dramatic function and significance.

Activity Alternatives

1. Write an analysis of the minor characters.

2. Sketch a series of "mug shots" of each character, accompanied by a brief police-like dossier of the character's activities.

3. Tape a radio talkshow, interviewing these characters. Tape their responses to your questions on their activities and importance.

Reporting Alternatives

1. Submit the composition to your teacher.

2. Present your "mug shots" and commentaries to a small group of classmates. Ask if they have seen or heard of similar types.

3. Play the tape for some of your classmates.

Resource Alternatives

Books

Alden, Raymond. *A Shakespeare Handbook.* New York: Crofts, 1925.

Bartlett, Henrietta. *Mr. William Shakespeare.* New Haven: Yale University Press, 1922.

Bate, John. *How to Find Out about Shakespeare.* New York: Permagon Press, 1968.

Berman, Ronald. *A Reader's Guide to Shakespeare's Plays.* Chicago: Scott, Foresman, 1965.

Bullough, Geoffrey. *Narrative and Dramatic Sources of Shakespeare,* vols. 1–6. London: Oxford University Press, 1957.

Campbell, Oscar J., ed. *The Reader's Encyclopedia of Shakespeare.* New York: Crowell, 1966.

Chute, Marchette. *An Introduction to Shakespeare.* New York: Dutton, 1951.

Dowden, Edward. *Shakespeare: A Critical Study of His Mind and Art.* London: Dent, 1960.

Ebisch, W., and Schucking, L. *Shakespeare Bibliography.* London: Murray, 1931.

Halliday, Frank. *A Shakespeare Companion.* New York: Funk & Wagnalls, 1952.

Mackenzie, A. *The Women in Shakespeare's Plays.* London: Oxford University Press, 1924.

Rabkin, Norman. *Approaches to Shakespeare.* New York: McGraw-Hill, 1964.

Stokes, Francis G. *Dictionary of the Characters and Proper Names.* New York: Grosset & Dunlap, 1960.

Wilson, H. S. *On the Design of Shakespeare's Tragedies.* New York: Harcourt, Brace & World, 1960.

Wilson, J. *Shakespeare's Happy Comedies.* London: Dent, 1962.

There are, of course, many other books about Shakespeare and his plays. You may use books other than the ones on this list to aid you in completing your objectives, but be certain to list them on the log provided for this purpose.

The following list consists of multimedia sources about Shakespeare's life and works. The numbers after each title are not a part of a standard cataloging system, but represent a numbering system used at one particular school in which the Shakespeare CAP is used.

Films — General

The Life of William Shakespeare 2H-23

Filmstrip — General

Shakespeare's Theatre 5F-11
Introduction to Shakespeare 5F-12
Styles in Shakespearean Acting, 1980–1950 73-22

Records — General

Scenes from Shakespeare: Tragedies 67
Shakespeare: The Soul of an Age 630
Songs from the Plays of Shakespeare (I) 888
Songs from the Plays of Shakespeare (II) 890

Films — The Plays

Hamlet: Age of Elizabeth (I) 254
Macbeth: Politics of Power (I) 258
Themes of Macbeth 259
Macbeth: The Secret'st Man 269
The Sense of Tragedy: Macbeth 383
Hamlet: The Poisoned Kingdom 450
Hamlet: The Readiness is All 451
What Happened in Hamlet 449

Filmstrip — The Plays

Julius Caeser: Part I 5E-44
Julius Caeser: Part II 5E-45
Hamlet 5F-13
Macbeth 5F-14
Romeo and Juliet 5F-15
Midsummer Night's Dream 5F-16
As You Like It 5F-17
Henry V 5F-18

Records — The Plays

Julius Caeser 44
Macbeth 171
Macbeth 172
Macbeth 832
Hamlet 504
Hamlet 505
Hamlet 507
The Merchant of Venice 749
The Merchant of Venice 750
The Merchant of Venice 751
The Merchant of Venice (Orson Welles) 846-869
Love's Labours Lost 757
Love's Labours Lost 748
Love's Labours Lost 759
Much Ado About Nothing 760
Much Ado About Nothing 761
Much Ado About Nothing 762
Romeo and Juliet 811
Romeo and Juliet 812
Romeo and Juliet 813

Midsummer Night's Dream 837
Midsummer Night's Dream 838
Midsummer Night's Dream 839
Othello 882
Othello 883
Othello 884
Othello 885
The Tempest 889
The Tempest 890
The Tempest 891
Twelfth Night 1031

STUDENT SELECTED RESOURCE ALTERNATIVES

_____

_____

_____

_____

_____

_____

_____

_____

_____

TEAM LEARNING

Team Members:

1. _____   4. _____

2. _____   5. _____

3. _____   6. _____

Recorder:_____

Objective

Be able to read Shakespeare closely and carefully in order to understand his language, which is so different from contemporary prose.

1   To be, or not to be, — that is the question: —
      Whether 'tis nobler in the mind to suffer
      The slings and arrows of outrageous fortune,
      Or to take arms against a sea of troubles,
5   And by opposing end them? — To die, — to sleep, —
      No more; and by a sleep to say we end
      The heart-ache, and the thousand natural shocks
      That flesh is heir to, 'tis a consummation
      Devoutly to be wisht. To die, — to sleep; —
10   To sleep! Perchance to dream: ay, there's the rub;
      For in that sleep of death what dreams may come,
      When we have shuffled off this mortal coil,
      Must give us pause: there's the respect
      That makes calamity of so long life;
15   For who would bear the whips and scorns of time,
      The oppressor's wrong, the proud man's contumely,
      The pangs of despised love, the law's delay,
      The insolence of office, and the spurns
      The patient merit of the unworthy takes,
20   When he himself might he quietus make
      With a bare bodkin? Who would fardels bear,
      To grunt and sweat under a weary life,
      But that dread of something after death, —
      The undiscover'd country, from whose bourn
25   No traveller returns, — puzzles the will,
      And makes us rather bear those ills we have
      Than fly to others that we know of?
      Thus conscience does make cowards of us all;
      And thus the native hue of resolution
30   Is sicklied o'er with the pale cast of thought;
      and enterprises of great pith and moment,
      With this regard, their currents turn awry,
      And lost the name of action.

                                (*Hamlet,* Act III, Scene I)

Assignment

1.   What action is Hamlet contemplating?

Why?

_____

2.   What does Hamlet mean when he says "To sleep! Perchance to dream: ay, there's the rub"?

_____

_____

_____

_____

3.   Why do people, according to Hamlet, continue to live?

_____

_____

_____

Quote the lines that support your answer.

_____

_____

4.   What common life experiences does Hamlet mention?

a. _____

b. _____

c. _____

d. _____

e. _____

f. _____

g. _____

5.   What does Hamlet decide to do?

_____

6.   Why does he make this decision?

_____

7.   What is Hamlet's attitude toward life?

_____

_____

List as many words as you can, from the text, that support your con-

clusion._____

_____

_____

_____

_____

8.   At what point in the soliloquy do Hamlet's "currents turn awry"?

_____

_____

CIRCLE OF KNOWLEDGE

Circle Members:

1. _____   4. _____

2. _____   5. _____

3. _____   6. _____

Recorder:_____

Name as many Shakespearean characters (proper names) as you can:

_____   _____

_____   _____

_____   _____

_____   _____

_____   _____

_____   _____

_____   _____

_____   _____

_____   _____

_____   _____

Circle of Knowledge

Circle Members:

1. _____   4. _____

2. _____   5. _____

3. _____   6. _____

Recorder:_____

What are the basic aspects of Shakespearean tragedy (or comedy)?

_____

_____

_____

_____

_____

GROUP ANALYSIS

Group Members:

1. _____   4. _____ _____

2. _____   5. _____

3. _____   6. _____

Recorder:_____

Subject: Conventions

Objectives

1. To enable you to identify and understand Shakespeare's use of conventions.

2. To enable you to identify and understand how conventions are used in literature and the media today.

Conventions, in one sense of the term, are necessary or convenient devices, widely accepted by the public, for solving the problems imposed by a particular artistic medium (play, television show, movie, novel) in representing reality. In watching a production of a play, for example, the audience accepts without question the convention by which a stage set with three walls (or if it is in the round, with no walls) represents a room with four walls. It also accepts the convention of characters uttering soliloquies and asides or the convention by which action presented on one set in three or so hours may represent events that take place in a great variety of places over a span of years.

In a second sense of the term, conventions are recurrent, identifiable elements of subject matter, types of characters (the braggart, the young lovers, the crotchety old man), plots, or diction and style. Often conventions become so stereotypical as to be corny.

Examine the sixteenth-century engraving "As the Poet Pictures His Sweetheart" (Exhibit 4-9).

1. What was your first reaction to this lady?

_____

2. Why?

Exhibit 4-9.

As the poet pictures his sweetheart

Feeling: Reason:

_____   _____

_____   _____

_____   _____

    3.   Take one feature at a time and describe verbally what you see in the picture.

_____

_____

_____

_____

_____

_____

    4.   Can you think of other conventions, in the same spirit, that are not represented in this particular picture? For example, "eyes like limpid pools."

_____

_____

_____

    5.   If the woman in question was a "heavy," what kind of conventions would be used?

_____

_____

_____

_____

6.   What are some current conventions applicable to women? What factors are common, for example, to sex symbols?

_____

_____

_____

_____

_____

_____

7.   Based on the conventions you have uncovered, recall as many as you can that are applicable to the heroines in your respective plays.

_____

_____

_____

_____

_____

_____

8.   Can you think of real or fictional women that run counter to these conventions?

Who   Why/How

_____   _____

_____   _____

_____   _____

_____   _____

9. Can you think of some conventions that would apply to "good" and "bad" male characters? For example, the hero in a western wears a white hat; how is the villain dressed?

_____

Other conventions	Type of character
_____	_____
_____	_____
_____	_____
_____	_____
_____	_____

10. Similar patterns occur in plots, too. Complications can arise, for example, from mistaken identity; or the problems of the "eternal triangle" love story. Discuss some current movies, television shows, or plays that you've seen, and list those that have plots or situations in common.

Title	Plot/Situation
_____	_____
_____	_____
_____	_____
_____	_____
_____	_____
_____	_____
_____	_____

11.   Discuss the plays you've read and list as many character types, plots, situations, or even viewpoints as you can that are common to all.

_____

_____

_____

_____

_____

12.   Form an opinion on the pros and cons of conventions in the arts.

_____

_____

_____

_____

_____

_____

_____

_____

_____

SELF-ASSESSMENT TEST

1.   Describe the plot, theme, and at least four (4) characters of the play you have selected.

Plot:

_____

_____

_____

_____

_____

Theme:

_____

_____

_____

Characters:

a.   _____

b.   _____

c.   _____

d.   _____

2.   List at least six (6) quotations from your play.

a.   _____

b.   _____

c.   _____

d.   _____

e. _____

f. _____
You're terrific if you can recall two more!

g. _____

h. _____

3. Analyze how Shakespeare effects characterization through the use of imagery for at least three (3) protagonists. (Consider his use of figurative language.)

a. _____

_____

_____

_____

b. _____

_____

_____

_____

c. _____

_____

_____

4. Identify the central conflict in your play.

_____

_____

_____

5.   Based on the female characters in your play, analyze Shakespeare's general view of women. Isolate those features that seem dated from those that persist to this day.

Analysis:_____

_____

_____

Some dated features:_____

_____

_____

Some current features:_____

_____

_____

6.   Determine at least three (3) biographical factors that influenced Shakespeare and, in turn, his play.

a.   _____

_____

_____

b.   _____

_____

_____

c.   _____

_____

_____

7. List, from the situations and actions occuring in your play, at least four (4) basic elements of Shakespearean comedy or tragedy.

a. _____

b. _____

c. _____

d. _____

8. Explain the dramatic function and significance of at least three (3) minor characters from your play.

a. _____

b. _____

c. _____

5

Designing Programmed Instruction Sequences to Respond to Individual Learning Styles

A second basic method for individualizing instruction is to program instructional material so that it may be learned in small, simple steps without the direct supervision of an adult. Like any other method, programmed instruction enhances only selected learning style characteristics, and, therefore, it should not be prescribed for all students. When administrators or teachers purchase commercially prepared programs for the population of an entire class or school, they reveal that they are not aware that individual youngsters require different methods and resources through which to learn.

Commercial programs are designed around preselected concepts and skills, called "objectives," that must be mastered by each student. Objectives range from the simple to the complex and are sequenced so that, after taking a pretest, students are assigned only those that they have not achieved prior to being exposed to the program. Each youngster is then introduced to the programmed materials at the point where the remaining objectives are either partially repetitive or introductory. All students proceed through the identical sequence but may pace themselves and use the program when and where they prefer to study. Programmed instruction is individualized only in terms of diagnosis, prescription, level, and, when used flexibly, selected aspects of learning style.

Programs that have been commercially produced have had only limited effectiveness because they are visual—similar to short workbooks—and therefore appeal to students who read fairly well and who can retain information by seeing. The firms that produce such programs maintain that cassettes and filmstrips occasionally supplement their resources. When multimedia materials are available, they should be used to facilitate the program's effectiveness for those youngsters who are auditory while serving as reinforcement for those who are visual.

In actual practice, students are each given a program for which they are responsible, and, as the various objectives and their related tests are completed, gradual progress is made toward completing the material. Unless learners need and seek assistance, they may be virtually isolated for long periods of instructional time. It is also possible for them to engage in hours of study without benefiting from either adult or peer interaction. There are youngsters who prefer to work alone,[1] but the Scribner and Durell studies conducted at Boston University and, more recently, the Poirier methods[2] instituted at the University of California verify that for many students, retention is increased after peer discussions of what is being learned. A teacher who chooses to use programmed materials for students who are peer-oriented may overcome the isolation factor, however, by incorporating selected small-group techniques into the programs—such as team learning, circle of knowledge, group analysis, case study, simulation, and brainstorming.[3]

Learning Style Characteristics Responsive to Programmed Instruction

Because programmed materials are used independently (alone) it is important that those students to whom this resource is assigned are motivated to learn the contents of the package. They should also be persistent, suggesting that they normally would continue using the materials until the program has been completed. Should they experience difficulty, they either will review the previous frames and continue to try to progress or they will seek assistance from appropriate persons. Programmed instruction also requires responsibility from students; should they daydream or neglect to work toward completion of the materials, they will be wasting valuable instructional time.

By organizing everything that should be learned so that only one item at a time is presented, the sequenced materials in each program provide a great deal of structure. A student cannot proceed until what must be achieved at each stage has been fully understood, as demonstrated through a short quiz at the end of each frame or page. Youngsters who prefer to be directed and told exactly what to do will feel at ease with programmed packages, while creative students may find them boring and, thus, irritating.

Programmed instruction is ideally suited to youngsters who *prefer to work alone* and to avoid the sounds, movement, and interaction of classmates. It is also a perfect match for students who learn best by seeing and for those who need to read, and, perhaps, reread materials before they can be absorbed.

Teachers who believe that selected students are not motivated, persistent, or responsible, but who recognize that they are slow achievers, visual learners, and in need of structure, should experiment with programmed instruction. Because this strategy presents concepts and skills simply, gradually, and repeatedly, and may be used alone—without causing either the embarrassment or pressure that emerges when one has difficulty achieving among one's peers—many youngsters often become motivated, persistent, or responsible when using a program. When the "right" method is matched correctly with the "right" student, increased academic achievement and improved attitudes toward learning are likely to result.

Learning Style Characteristics to Which Programmed Instruction Can Be Accommodated

Because a program may be used in a classroom, in a library, in a corridor, or in an instructional resource center as well as at home, it can accommodate each student's environmental and physical preferences. For example, the package can be taken to a silent area if quiet is desired or it may be used in the midst of classroom activity when the learner can block out sound. It can be moved to either a warm section of a room—near a radiator perhaps, or to a cool area. It can be studied at a desk or on a carpet, in either a well-lit area or away from the bright sunshine. A student may snack or not as he or she works, may use the package at any time of day that is convenient, and may "take a break" or two if mobility is necessary. Since the program is visual, it will utilize the perceptual strengths of students who learn best by reading or seeing. For auditory youngsters, a teacher should add a tape that repeats orally what the text teaches visually. When students are either tactual or kinesthetic learners, the teacher should add games that introduce the program's objectives through those senses. For students who learn slowly or with difficulty, it is wise to supplement a visual programmed sequence with three other types of perceptual resources—auditory, tactual, and kinesthetic.

Case Studies Describing Students Whose Learning Styles Are Complemented by Programmed Instruction

1. Only the sound of his own name was able to break through into his thoughts. As Mrs. Diamond's voice repeated the question, Kerry sat up in his seat. He had been so engrossed in contemplating

the effects of the Civil Rights Movement—an item on which the teacher had been focusing ten minutes earlier—that his imagination had carried from the advent of slavery in the United States to the psychological implications of being a despised minority in a majority culture.

Mrs. Diamond's voice was sympathetic. "Do you know the answer?" Kerry sat up quickly in embarrassment. "I'm sorry," he answered. "I was thinking about something else." "What?" she asked. He merely shrugged. He was reluctant to reveal that he was mentally involved with an item that had been discussed a while before—one only tangentially related to what the class was studying. "Please keep up with us," the teacher urged, and slowly shook her head in exasperation.

Students who are motivated to learn but who need more time to consider items or to concentrate than is usually permitted by group instruction may learn more effectively through programmed instruction.

2. Mark could not work out the fifth example. He pulled his text out from the desk and fingered through its pages until he found the chapter that explained how to convert fractions. He read the section related to that process and was still not certain of how to apply the rule. He leaned over toward a classmate and asked for assistance. When the directions for solving the problem were clear to him, he turned back to the papers on his desk and continued working.

Students who are persistent—who continue working toward the completion of an assignment and find ways to do so—usually respond well to programmed instruction.

3. Barbara's elbow was on her desk, her forehead rested on the fingers of her clenched hand, and her eyes had just closed tightly. She was trying to reconstruct the page she had read, which described how Shakespeare had used characters to depict human frailty. Suddenly she recalled the lower left section of the page and was able to "see" the listing of examples. She relaxed, picked up her pen, and began to answer the test question.

Students who are visual learners—who remember more by reading and seeing than they do by listening—usually respond well to programmed instruction.

4. Tim was having a great time with the kids on his committee. As members tried to find the information for their assignment, he collected their pens, pencils, and notes and hid them inside his

desk. When the boys reconvened to decide on how they would present their report, Tim alternated between wandering around the room and tipping his chair to see how far back it could go without falling. When the teacher cautioned him to settle down and work with the group, he picked up a pencil and began to organize the presentation.

Students who do not work well in groups may work better alone knowing that they, personally, are responsible for completing an assignment. Such youngsters may respond well to either programs, contracts, or instructional packages.

5. Claire was at her teacher's side again. "Mr. Dawes, am I doing this right?" she asked. "You asked the same question five minutes ago!" the teacher responded. "I know,"Claire answered, "but I want to be sure!"

Students who require structure—who need to know exactly what to do and how to do it—usually respond well to programmed instruction.

Programmed Instruction: Controversy and Criticisms

At one time or another, all instructional methods have been criticized. Few people recognize that no one strategy is effective for everyone and that few methods will ensure academic achievement for a majority of learners. The controversy surrounding programmed instruction has had many dimensions, but it is important to recognize that in no published research studies concerning this strategy have students' learning styles been identified prior to their assignment to programmed materials. Therefore, in all the investigations, achievement results were analyzed with no reference to whether this method could be an effective way of learning for the individual students involved in the studies.

Ideally, students should be analyzed to determine their learning styles. Those whose data indicate that they could function well with programmed learning—those who are motivated, persistent, responsible, and in need of structure, and who prefer learning alone and are visually oriented—should be assigned a programmed package. For those students, academic achievement should be excellent. It is fallacious to assign programmed materials indiscriminately and then to compare the results of that experiment, for the youngsters whose learning style cannot be complemented by programming cannot learn well through that method.

It is this major deficiency that diminishes the findings of researchers who in the past conducted investigations into the effects of programmed materials. For example, Roderick and Anderson[4] found that achievement levels of undergraduates who used a programmed psychology unit were no different from the scores achieved by students who used a written summary presented in conventional textbook form. These researchers noted, too, that it took four times longer to complete the program than to read the summaries, but they ignored the importance of the program strategy that required that, in addition to reading the material, the students had to consider each item, respond to questions concerning it, and could not advance without complete mastery of each previous phase. Obviously such a procedure takes longer, but numerous studies verify that it also helps students to internalize the information and to increase retention.

To his credit, Kress[5] appears to have recognized that only students who prefer to learn by themselves will do well with programmed materials. As early as 1966 he cautioned that learners who lacked the necessary independent study skills to work with programs under individual, self-paced conditions should not be permitted to do so. Gotkin's observations of boredom among youngsters who worked on programs in isolation for prolonged periods of time[6] may also have been related to the concept that some students prefer to learn alone, while others, in contrast, prefer to study with peers. Had the learning styles of the students in these studies been tested, the data might have revealed that those who preferred to work alone were not bored, whereas those who preferred either paired or grouped learning or, possibly, adult instruction, could not be successful with this type of method unless it were revised to permit such options.[7]

In addition, students who are neither motivated nor persistent will find it difficult to acquire the focusing strategy required of those who learn successfully through programming.[8] Indeed, researchers contend that under certain circumstances stereotyped and repetitious use of prompted frames can impair the effectiveness of the materials themselves.[9] This research suggests that students often begin to respond on the basis of the prompt alone and do not actually pay attention to the content. Finally, programmed learning should be recognized as a strategy that appeals to visual learners, and that those who require auditory, tactual, or kinesthetic techniques will benefit from a program only after these supplements have been added (see Chapter seven for directions for developing such materials).

Basic Principles of Programmed Instruction

Programmed instruction is designed on the basis of several important principles that tend to facilitate academic achievement for students with selected learning style elements.[10] All programs tend to follow a similar pattern, which includes each of the following characteristics:

1. *Only one item is presented at a time.*
A single concept or skill that should be mastered is introduced through a simple written statement. After reading the material, the learner is required

to answer a question or two to demonstrate that what has been introduced on that frame (page, section) has been understood. This procedure prevents the lesson from advancing faster than the student, and it does not permit the student to fall behind. The youngster may learn as quickly as he or she is capable of comprehending the material, or as slowly and with as much repetition as may be needed. No one may continue into a subsequent frame or phase of the program until each previous one has been mastered.

Presenting one item at a time is effective for the youngster who wants to learn (is motivated), who will continue trying (is persistent), and who wants to do what is required (is responsible). For students in need of structure, being exposed to one item at a time breaks the content into small phases and the process into short steps that can be mastered gradually. Understandably, this process is not effective for the student who needs to be exposed to a gestalt of the information, who, rather than piecing a totality together bit by bit, prefers to develop an overall view of the end product. It is also inappropriate for those who cannot continue to work with the same set of materials for any continuing amount of time and who need diversity and variety. In addition, it appears to be a method that does not attract and hold creative students who want to add their own knowledge and special talents to what is being learned before they have accomplished the entire task.

2.   *The student is required to be an active, rather than a passive, learner.*

Unlike large-group instruction, where a student may merely sit and appear to be listening, programming requires that a response be made to questions related to each introduced item. Youngsters cannot progress through the program without responding, and only accurate answers permit continuation of this learning process.

3.   *The student is immediately informed of the correctness of each response.*

As soon as a youngster has read the frame, he or she is required to answer a question based on the material that has just been read. The moment that the student's response has been recorded, the youngster may turn to a section in the program where the correct answer is stated. The student, therefore, is immediately made aware of the accuracy or inaccuracy of the response. This technique of "immediate reinforcement" is a highly effective teaching strategy with most learners.

4.   *The student may not continue into the next phase of a program until each previous phase has been understood and mastered.*

When the program reveals that a student's response to the questions related to each frame are correct, the student is directed to continue into the next section (frame, page, or phase). When students' responses are not correct, they are directed either to restudy the previously read frames or to turn to another section of the program that will explain in a different way the material that has not been understood. Because each phase of the program must be mastered before students are permitted to continue into the next phase, learners do not move ahead aimlessly while grasping only parts of a concept or topic. Their base of knowledge is solid before they are exposed to either new ideas or related ones.

5. *The student is exposed to material that gradually progresses from the easy to the more difficult.*

Frames are written so that the first few in a series introduce what should be learned in an uncomplicated, direct manner. Gradually, as the student's correct answers demonstrate his or her increasing understanding of what is being taught, more difficult aspects of the topic are introduced. Through this technique, students are made to feel both comfortable and successful with the beginning phases of each program and their confidence in their own ability to achieve is bolstered. Youngsters who find themselves achieving are likely to continue in the learning process.

6. *As the student proceeds in the program, fewer hints and crutches are provided.*

Programming uses a system of "fading," or gradually withdrawing easy questions or hints (repeated expressions, illustrations, color-coding, and similar crutches) so that the student's developing knowledge is tested precisely. This technique enables the teacher to accurately assess the youngster's progess and mastery of the material.

Step-by-step Guide to Designing a Programmed Learning Sequence

Developing a program is not difficult, but it does require that you organize the topic that will be taught into a logical, easy-to-follow sequence. Begin with Step 1 and gradually move through each of the remaining steps until you have completed your first program. Each consecutive program will become easier and easier to design. By their questions and responses, students will provide direct feedback on how to revise and improve your initial efforts. Subsequent programs will require fewer revisions.

Step 1 Begin by identifying a topic, concept, or skill that you want to teach. A good choice would be something that most youngsters in your classes need to learn. Since all students are not capable of learning at the same time, in the same way, and with the same speed, a program is one way of permitting individuals to self-pace themselves with materials whenever they are ready to achieve. Thus, some youngsters may use this program early in the semester while others will use it later. Some will use it to learn before the remainder of the class is exposed to a new idea, and others will use it to reinforce an idea that you have already taught—but which they did not master.

Step 2   Write the name of the topic, concept, or skill that you have decided to teach as a heading at the top of a blank sheet of paper.

Step 3   Translate the heading that you have written at the top of the sheet into an introductory sentence that explains to the youngsters using the program exactly what they should be able to do after they have mastered what the materials are designed to teach.

Examples

• By the time you finish this program, you will be able to recognize *adjectives* and identify the *nouns* that each of the adjectives modifies.

• When you have completed this program, you should be able to explain at least five (5) ways in which your life is *different* from a desert child's life and at least five (5) ways in which your lives are *similar.*

• This program will teach you to recognize at least five (5) geometric shapes and to spell each of their names correctly. You will also be able to draw each of the different shapes.

• I am so pleased that you are going to work with this program, because it will teach you how to:

1.   Punctuate a sentence correctly, and

2.   Write a series of correctly punctuated sentences to form a paragraph.

Step 4   List all the prerequisites for using the program effectively.

Examples

• Before you use this program, you should be familiar with the meanings of each of the following words: desert, nomad, oasis, arid, mirage.

• Be certain that you begin using this program either on or near a large table so that you will have ample room to use these materials and the tape recorder at the same time.

Since you may recognize that certain knowledges or skills are, indeed, prerequisite after you have moved beyond Step 4, leave space on your paper so that you may insert additions as they come to mind.

Step 5   Decide which of the two basic types of programming you will use.

Type 1: Linear Programming

This type of programming presents material in a highly structured sequence. Each part of the sequence is called a "frame," and each frame builds upon the one immediately preceding it. Each frame ends with an item that requires an answer—either in completion or multiple choice formats. Prior to the introduction of each subsequent frame, the answer to the previous frame is supplied. Program efficiency increases when the correct answer is accompanied by an explanation. Additional comprehension is developed when the incorrect answers also are accompanied by explanations.

Example

Frame 1

Read the paragraph below. Then write the correct answer on the line at the end of the paragraph.

Richard, Robert, and Randy are similar in many ways. They are all boys, they are all good baseball players, and they are all on the same _____team.

football   baseball   basketball

Back of Frame 1

Answer: baseball

The paragraph tells us that the three boys are good *baseball* players. It does not tell us whether or not they play football or basketball.

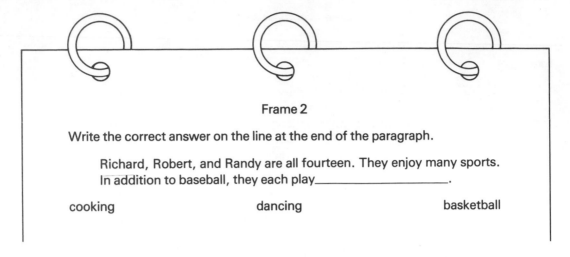

Frame 2

Write the correct answer on the line at the end of the paragraph.

Richard, Robert, and Randy are all fourteen. They enjoy many sports. In addition to baseball, they each play_____.

cooking   dancing   basketball

Back of Frame 2

Answer: basketball

Boys can cook or dance, but we do not say that anyone can "play cooking" or "play dancing." Also, the paragraph stated that they enjoy sports, and basketball is a sport; cooking and dancing are not.

Type 2: Intrinsic Programming

Intrinsic programming also presents material in a highly structured sequence, but the major difference between linear and intrinsic types is that the intrinsic does not require that each student should complete every frame. Intrinsic programming recognizes that some youngsters can move through learning experiences faster than others can, and it permits those who score correct answers to skip over some of the reinforcement frames.

When students may bypass frames that teach the same aspect of a subject, the system is called "branching." Branching, in effect, permits a faster rate of self-pacing.

When a student answers a question incorrectly, he must continue from one frame to the next, to the next, and so on until every frame in the entire program has been completed. When a student studies several introductory frames and then answers the questions correctly, he may branch over additional reinforcement frames if the program is an intrinsic one.

Example

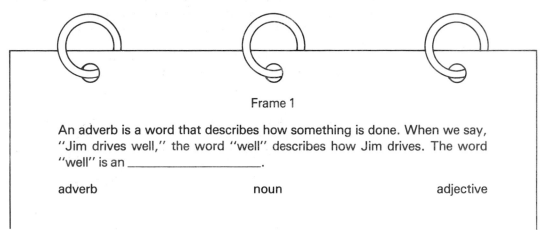

Frame 1

An adverb is a word that describes how something is done. When we say, "Jim drives well," the word "well" describes how Jim drives. The word "well" is an _____.

adverb   noun   adjective

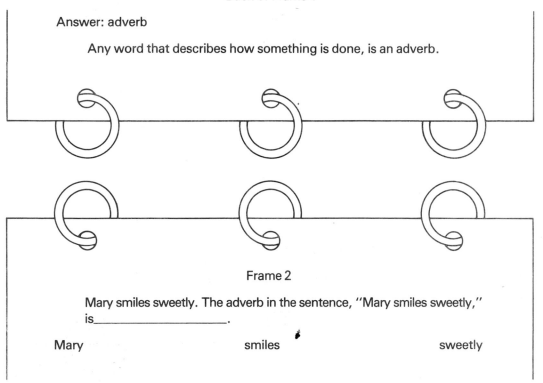

Back of Frame 1

Answer: adverb

Any word that describes how something is done, is an adverb.

Frame 2

Mary smiles sweetly. The adverb in the sentence, "Mary smiles sweetly," is_____.

Mary   smiles   sweetly

Back of Frame 2

Answer: sweetly

"Sweetly" tells how Mary smiles. Mary is a girl's name. Mary is a noun. "Smile" is what Mary does. Smile is a verb. If you wrote that "sweetly" is an adverb, you understand how to recognize some words that are adverbs.

Turn to Frame 5. You may skip Frames 3 and 4. If you did not write that "sweetly" is an adverb, turn to Frame 3 for more practice in recognizing adverbs.

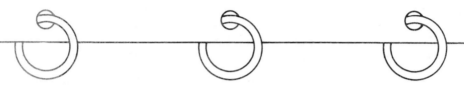

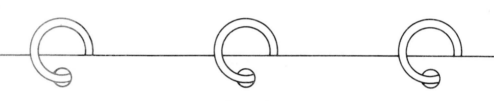

Frame 3

John walks quickly.

Circle the adverb in the sentence above.

Back of Frame 3

Answer: quickly

"Quickly" tells how John walks.
"John" is the boy's name." "John" is a noun.
"Walks" is what John does. "Walks" is a verb.

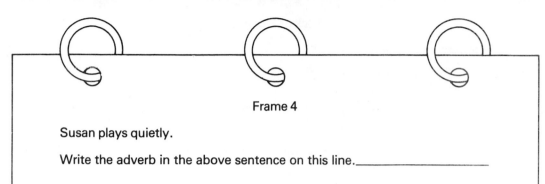

Frame 4

Susan plays quietly.

Write the adverb in the above sentence on this line._____

Back of Frame 4

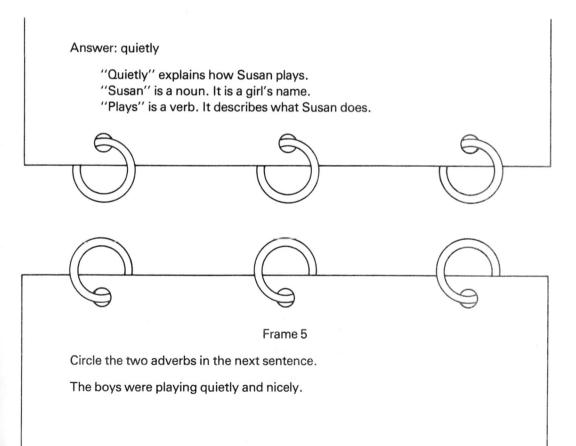

Answer: quietly

"Quietly" explains how Susan plays.
"Susan" is a noun. It is a girl's name.
"Plays" is a verb. It describes what Susan does.

Frame 5

Circle the two adverbs in the next sentence.

The boys were playing quietly and nicely.

Back of Frame 5

Answers: quietly and nicely

"The" is an article.
"Boys" is a noun.
"Were" and "playing" are verbs. They tell what the boys were doing.
"And" is a conjunction.

If you had both answers correct, turn to Frame 8. If you did not have both "quietly" and "nicely" correct, turn to Frame 6.

Step 6   Outline how you plan to teach the topic. Use short, simple sentences, if possible.

Most people have two different vocabularies: one is used for speaking, the other for writing. When you begin to outline your program, make believe that you are speaking to the student who will have the most trouble learning this material. Use simple words and sentences. Then write exactly the words that you use when you act out the way you would teach this material if you were actually talking to that youngster. In other words, use your speaking vocabulary rather than your professional writing vocabulary to develop the program.

Step 7   Divide the sentences in your outline into frames.

Frames are small sections of the topic that teach part of the idea, skill, or information. After listing the sentences that teach, ask a question that relates to the material. The student's answer will demonstrate his or her growing understanding of the subject. Think small! Most people who begin to write programs try to cover too much in a frame. Keep it a simple, small part of the total knowledge represented by your instructional objectives. In some cases you may wish to start with a simple generalization and move to specific examples and applications.

Pose fairly easy-to-answer questions in the first two or three frames to:

- Build a student's self-confidence;
- Demonstrate to the student that he or she can learn independently through the program; and

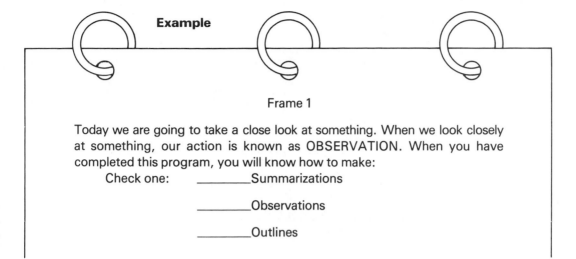

Example

Frame 1

Today we are going to take a close look at something. When we look closely at something, our action is known as OBSERVATION. When you have completed this program, you will know how to make:

Check one: _____Summarizations

_____Observations

_____Outlines

- Provide the student with a couple of successful experiences by using the process of programmed learning.

Step 8   Using a five-by-seven-inch index card to represent each frame, develop a sequence that teaches a subject and, simultaneously, test the student's growing knowledge of it.

Step 9   Refine each index card frame.

1.   Review the sequence to be certain that it is logical and does not teach too much on each frame.

2.   Check the spelling, grammer, and punctuation of each frame.

3.   Examine the vocabulary to be certain that it is understandable by the slowest youngsters that may use the program. Avoid colloquialisms that are acceptable in conversation but are less than professional in written form. But remember to use good oral language as opposed to good written language.

4.   Reread the entire series to be certain that each frame leads to the next one, and so on.

Step 10   When you are satisfied with the content, sequence, and questions on the frames, add colorful illustrations to clarify the main point on each index card.

If you do not draw, use magazine cutouts or gift wrapping paper to graphically supplement the most important sections of the text.

Step 11   Read the written material on each frame onto a cassette so that poor readers may use the program by listening to the frames being read to them as they simultaneously read along. (See Chapter six for directions for making a tape.)

Step 12   Ask three or four of your students to try the program, one at a time.

Observe each youngster using the material and try to identify whether any errors, omissions, or areas of difficulty exist. Correct anything that requires improvement.

Step 13   If necessary, revise the program based on your observations of student usage.

Step 14   Laminate each of the index cards that comprise the program or cover them with clear Con-tact.

Student use will cause the index cards to deteriorate unless they are protected by a covering. Laminated programs have lasted for years and can be cleaned with warm water and soap. They can be written on with grease pencils and then erased for use by another youngster.

Step 15 (Optional)   Add a tactual activity in game form for reinforcement of the most important information in the program. (See Chapter seven.) The program, as designed through Step 14, will respond only to youngsters who learn through either their visual or auditory senses. If you can add tactual reinforcement through materials such as task cards, learning circles, or an electroboard, you will be providing youngsters who need to learn through their sense of touch with a method appropriate for them. You thus will be adding to the effectiveness of the program and increasing the number of students who can learn successfully through it.

Step 16   Ask additional students to use the program.

Step 17   When you are satisfied that all the "bugs" have been eliminated, add a front and back cover.

Place the title of the program on the front cover, and, if possible, illustrate the cover to represent the subject matter. Bind the covers to the index card frames. You may use notebook rings, colored yarn, or any other substance that will permit easy turning of the index cards. Be certain that the answers to each frame, which appear on the back of the previous frame, are easily readable and are not upside down. When the program has been completed, make it available to students whose learning styles are complemented by this resource.

Step 18   Design a record-keeping form so that you know which students are using and have used the program and how much of it they have completed successfully. (See Exhibit 5-1.)

LANGUAGE ARTS PROGRAMS COMPLETED

Student	Adjectives	Test Score	Adverbs	Test Score	Pronouns	Test Score	Recommended Prescriptions
Adams, William	3/17	87	3/25	88	3/29	90	Continue programs.
Altman, Susan	3/9	94	3/10	93	3/15	98	Continue programs; try a contract.
Baron, Mary	3/15	82	3/21	80	3/10	85	Supplement adverbs program with games.
Brice, Amy	3/9	89	3/20	81	3/23	86	Supplement adverbs program with games.
Caldor, John	3/10	76	3/15	75	3/20	75	Try instructional packages.
Friedman, Joan	3/10	96	3/12	98	3/17	100	Continue programs; alternate with small groups; try a contract or two.

Exhibit 5-1.   Record-keeping form for programmed learning.

Step 19 Begin the process again and design a new program to teach another topic in this way!

SAMPLE PROGRAMS

Following are several samples of programs (Exhibits 5–2 through 5–5) developed by teachers and used successfully at different levels with children whose learning styles matched the approach intrinsic to programmed learning.

Primary Level: Shapes[11]

This program (Exhibit 5–2) should be taped for young students who are not yet reading well. They can listen as they follow the printed directions and explanations. Reinforcement can include games, cutouts of the shapes, and manipulative puzzles (see Chapter 7). Slower students who do not respond may do well with instructional packages (see Chapter 6). This type of step-by-step sequence is most effective with youngsters who require explicit directions and structure. It permits rereading and redoing, if necessary.

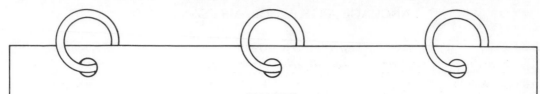

SHAPES

INTRODUCTION:

Mark each correct answer by placing an X in the box next to the answer that you choose.

In certain questions you may be asked to fill in missing letters or words or numbers.

When you have completed the entire program, wipe your answers off each frame.

The answers to each frame are found on the back of each card. Remember to mark only one answer unless you have to fill in missing letters or words or numbers.

NEW WORD CARD:

SQUARE:	(skwãr)	□
RECTANGLE:	(rek ´tang gel)	▭
TRIANGLE:	(tri ´ang gel)	△
CIRCLE:	(ser ´kel)	○

Frame 1

Today we are going to work on a program that will teach you about shapes.

By the time you finish this program you will be able to recognize at least three (3) geometric shapes, draw each of them, and correctly spell each of their names.

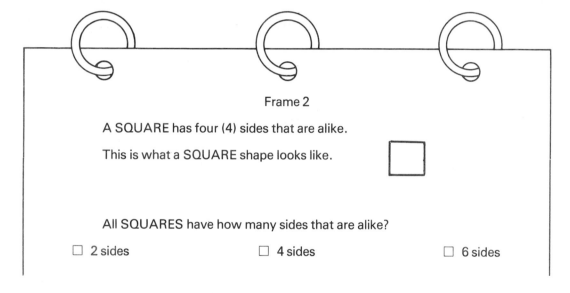

Frame 2

A SQUARE has four (4) sides that are alike.

This is what a SQUARE shape looks like.

All SQUARES have how many sides that are alike?

☐ 2 sides ☐ 4 sides ☐ 6 sides

Back of Frame 2

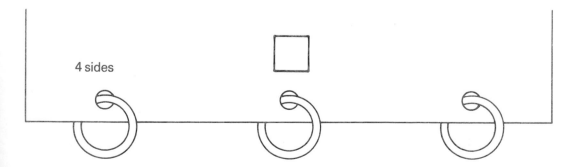

4 sides

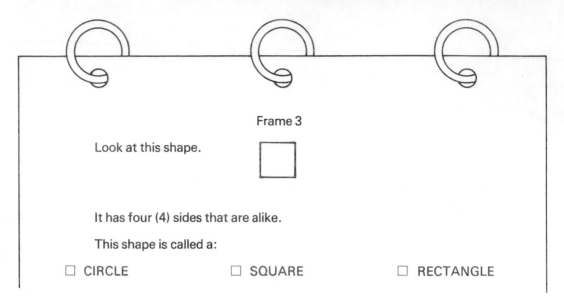

Frame 3

Look at this shape.

It has four (4) sides that are alike.

This shape is called a:

☐ CIRCLE   ☐ SQUARE   ☐ RECTANGLE

Back of Frame 3

SQUARE

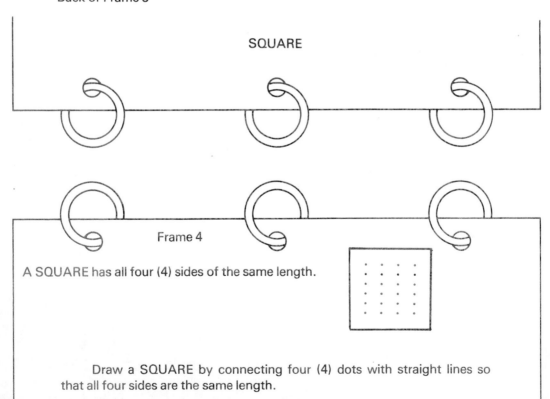

Frame 4

A SQUARE has all four (4) sides of the same length.

Draw a SQUARE by connecting four (4) dots with straight lines so that all four sides are the same length.

Back of Frame 4

You can make a SQUARE shape with any of the dots. Your shape may be bigger or smaller than this SQUARE.

Remember a SQUARE has four (4) sides that are alike. They are all the same length.

Frame 5

A RECTANGLE has two (2) sides that are the same length and another two (2) sides that are equal to each other but of a different length from the first two sides.

This is a rectangular shape.

How many sides do all RECTANGLES have?

☐ 4 sides ☐ 2 sides ☐ 3 sides

Back of Frame 5

4 sides

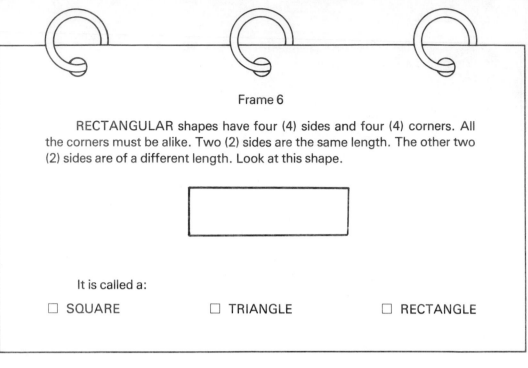

Frame 6

RECTANGULAR shapes have four (4) sides and four (4) corners. All the corners must be alike. Two (2) sides are the same length. The other two (2) sides are of a different length. Look at this shape.

It is called a:

☐ SQUARE   ☐ TRIANGLE   ☐ RECTANGLE

Back of Frame 6

RECTANGLE

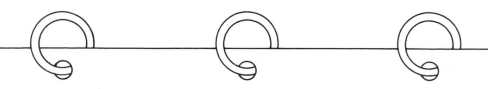

Frame 7

All the shapes in this drawing are R _ C _ A _ G _ L _ R. Fill in the missing letters.

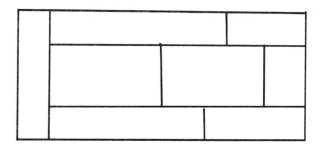

Back of Frame 7

RECTANGULAR

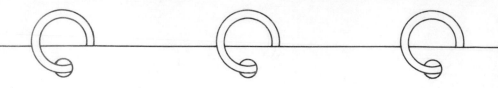

Frame 8

Return to FRAME 7 and count the RECTANGULAR shapes in the picture.

How many RECTANGULAR shapes can you find?

Write your answer on this line.   _____

Back of Frame 8

You should find at least 8 RECTANGULAR shapes in Frame 7.

If you put two (2) RECTANGLES together, you may find some more RECTANGLES here.

Did you count the drawing itself as a RECTANGLE too?

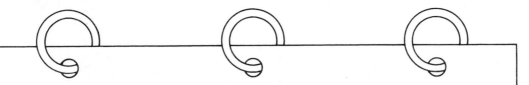

Frame 9

A RECTANGLE has two (2) sides that are the same length and another two (2) sides that are a different length from the first 2 sides, but equal to each other. Complete the drawing to make a RECTANGLE.

Back of Frame 9

To make a RECTANGLE you have to draw in another long side and another short side to match the first two in length.

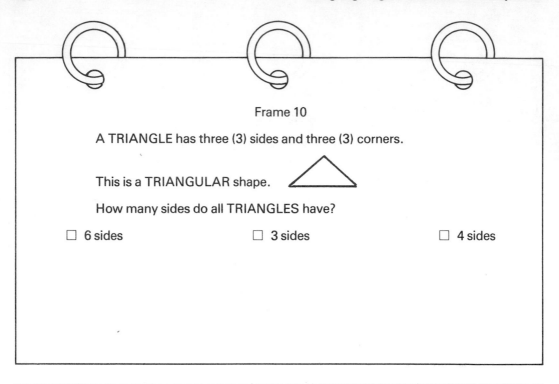

Frame 10

A TRIANGLE has three (3) sides and three (3) corners.

This is a TRIANGULAR shape.

How many sides do all TRIANGLES have?

☐ 6 sides   ☐ 3 sides   ☐ 4 sides

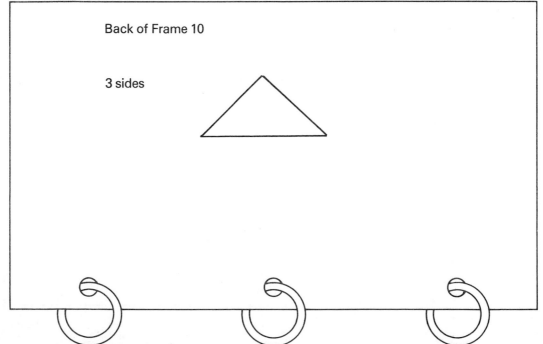

Back of Frame 10

3 sides

Frame 11

The three (3) sides of a TRIANGULAR shape may be the same, or they may be different.

The three (3) corners may be the same, or they may be different.

Look at this shape.

It is called a:

☐ SQUARE   ☐ TRIANGLE   ☐ RECTANGLE

Back of Frame 11

TRIANGLE

Frame 12

All the shapes in this drawing are T__I__N__U__A__.
Fill in the missing letters.

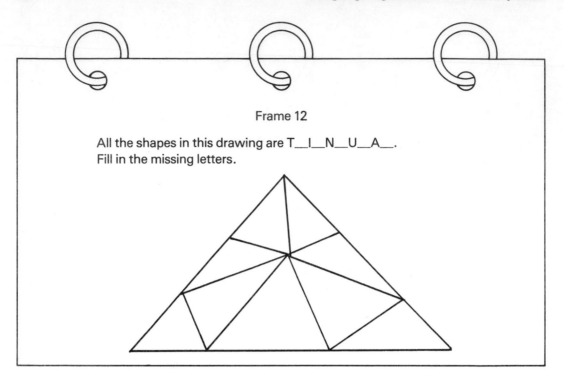

Back of Frame 12

T R I A N G U L A R

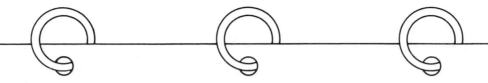

Frame 13

    Return to FRAME 12 and count the TRIANGULAR shapes in the drawing.

    How many TRIANGULAR shapes can you find?

Back of Frame 13

    You should find at least <u>9</u> TRIANGULAR shapes in Frame 12.

    If you put two (2) TRIANGLES together, you may find some more TRIANGLES.

    Did you count the drawing itself as a TRIANGLE too?

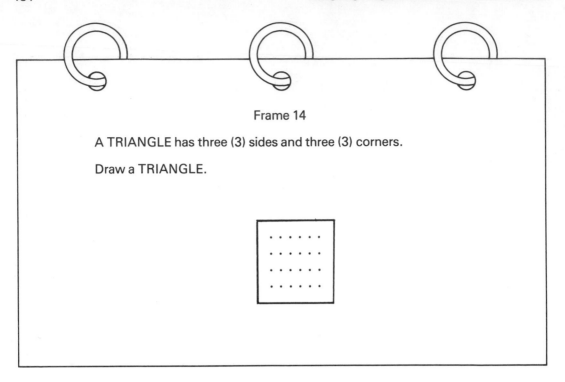

Frame 14

A TRIANGLE has three (3) sides and three (3) corners.

Draw a TRIANGLE.

Back of Frame 14

You can make a TRIANGLE with any of the dots.
Your shape may be bigger or smaller than this TRIANGLE.

Remember a TRIANGLE has three (3) sides and
three (3) corners.

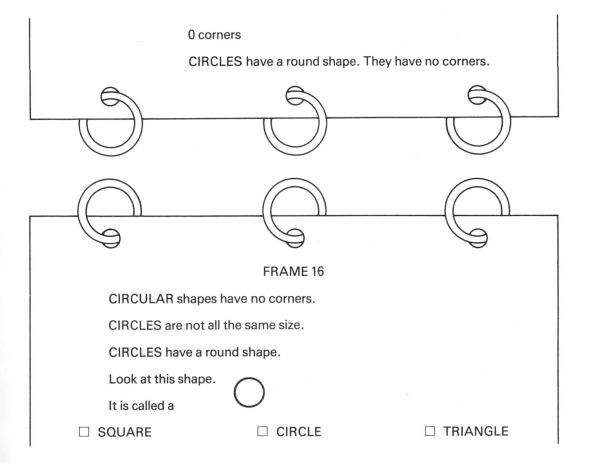

Frame 15

A CIRCLE has no corners. This is a CIRCULAR shape.

How many corners do all circles have?

☐ 2 corners   ☐ 0 corners   ☐ 4 corners

Back of Frame 15

0 corners

CIRCLES have a round shape. They have no corners.

FRAME 16

CIRCULAR shapes have no corners.

CIRCLES are not all the same size.

CIRCLES have a round shape.

Look at this shape.

It is called a

☐ SQUARE   ☐ CIRCLE   ☐ TRIANGLE

Back of Frame 16

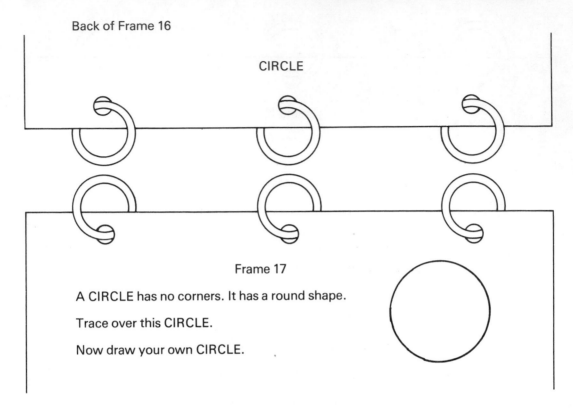

CIRCLE

Frame 17

A CIRCLE has no corners. It has a round shape.

Trace over this CIRCLE.

Now draw your own CIRCLE.

Back of Frame 17

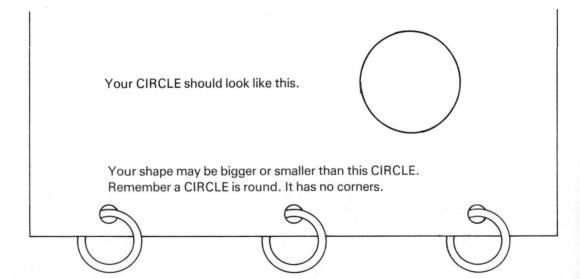

Your CIRCLE should look like this.

Your shape may be bigger or smaller than this CIRCLE.
Remember a CIRCLE is round. It has no corners.

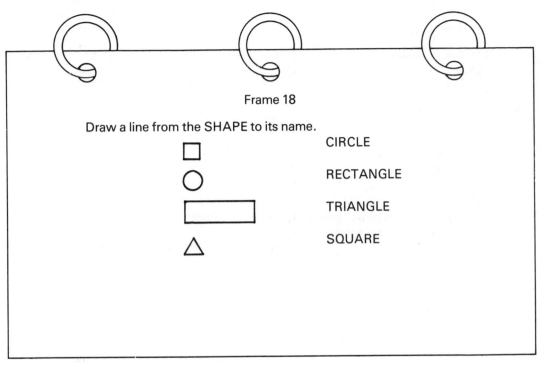

Frame 18

Draw a line from the SHAPE to its name.

CIRCLE

RECTANGLE

TRIANGLE

SQUARE

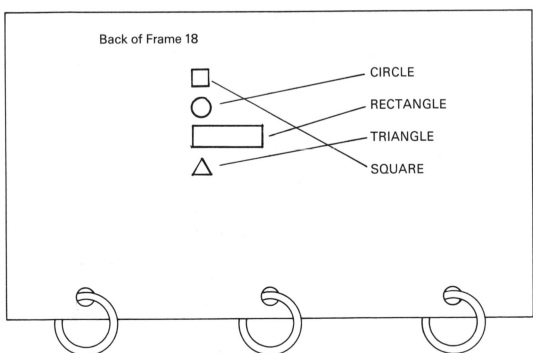

Back of Frame 18

CIRCLE

RECTANGLE

TRIANGLE

SQUARE

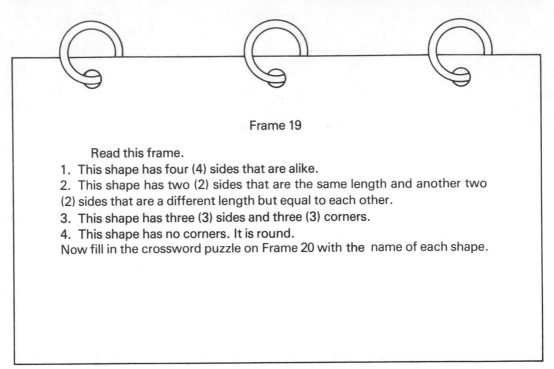

Frame 19

Read this frame.
1. This shape has four (4) sides that are alike.
2. This shape has two (2) sides that are the same length and another two
(2) sides that are a different length but equal to each other.
3. This shape has three (3) sides and three (3) corners.
4. This shape has no corners. It is round.
Now fill in the crossword puzzle on Frame 20 with the name of each shape.

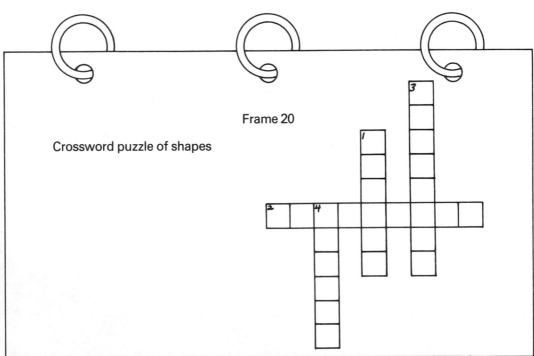

Frame 20

Crossword puzzle of shapes

Back of Frame 20

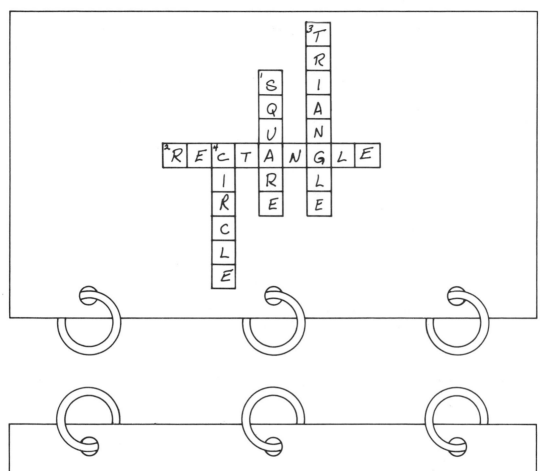

Frame 21

On the next FRAME (FRAME 22) draw and <u>write the name</u> of each of the four (4) SHAPES you learned about in this program. When you have drawn and named the SHAPES, show FRAME 22 to your teacher.

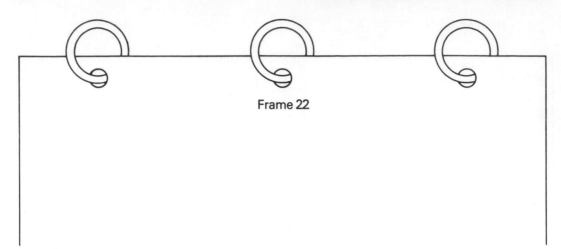

Frame 22

Back of Frame 22

Check your drawings and the spelling of each SHAPE against the drawings in FRAME 18. Correct anything that needs changing.

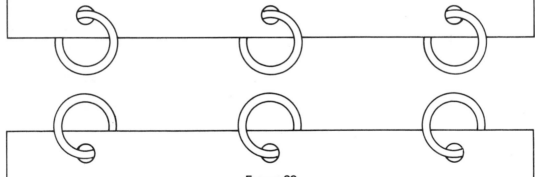

Frame 23

Now that you have finished this program, look at the back of the front cover again.

Name all the SHAPES and spell each of their names correctly—without looking.

If you can do this, CONGRATULATIONS!

If you have trouble doing this, then go back and do all or part of this program again! If your answers were correct, ask your teacher for the posttest on SHAPES.

Elementary Level: Life Cycle of the Frog[12]

Appealing drawings and the liberal use of color will attract elementary school children to a variety of instructional resources. Programmed learning booklets should be designed to be attractive and long-lasting. Laminate the heavy oaktag or cardboard pages and the programs can be used indefinitely.

Note that this program (Exhibit 5-3) concludes with a matching game. Several follow-up activities may be designed for reinforcement such as (1) fishing for frog's eggs, tadpoles with tails, or young frogs with magnet "nets" and placement in a diorama pond, (2) creating a story poster for the classroom, and (3) writing poems and drawings.

Youngsters who like to work quietly and alone or who prefer orderly directions and like to build knowledge, will gradually do well with this type of program.

Exhibit 5-3.   Sample elementary level program: Life Cycle of Freddy Frog.

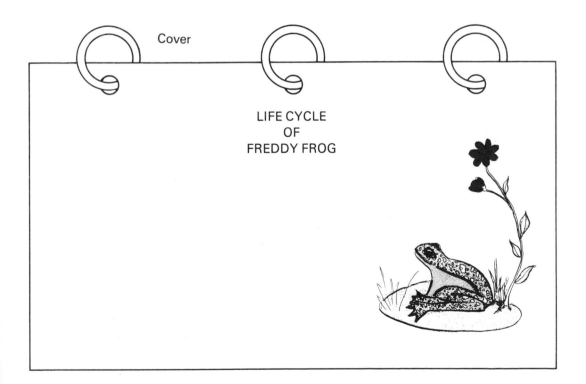

Back of Cover

When you complete this program, you will be able to identify the stages in the life cycle of a frog and explain each stage.

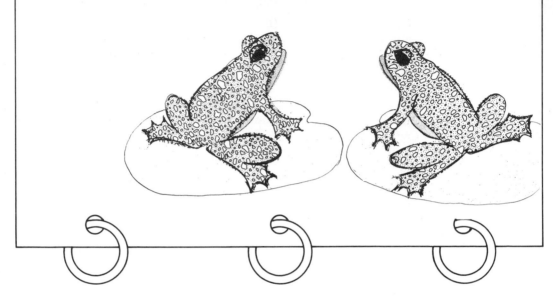

Front of Introductory Frame

VOCABULARY

You will need to know the meanings of these words to complete this program:

CLUMP — a group
DEVELOP — to grow
FERTILIZE — to give an egg cell power to grow by combining with a male cell
GILLS — part of a fish's body that is used for breathing under water
HATCH — to come out of a shell
POLLIWOG — a tadpole
TADPOLE — a stage of growth in a frog

Back of Introductory Frame

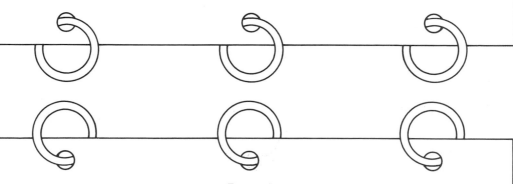

Read each paragraph. Then write the correct answer on the line at the end of the paragraph with the special pen tied to this program. Check your answers on the back of each frame. The answers will be written in ORANGE ink.

When you finish this program, be certain to wipe off all your answers with a damp tissue. Then someone else can use this book when you are finished.

Frame 1

It was a beautiful spring day. The sun was shining brightly. Birds were chirping and flying about building their nests.

The season was_____.

summer   spring   winter

Back of Frame 1

Answer: spring

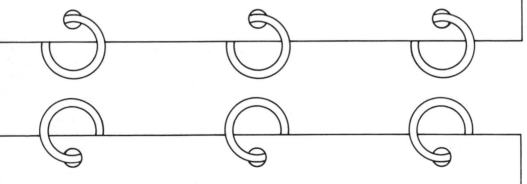

Frame 2

Mother and Father Frog woke up from their winter's sleep.
"Ribid", said Mr. Frog.
"Ribid, ribid," answered Mrs. Frog.
It was time to leave the hole. They hopped down to a nearby pond so that Mrs. Frog could lay her eggs.
Mrs. Frog laid her_____in the pond.

Back of Frame 2

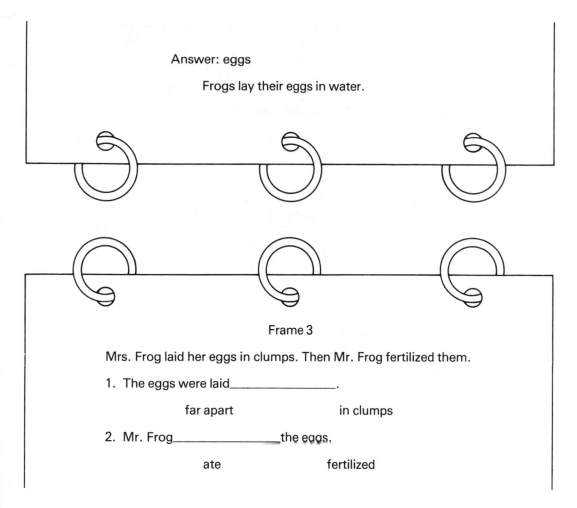

Answer: eggs

Frogs lay their eggs in water.

Frame 3

Mrs. Frog laid her eggs in clumps. Then Mr. Frog fertilized them.

1. The eggs were laid_____.

        far apart   in clumps

2. Mr. Frog_____the eggs.

        ate   fertilized

Back of Frame 3

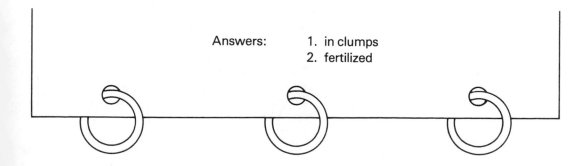

Answers: 1. in clumps
                  2. fertilized

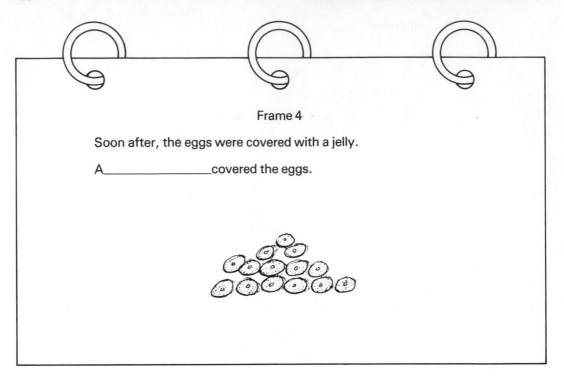

Frame 4

Soon after, the eggs were covered with a jelly.

A_____covered the eggs.

Back of Frame 4

Answer: jelly

The jelly helps to keep the eggs safe.

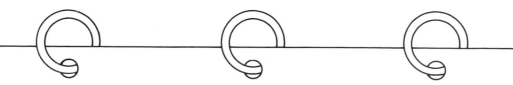

Frame 5

Mr. and Mrs. Frog hopped away in search of insects. They knew that soon their children would be born. The eggs would hatch in from four (4) to fifteen (15) days after they were laid.

The eggs would_____in from four (4) to fifteen (15) days after they were laid.

Back of Frame 5

Answer: hatch

The temperature of the water affects the speed at which eggs hatch.

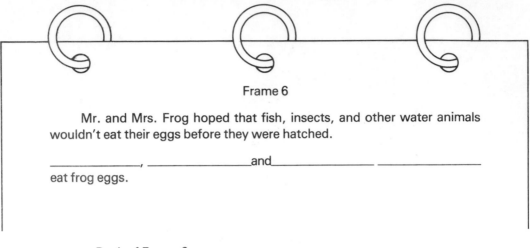

Frame 6

Mr. and Mrs. Frog hoped that fish, insects, and other water animals wouldn't eat their eggs before they were hatched.

_____, _____and_____ _____

eat frog eggs.

Back of Frame 6

Answer: fish, insects, and water animals

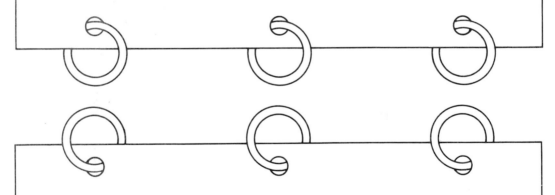

Frame 7

After eight (8) days, one egg hatched and out came Freddy. He was a funny looking creature.

Freddy didn't look at all like Mr. or Mrs. Frog. He had a big round head joined to his body and a tail. He looked like a tiny fish. He breathed through his gills, as fish do.

Freedy breathed through his_____.

Back of Frame 7

Answer: gills

Frame 8

At this time in his life Freddy was known as a tadpole.
The animal that was hatched was named "Freddy". He was known as
a _____at this time in his life.

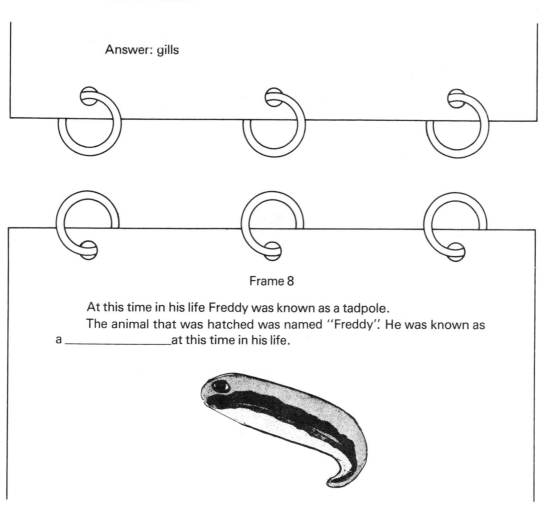

Back of Frame 8

Answer: tadpole

Some people call tadpoles "polliwogs."

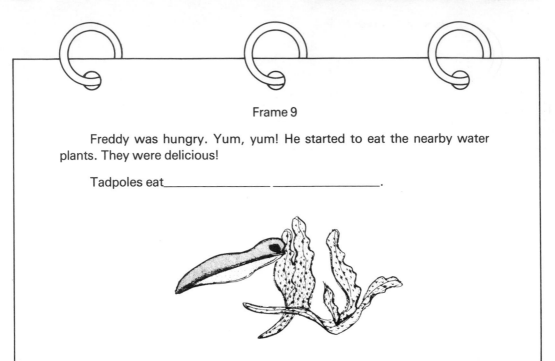

Frame 9

Freddy was hungry. Yum, yum! He started to eat the nearby water plants. They were delicious!

Tadpoles eat_____ _____.

Back of Frame 9

Answer: water plants

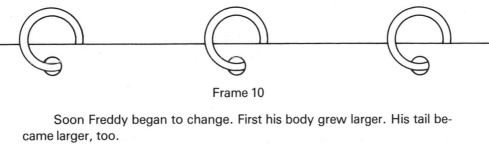

Frame 10

Soon Freddy began to change. First his body grew larger. His tail became larger, too.

The tadpole changed. First his_____and_____grew larger.

gills   body   head   tail

Back of Frame 10

Answer: body and tail

A tadpole's big tail helps him to swim about and capture food.

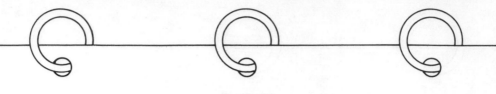

Frame 11

Freddy felt strange. Something new seemed to be happening to his body. Freddy didn't know it, but his hind legs were beginning to develop.

Next a tadpole's_____ _____develop.

Back of Frame 11

Answer: hind legs

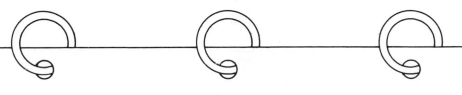

Frame 12

Freddy's hind legs grew longer, and
longer and
longer.

Then more legs came out. These were his front legs.

Tadpoles develop_____legs first.

Back of Frame 12

Answer: hind

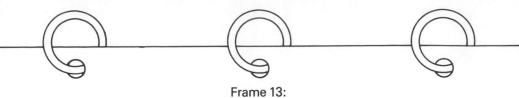

Frame 13:

That wasn't all that happened to Freddy. His lungs were growing, and his gills began to shrink.

Freddy's gills began to shrink as his_____began to grow.

head   tail   lungs

Back of Frame 13

Answer: lungs

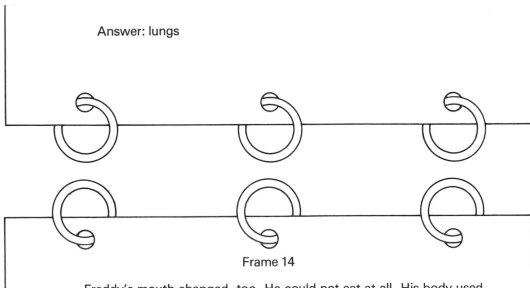

Frame 14

Freddy's mouth changed, too. He could not eat at all. His body used the food that was stored in his tail.

When the tadpole's mouth changed, his body used the food stored in

his_____.

tail   legs   lungs

Back of Frame 14

Answer: tail

Frame 15

Now Freddy's tail got s h o r t e r and
                                    s h o r t e r and
                                              shorter . . .

Until there was no tail at all.

The last change to happen to Freddy as a tadpole was that his_____

got shorter and shorter until there was no_____at all.

Back of Frame 15

Answer: tail
          tail

How well did you learn about Freddy as a tadpole? If you answered all the questions correctly, you are wonderful!

If you had more than two (2) incorrect answers, go back to Frame 7 and review the story about Freddy the tadpole.

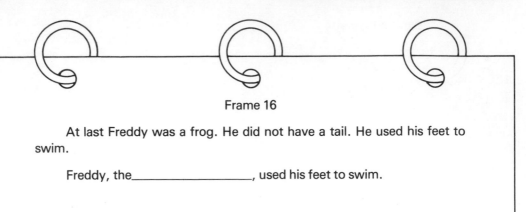

Frame 16

At last Freddy was a frog. He did not have a tail. He used his feet to swim.

Freddy, the_____, used his feet to swim.

Back of Frame 16

Answer: frog

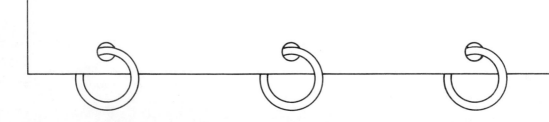

Frame 17

Freddy doesn't drink water. Frogs get water through their skin.

Frogs get water through their_____.

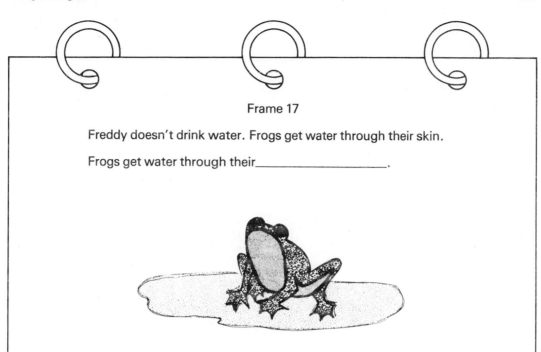

Back of Frame 17

Answer: skin

    A frog will sit in the water or on wet ground to get water.

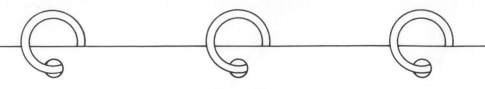

Frame 18

Freddy used his lungs to breathe air, for now he had no gills. he could not swim under water for a long time. He had to come up for air.

Freddy the frog used his_____to breathe in air.

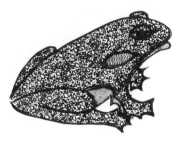

Back of Frame 18

Answer: lungs

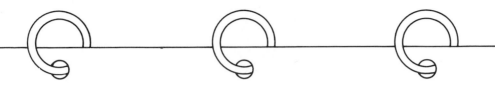

Frame 19

Freddy did not need to stay in the water all the time now. With his nice strong legs he hopped all over the ground.
Hop!
Hop! went Freddy.

The frog could_____to move all over the ground.

Back of Frame 19

Answer: hop

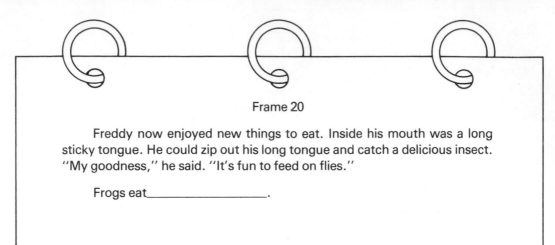

Frame 20

Freddy now enjoyed new things to eat. Inside his mouth was a long sticky tongue. He could zip out his long tongue and catch a delicious insect. "My goodness," he said. "It's fun to feed on flies."

Frogs eat_____.

Back of Frame 20

Answer: If you thought "insects" or "flies," you are correct.

Frogs are helpful to man because they eat flies and mosquitoes as well as other harmful insects.

Frame 21

Freddy ate lots of insects. He ate flies. He ate mosquitoes.
He grew
and g r e w
and GREW!

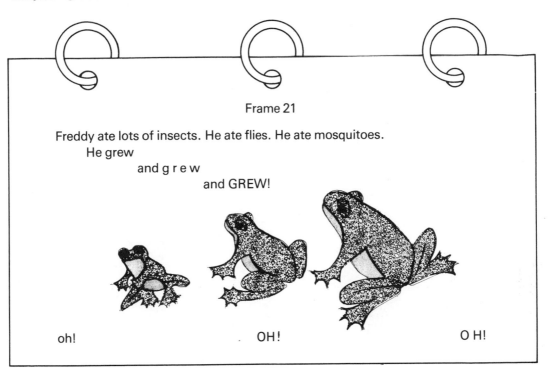

oh!   OH!   O H!

Frame 22

Pull! pull! pull! Freddy pulled off his old skin. A new skin grew under the old one. This new skin fit. Freddy was happy.

The frog pulled off his old skin. A new＿＿＿＿＿＿＿grew under the old one.

Back of Frame 22

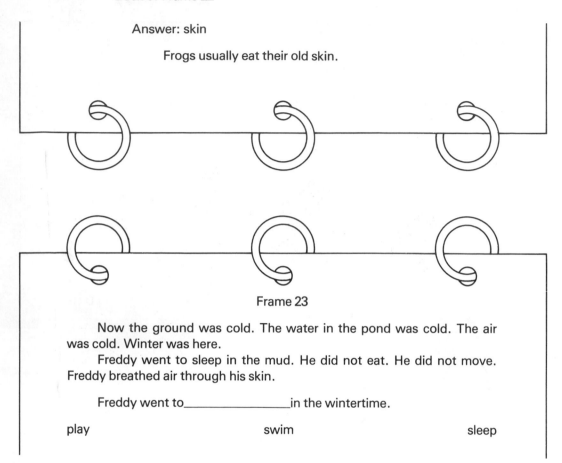

Answer: skin

Frogs usually eat their old skin.

Frame 23

Now the ground was cold. The water in the pond was cold. The air was cold. Winter was here.

Freddy went to sleep in the mud. He did not eat. He did not move. Freddy breathed air through his skin.

Freddy went to_____in the wintertime.

play   swim   sleep

Back of Frame 23

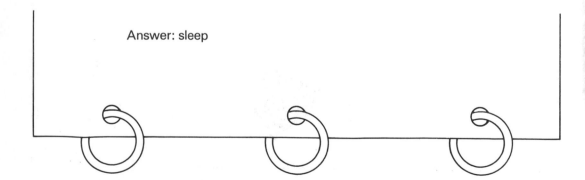

Answer: sleep

Frame 24

One morning Freddy woke up. He felt the warm sun. It was a beautiful spring day. The sun was shining brightly. Birds were chirping and flying about while building their nests.

Freddy woke up when _____ came.

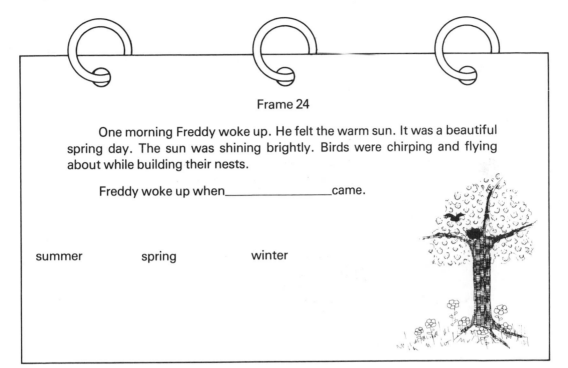

summer   spring   winter

Back of Frame 24

Answer: spring

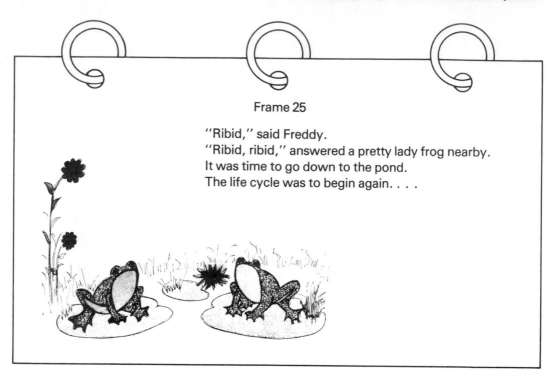

Frame 25

"Ribid," said Freddy.
"Ribid, ribid," answered a pretty lady frog nearby.
It was time to go down to the pond.
The life cycle was to begin again. . . .

At the end of the program Life Cycle of Freddy Frog is an attached matching game. Colorful pictures of frogs in various stages were drawn on cards. A description of each stage was typed onto other cards of the same size. The back of each drawing and its matching answer were color-coded and then laminated to make them durable. Directions for playing this matching game were then typed onto an envelope, which was also laminated or covered with a clear plastic. The deck of cards was mixed and placed in the envelope. Students could test their knowledge of the life cycle of a frog either by matching the correct cards and checking their answers by turning them over to see whether the colors matched too or by matching the colors and then turning over the cards to learn which answer was correct for each drawing.

Directions

Open the envelope and take out all the cards. Try to match each drawing with its correct description. When you have finished, turn over the pairs that you matched to learn if you were correct. After you have matched all the cards correctly, carefully place them back into the envelope. Then return the program and the matching game to the learning station.

Examples of Matching Cards

Middle or Junior High School Level: Uni- Bi- Tri- Made as Simple as 1, 2, 3[13]

Although some students thrive when taught directly by a teacher in either large or small groups, others learn faster and with less tension when they study either alone or with a friend. The following program (Exhibit 5-4) is one that might be used with youngsters in many grades but which was designed originally for middle or junior high school learners. Most programs can be effective with different aged students, depending on the learning style and achievement level of the individual.

COVER

Exhibit 5-4.   Sample middle or junior high school level program.

uni-

bi-

tri-

Made as simple as

1 2 3

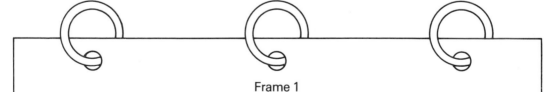

Frame 1

As you read you may come to new words that you do not understand. You can discover the meaning of some of these words if you know what the different parts of the word mean.

You are going to learn about three word-beginnings and what they mean when they are put in front of a word. When you finish this program, you will be able to discover the meanings of many new words that begin with uni-, bi-, and tri-.

Frame 2

VOCABULARY

Base: The main part of a word that holds most of its meaning.

Prefix: A group of letters added to the beginning of a base to change its meaning.

Uni-:   A prefix that means "one."

Bi-:   A prefix that means "two."

Tri-:   A prefix that means "three."

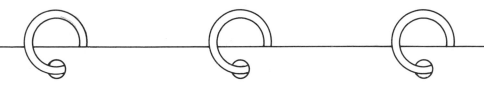

Frame 3

The main part of a word is called a base. It tells us most of the meaning of the word.

The main part of a word is called its_____.

Back of Frame 3

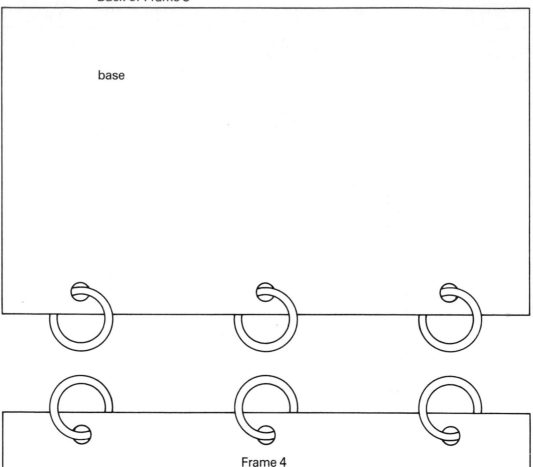

base

Frame 4

Sometimes a group of letters is placed in front of a base to change its meaning. We call these letters a prefix.

When a prefix changes or adds to the meaning of a base, a new word is formed.

PREFIX   +   BASE   =   NEW WORD

A_____is a group of letters added to the beginning of a base to change its meaning.

Back of Frame 4

prefix

Frame 5

TRI + ANGLE = TRIANGLE

Tri- is a prefix.
Angle is a base.
Together they form the word triangle.

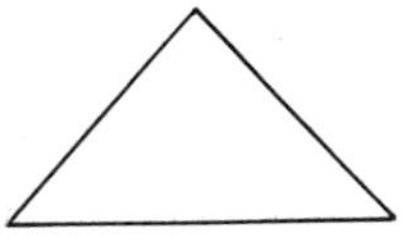

In the word biceps, bi- is a_____and -ceps is a_____.

Back of Frame 5

prefix
base

Frame 6

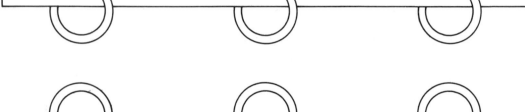

Sometimes the base is a word by itself. For example, the word angle is a base in the word triangle. Angle can be a word all by itself, even when it has no prefix.

This is a tricolor flag.

The base in the word tricolor is a_____all by itself.

The base in the word "tricolor" is_____.

Back of Frame 6

word
color

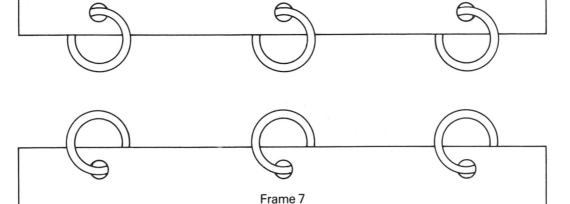

Frame 7

But sometimes a base needs help and cannot be a word unless something else is attached to it. For example, the -ceps in the word biceps is a base, but this base cannot stand alone as a word.

Choose (a) or (b).

If we take off the prefix tri- in the word triplet, the base that is left (a) can (b) cannot stand alone as a word.

Back of Frame 7

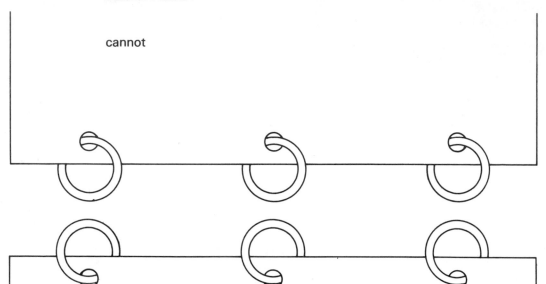

cannot

Frame 8

There are many different prefixes in the English language. Each time you learn a new prefix, you are learning a little more about your language. You often can discover the meaning of a word if you know the meaning of the prefix with which it begins.

It is good to learn many new prefixes because you often can discover the meaning of a new_____if you know the meaning of the prefix at its beginning.

Back of Frame 8

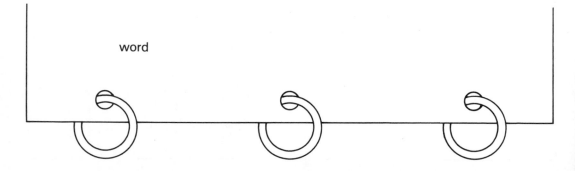

word

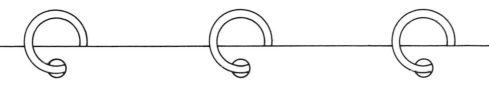

Frame 9

The prefix uni- means one. When you see the prefix uni- at the beginning of a word, it tells you that the meaning of the word has something to do with one.

A unicycle is a vehicle that has only one wheel.

A uniform way of doing something is having only one way of doing it.

The word unicorn comes from the Latin word for horn, which is "cornu." A unicorn is an animal that has _____ _____ on its head.

Back of Frame 9

one horn

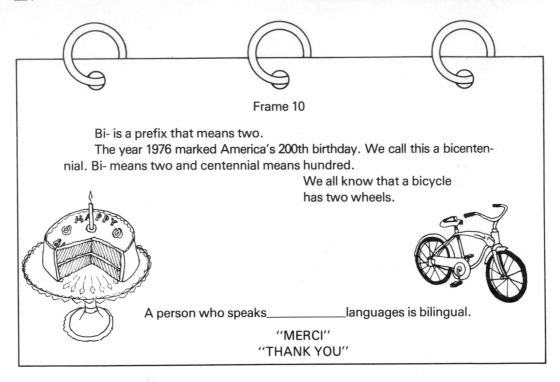

Frame 10

Bi- is a prefix that means two.

The year 1976 marked America's 200th birthday. We call this a bicentennial. Bi- means two and centennial means hundred.

We all know that a bicycle
has two wheels.

A person who speaks_____languages is bilingual.

"MERCI"
"THANK YOU"

Back of Frame 10

two

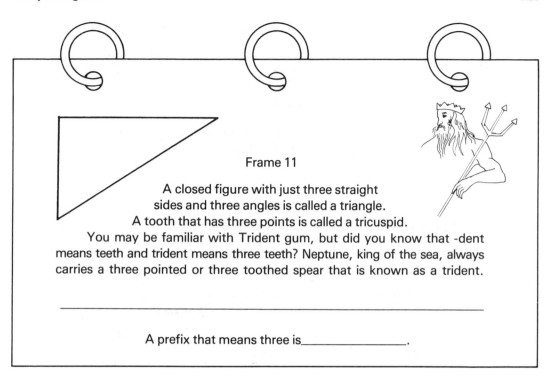

Frame 11

A closed figure with just three straight
sides and three angles is called a triangle.
A tooth that has three points is called a tricuspid.
You may be familiar with Trident gum, but did you know that -dent
means teeth and trident means three teeth? Neptune, king of the sea, always
carries a three pointed or three toothed spear that is known as a trident.

A prefix that means three is_____.

Back of Frame 11

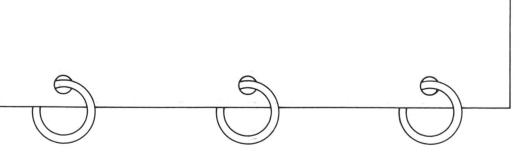

tri-

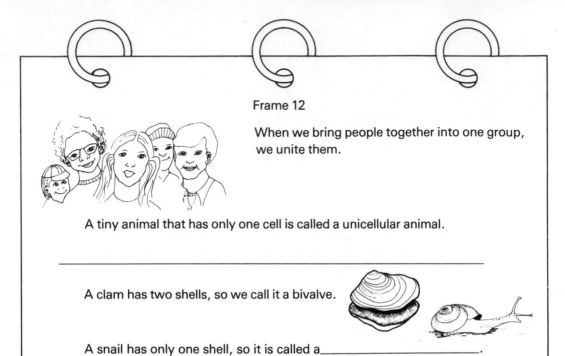

Frame 12

When we bring people together into one group, we unite them.

A tiny animal that has only one cell is called a unicellular animal.

A clam has two shells, so we call it a bivalve.

A snail has only one shell, so it is called a_____.

Back of Frame 12

univalve

Frame 13

When we cut something into two parts we <u>bi</u>sect it.

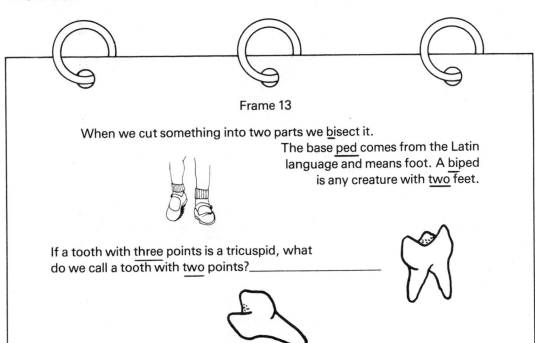

The base <u>ped</u> comes from the Latin language and means foot. A <u>bi</u>ped is any creature with <u>two</u> feet.

If a tooth with <u>three</u> points is a tricuspid, what do we call a tooth with <u>two</u> points?_____

Back of Frame 13

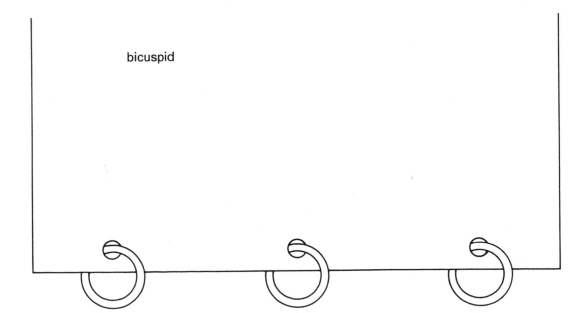

bicuspid

Frame 14

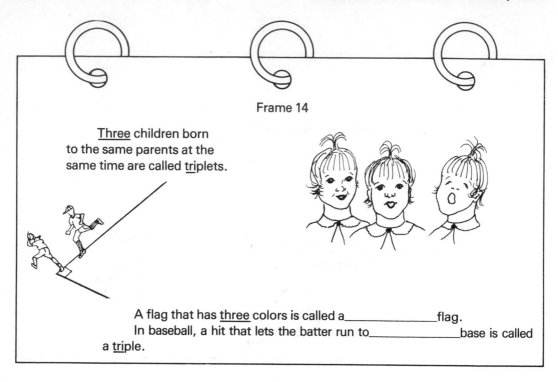

Three children born
to the same parents at the
same time are called triplets.

A flag that has three colors is called a_____flag.

In baseball, a hit that lets the batter run to_____base is called
a triple.

Back of Frame 14

tricolor
third

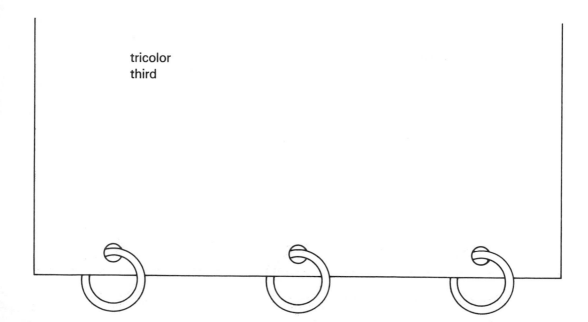

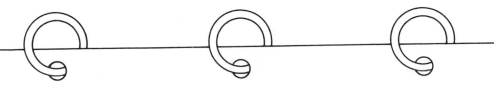

Frame 15

When you read three books and each one is a continuation of the book before it, we call the set of books a trilogy.

A muscle that is said to have two heads is called a bicep.

A trio is formed when_____ people sing together.

Annual means every year. Biannual means_____times a year.

Back of Frame 15

three
two (twice)

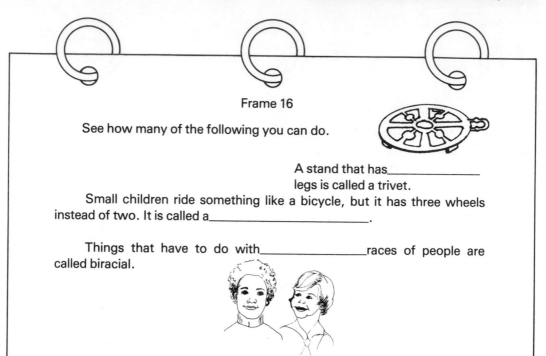

Frame 16

See how many of the following you can do.

A stand that has_____
legs is called a trivet.

Small children ride something like a bicycle, but it has three wheels instead of two. It is called a_____.

Things that have to do with_____races of people are called biracial.

Back of Frame 16

three
tricycle
two

TEST YOURSELF

1. The main part of a word is called its _____.

2. A_____is a group of letters added to the beginning of a base to change its meaning.

3. In the word biceps, bi- is a_____and -ceps is a _____.

4. The base in the word tricolor is a_____all by itself.

5. The base in the word tricolor is_____.

6. Choose (a) or (b). If we take off the prefix tri- in the word triplet, the base that is left (a) can (b) cannot stand alone as a word.

7. It is good to learn many new prefixes, because you often can discover the meaning of a new_____if you know the meaning of the prefix at its beginning.

8. A prefix that means three is_____.

9. A prefix that means one is_____.

10. A prefix that means two is_____.

11. The word unicorn comes from the Latin word for horn, which is "cornu." A unicorn is an animal that has _____ _____on his head.

12. A person who speaks_____languages is bilingual.

13. A clam has two shells, so we call it a bivalve. A snail has only one shell, so it is called a_____.

14. If a tooth with three points is a tricuspid, what do we call a tooth with two points?_____

15. A flag that has three colors is called a_____flag.

16. In baseball, a hit that lets the batter run to_____base is called a triple.

17. A trio is formed when_____people sing together.

18. Annual means every year. Biannual means _____times a year.

19. A stand that has _____legs is called a trivet.

20. Small children ride something like a bicycle, but it has three wheels instead of two. It is called a_____.

21. Things that have to do with_____races of people are called biracial.

ANSWERS FOR TEST

1.	base	11.	one horn
2.	prefix	12.	two
3.	prefix, base	13.	univalve
4.	word	14.	a bicuspid
5.	color	15.	tricolor
6.	cannot	16.	third
7.	word	17.	three
8.	tri-	18.	two
9.	uni-	19.	three
10.	bi-	20.	tricycle
		21.	two

How many of the answers on your self-test were correct?

If you had all twenty-one correct, you may find some friends and play the game on the next page. If you had one or two wrong answers, go back and see if you can figure out why they were wrong. You may have to reread a few frames. If you can't understand why they were wrong or if you had three or more wrong, then talk to your teacher about your answers.

WORD BINGO AT END OF PROGRAM

You will need one person to be caller and two or more players.

Each player receives a card and twenty-one prefix markers, seven of each prefix. The caller gets the pack of definition cards, shuffles them, and picks up the top card. He or she reads the word on the card and its definition. Each player must place the right prefix marker over the correct base on his or her card to form the word being read.

The first player to cover five bases horizontally, vertically, or diagonally wins. Be certain to have the caller check the winning card to see if all the words have been called.

SAMPLE WORD BINGO GAME CARDS

-ped	-vet	-color	-racial	-cep
-plet	-plet	-annual	-cuspid	-cellular
-form	-angle	FREE	-dent	-ple
-logy	-te	-corn	-sect	-cep
-o	-lingual	-valve	-centennial	-cycle

-plet	-centennial	-o	-ped	-sect
-logy	-ple	-plet	-dent	-cellular
-valve	-cuspid	FREE	-lingual	-color
-cycle	-vet	-racial	-form	-valve
-corn	-annual	-te	-angle	-cep

MARKERS FOR WORD BINGO (TO BE CUT OUT)

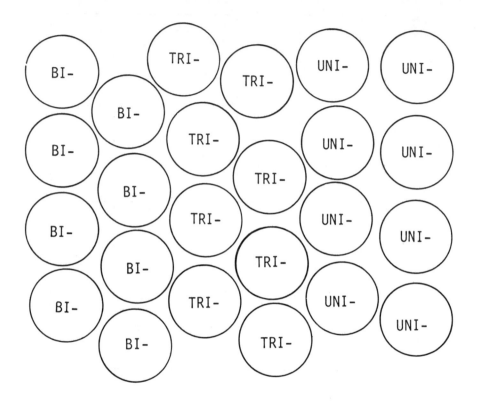

EXAMPLES: QUESTIONS CARDS FOR WORD BINGO

triangle—a closed figure
           with three straight
           sides and three
           angles.

bilingual—able to speak
            two languages.

EXAMPLES: QUESTION CARDS FOR WORD BINGO

bicentennial — a 200th
birthday or
anniversary.

trilingual — able to
speak three
languages.

biracial — having to do
with two races.

univalve — an animal that
has one shell, for
example, a snail.

bicuspid — a tooth with
two points.

tricorn — having three
horns.

tricolor — having three
colors.

trilogy — three stories
that have to do
with each other.

EXAMPLES: QUESTION CARDS FOR WORD BINGO

trisect — cut into three equal parts.	**triplets** — three children born to the same parents at the same time.
bicorn — having two horns.	**tricep** — a muscle having three heads or points.
triform — having three forms.	**biped** — an animal with two feet.
triple — having three parts, for example, in baseball a three base hit.	**bicep** — a muscle having two heads or points.

EXAMPLES: QUESTION CARDS FOR WORD BINGO

tricycle — a pedaled vehicle with three wheels.

biannual — twice a year.

unite — to bring together.

tricentennial — a 300th birthday or anniversary.

bicolor — having two colors

trio — three people who sing together or any three people or things that are joined in some way.

uniform — always the same.

trivet — a stand that has three legs.

EXAMPLES: QUESTION CARDS FOR WORD BINGO

---

unicorn — a make-believe
animal with one horn
growing out of its head.

High School Level: Exponents[14]

Many high school students are bored or easily distracted when the teacher explains a new topic by lecturing or a chalk-talk. These students may be tactual or kinesthetic learners and may be unable to learn through their auditory-visual senses. Even if they can, their rate of learning may be slower (or faster) than the pace of the instructor's talking. They may prefer to work alone and may be distracted by the noise and shuffling present to some degree in whole-class or large-group instruction.

This program on exponents may closely follow a teacher's sequential chalkboard presentation, but it is now permanently inscribed in an attractive booklet with visuals and immediate feedback to a student's answers. The student is actively involved in reading, answering, and checking his or her work. For some students and topics this approach will prove to be a perfect match of method and learning style.

Exhibit 5-5.   Sample high school level program: Exponents

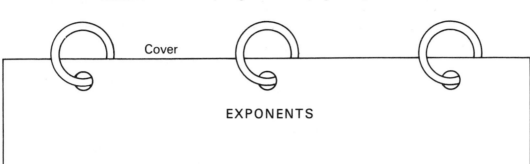

Cover

EXPONENTS

$x^3 = x \bullet x \bullet x$

$4^3 = 64$

$3^1 = 3$

Frame 1

PLEASE START THE TAPE RECORDER

    Throughout this program, questions you are asked to answer will appear on one side of the card. Each card is called a frame. The answer to the question appears on the back of the card. If you are using the tape recorder, you may wish to stop the tape if you need more time before going on to the next frame. Start the tape when you are ready by pressing the PLAY button.

PLEASE TURN TO THE NEXT FRAME

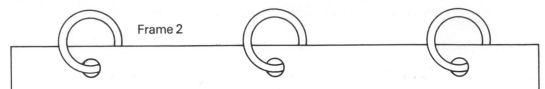

Frame 2

Please compare your answer with the answer that you find on the back of each card. If your answer is the same, go on to the next frame; if your answer is different, take the time to study the frame and learn what your error was. It is important that you understand each frame before going on to the next frame.

PLEASE TURN TO NEXT FRAME

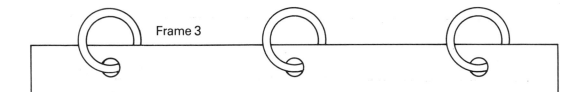

Frame 3

VOCABULARY

When we multiply two or more numbers, the result is the product. The numbers are called factors.

We can express products with like factors by using exponents. An exponent is a small numeral that indicates how many times a number (called the base) is used as a factor in finding a product. The product is called a power of the number that is the base.

PLEASE TURN TO NEXT FRAME

Front of Frame 4

   Consider the product of three (3) fives.

$5 \times 5 \times 5 = 5^3 \longleftarrow$ exponent
$\qquad \qquad \qquad \searrow$ base

   The base, 5, tells us the like factors being multiplied. The exponent, 3, tells us the number of like factors multiplied. So, 5^3 means the product of three (3) fives.

   In the expression 4^2 , the base is_____and the exponent is _____.

Back of Frame 4

the base is 4
the exponent is 2

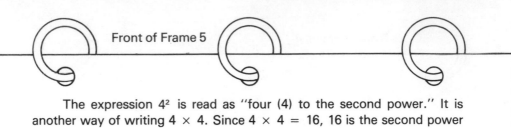

Front of Frame 5

The expression 4^2 is read as "four (4) to the second power." It is another way of writing 4×4. Since $4 \times 4 = 16$, 16 is the second power of 4.

In the expression 5^4, 5 is the_____and 4 is the_____.

CHECK YOUR ANSWERS PLEASE

Back of Frame 5

5 is the base
4 is the exponent

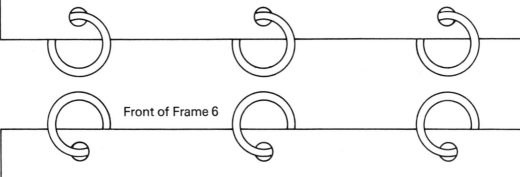

Front of Frame 6

In the expression x^4 (x to the fourth power), the base is_____
and the exponent is_____.

CHECK YOUR ANSWERS PLEASE

Back of Frame 6

base is x
exponent is 4

Front of Frame 7

The expression x^1 is written x, and $2^1 = 2$.
In the expression 2, then, the base is_____and the exponent is_____.

Back of Frame 7

base is 2
exponent is 1

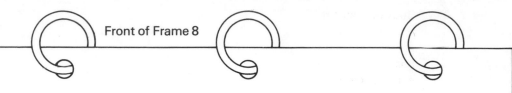

Front of Frame 8

The expression y^3 is read as "y to the third power." An expression that reads "x to the fourth power" may be written as_____.

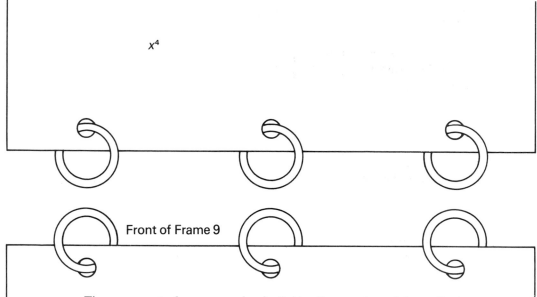

Back of Frame 8

x^4

Front of Frame 9

The exponent of an expression indicates the number of times the base is used as a factor.

$b^5 = b \cdot b \cdot b \cdot b \cdot b$ (• is a multiplication sign)

$t^4 = $ _____(Write as factors.)

Back of Frame 9

$t \bullet t \bullet t \bullet t$

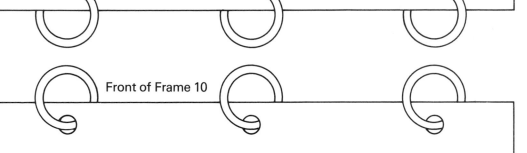

Front of Frame 10

t^4 is the short form and is equivalent to $t \bullet t \bullet t \bullet t$, the expanded form
Write in the short form: $y \bullet y \bullet y \bullet y \bullet y =$ _____

Back of Frame 10

y^5

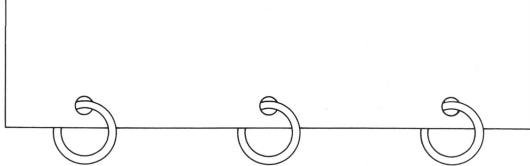

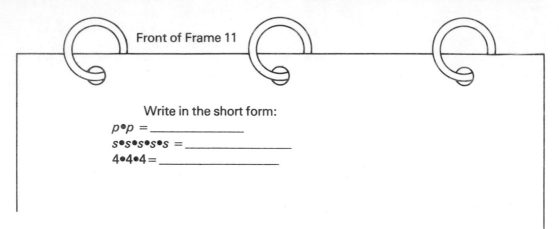

Write in the short form:

$p \bullet p =$ _____

$s \bullet s \bullet s \bullet s \bullet s =$ _____

$4 \bullet 4 \bullet 4 =$ _____

Back of Frame 11

p^2

s^5

4^3

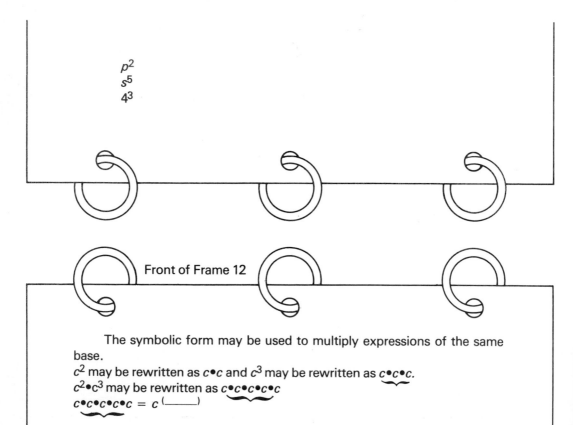

Front of Frame 12

The symbolic form may be used to multiply expressions of the same base.

c^2 may be rewritten as $c \bullet c$ and c^3 may be rewritten as $c \bullet c \bullet c$.

$c^2 \bullet c^3$ may be rewritten as $c \bullet c \bullet c \bullet c \bullet c$

$c \bullet c \bullet c \bullet c \bullet c = c^{(\_\_\_\_\_)}$

Back of Frame 12

c^5

Front of Frame 13

$$\frac{\overbrace{a \bullet a \bullet a \bullet a \bullet a}}{a \bullet a \bullet a \bullet a} = a^5$$

$a^3 \bullet a^2 = $ _____

Back of Frame 13

a^5

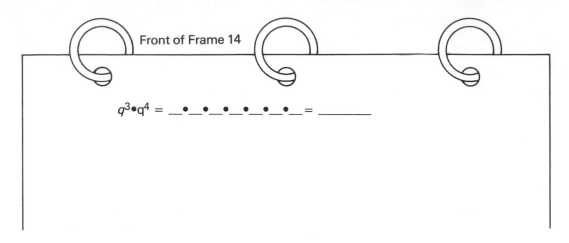

Front of Frame 14

$$q^3 \bullet q^4 = \_\_\bullet\_\_\bullet\_\_\bullet\_\_\bullet\_\_\bullet\_\_\bullet\_\_ = _____$$

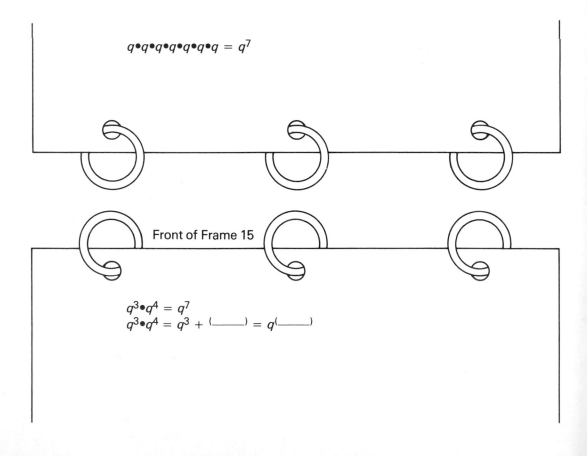

Back of Frame 14

$$q \bullet q \bullet q \bullet q \bullet q \bullet q \bullet q = q^7$$

Front of Frame 15

$$q^3 \bullet q^4 = q^7$$
$$q^3 \bullet q^4 = q^3 + {}^{(\underline{\hspace{1cm}})} = q^{(\underline{\hspace{1cm}})}$$

Back of Frame 15

$$q^{3 + 4} = q^7$$

Front of Frame 16

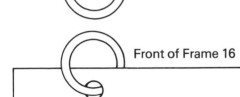

Multiply:
$$5^2 \cdot 5^3 = \underline{\hspace{1cm}}\ \underline{\hspace{1cm}}\ \underline{\hspace{1cm}}\ \underline{\hspace{1cm}}\ \underline{\hspace{1cm}}$$
$$= 5^{(\underline{\hspace{1cm}})}$$
$$c^2 \cdot c^5 = \underline{\hspace{2cm}}$$

Back of Frame 16

$$5 \cdot 5 \cdot 5 \cdot 5 \cdot 5$$
$$5^5$$
$$c^2 \cdot c^5 = c^{2 + 5} = c^7$$

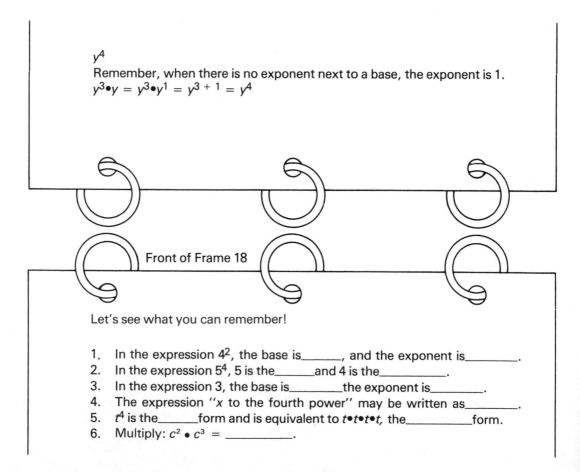

Front of Frame 17

Multiply:
$y^3 \cdot y =$ _____

Back of Frame 17

y^4
Remember, when there is no exponent next to a base, the exponent is 1.
$y^3 \cdot y = y^3 \cdot y^1 = y^{3+1} = y^4$

Front of Frame 18

Let's see what you can remember!

1.   In the expression 4^2, the base is_____, and the exponent is_____.
2.   In the expression 5^4, 5 is the_____and 4 is the_____.
3.   In the expression 3, the base is_____the exponent is_____.
4.   The expression "x to the fourth power" may be written as_____.
5. t^4 is the_____form and is equivalent to $t \cdot t \cdot t \cdot t$, the_____form.
6.   Multiply: $c^2 \cdot c^3 =$ _____.

Back of Frame 18

1. base is 4, exponent is 2
2. base, exponent
3. base is 3, exponent is 1
4. x^4
5. short, expanded
6. $c^{2+3} = c^5$

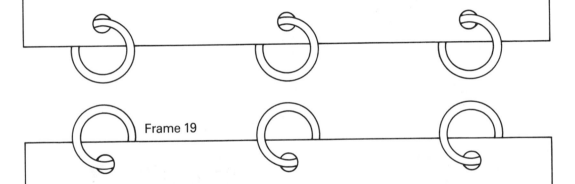

Frame 19

CONGRATULATIONS!
You have finished the first program on exponents.
Please rewind the tape so that it will be ready for the next person.
Please return the program, tape, and tape recorder to the math lab.
Next, take the game, *Exponent Rummy* from the math lab and try your hand at matching each expression with its correct symbolic form. When you have completed the task, ask your teacher to check your answers, then return the game to the lab.

GAME CARDS FOR EXPONENT RUMMY

d^4	$d \cdot d^3$
$y \cdot y^3 \cdot y^3$	x^6
Y^7	$x^2 \cdot x^2 \cdot x^2$
$y^2 \cdot y^2 \cdot y^3$	$c \cdot c^2$

GAME CARDS FOR EXPONENT RUMMY

$x^3 \cdot x^4$	$t \cdot t^4$
$y^3 \cdot y^4$	c^3
$t \cdot t \cdot t \cdot t \cdot t$	$y \bullet y \bullet y \bullet y \bullet y \bullet y \bullet y$
$c \cdot c \cdot c$	$t^3 \cdot t^2$

GAME CARDS FOR EXPONENT RUMMY

$$y^5 \cdot y^2$$

$$d^2 \cdot d^2$$

$$t^2 \cdot t^2 \cdot t$$

$$x \cdot x \cdot x \cdot x \cdot x \cdot x$$

$$x^3 \cdot x^3$$

$$d \cdot d \cdot d \cdot d$$

$$d \cdot d \cdot d^2$$

$$t^5$$

A Final Word on Programs

As with any successful technique, programs should not be prescribed to the point where continual use of the method causes boredom. This mistake was often made during the 1960s when much heralded teaching machines failed, at least in part, because of the uncreative, repetitious, and sometimes inferior programs to which youngsters were subjected for hours at a time, day after day, regardless of their learning styles.

Selective use of this technique with students who are motivated, persistent, and responsible, who need structure, prefer to work alone, and are visually oriented in learning will prove rewarding to them and to you. Do not, however, use it exclusively; vary your approaches based on learning style diagnoses and encourage alternative methods for those youngsters who would benefit from them.

6

Designing Multisensory Instructional Packages to Respond to Individual Learning Styles

Instructional packages are especially appealing to students who find it difficult to sit quietly for long periods of time or who cannot listen to a teacher without frequently interrupting or losing attention. Using a package, these youngsters can concentrate for the amount of time that suits them, take breathers whenever they wish, and then continue with their work. Instructional packages are not as effective for students who need continual direct interaction with either adults or peers; but very often they may be suitable for several learners at the beginning of a semester, for others a few weeks later, for others at midterm, and so on. They also may be designed so that one or two of the multisensory activities may be bypassed if less concentration on the topic is necessary.

Instructional packages are a boon to teachers who want to individualize instruction through direct appeal to personal learning styles but who cannot stretch themselves thin enough for a class full of children with a variety of needs and problems. Because students work independently (or with a friend) and the materials are self-corrective, the packages can meet the needs of learners on several academic levels—youngsters with learning disabilities who require special attention; slow learners who need more time to grasp new material; average youngsters who prefer working on their own or for shorter or longer blocks of time; advanced students who are capable of progressing faster than their peers; and any interested student who wants to·

learn about a topic, concept, or skill at the moment when he or she desires, not when the teacher is able to get to the subject. The packages don't take up much classroom space, and they are particularly well suited to home study (see Exhibit 6–1.)[1]

As an example of what is possible in a single classroom, one student might be working on a time-telling lesson while another, in a different section of the room, could be mastering the concept of halves. As the first manipulates movable hands, the second separates multicolored eggs. A third youngster may be hopping on a large plastic sheet that has been separated into sections and organized into a game that reviews parts of speech. The teacher moves among several small groups, pairs, and individuals while the instructional packages completely absorb the students using them.

Learning Style Characteristics Responsive to Instructional Packages

Because of their multisensory activities, instructional packages are very motivating to slow learners, who usually require repetition and varied approaches through many senses before they are motivated to acquire and retain new knowledge and skills. The tape, written script, tactual and kinesthetic materials may be used over and over again until the youngster masters the objectives of the package.

Each instructional package focuses on a single objective or concept to be taught. This isolated goal is well suited to the recalcitrant learner who often finds it difficult to concentrate on more than one thing at a time. Conversely, unless the material in the package is extremely challenging, it is unlikely to interest high achievers who quickly become bored by repetition.

Instructional packages are especially appropriate for those youngsters who require structure. The step-by-step procedures provide clear, sequenced directions that are repeated in a variety of ways until success is achieved.

Students who prefer working alone usually enjoy this multisensory method immensely. They can take the materials to an instructional area in the room, to the library, or even to their homes to work on intensively and without the distractions of the classroom and their peers.

Sound, in the form of your recorded voice, music, or other taped effects, can be provided or modulated through earphones or a cassette player.

All perceptual strengths are appealed to: by definition, instructional packages include visual, auditory, tactual, and kinesthetic activities. Even when a student has only a single perceptual strength, he or she is likely to learn and to complete objectives because everything that is taught is introduced and reinforced through the four major learning senses.

Teachers should be aware of those youngsters who prefer instructional packages but who lack responsibility. Encouragement and piecemeal success on portions of the package should be promoted. Careful monitoring

Exhibit 6–1.   Instructional packages may be signed out for home study. Instructions on teacher-made tapes guide students through each or all of four multisensory activities—auditory, visual, tactual, and kinesthetic. This package describes how nouns and verbs form sentence patterns. (Photographs courtesy of the Department of Curriculum and Teaching, St. John's University, Grand Central Parkway, Queens, New York.)

will aid those students in building responsibility. At times it may be necessary for the teacher or selected peers to work with those youngsters who respond well to instructional packages but who also require interaction with an authority figure or friends to stimulate learning.

Generally speaking, instructional packages are ideal for slower students who require structure and who can be sufficiently motivated by their multisensory activities to progress independently and successfully.

Learning Style Characteristics To Which Instructional Packages Can Be Accommodated

Instructional packages can be taken to wherever the light, temperature, and design of the physical environment are exactly as the student wishes them to be. Because instructional packages are portable and may be worked on alone, the choice of where to use these resources belongs to the student, who may select the amount of light, the degree of temperature, and the kind of design in which he or she feels most comfortable.

Motivation is often developed or stimulated through these packages because of (1) the choice that students have in their selection or in the topic that will be studied, (2) the way the packages accommodate to the environmental and physical elements of learning style, (3) the control that youngsters exercise over the amount and pace of learning in which they engage at a given time, and (4) the academic progress that is virtually assured by the package's multisensory repetition.

Three other important aspects of learning style—intake, time of day, and mobility—are accommodated by instructional packages.

It is easy to take advantage of intake while working independently on an instructional package. Raw vegetables, nuts, raisins, or other nutritious foods can be available in a bowl wherever the youngster is working, provided that rules have been established beforehand for access, eating, discarding, and the care of the premises.

Packages may be used at any time of the day or night without interfering with others and without interrupting other scheduled activities. Therefore, students can select the most appropriate and effective time to complete a package.

Many growing youngsters cannot sit still or work in one place for a long time. Packages allow total mobility. A student may take the package with him, spread it out, walk away, then come back, sprawl, kneel, or just sit. Since the activities themselves provide action and movement, mobility is well served by this method.

Case Studies Describing Students Whose Learning Styles Are Complemented by Instructional Packages

1. Ben looked around. He couldn't seem to follow the instructions. They were printed on a sheet but they didn't make sense to him. He turned to his neighbor, Ed, and asked what he was supposed to do after finishing the second problem. Before Ed could respond, the teacher called out impatiently, "Ben, the directions are printed for you. All you have to do is read them!"

Auditory students may need to hear instructions or directions; the printed word may not be effective for them. Instructional packages provide a taped version of the written instructions.

2. Amy was very creative. She liked to put things together and often ignored the item's directions. Most of the time she was successful, but occasionally she had ruined toys by not reading instruction sheets. She repeated this pattern at school, where she often plunged ahead on a test and answered questions that she had not carefully read. Her projects, too, although inspired, frequently contained many errors or were not completed because of Amy's cavalier approach to directions.

Students who require structure, concentration, concise direction, sequences, a single focus, and logical steps will benefit from the use of instructional packages.

3. John slammed his book down. The others looked at him. The teacher called John to her and asked what was wrong. "It's the kids, I guess," explained John. "Every time I start to do my work, the others ask questions or talk to me. I can't stand the interruptions when I'm working."

Students who work best alone may find instructional packages to their liking.

4. Susie smiled. She played the tape again; her fingers traced the words in the written script as she listened. She understood perfectly! For the first time, reading had become fun. After she finished the touching and feeling game with ease, she began to build the map with the pieces in the package. She told the teacher that she wanted a new package tomorrow.

Instructional packages are ideal for those who need to learn through a perceptual strength that is not usually appealed to in the classroom and for those who require reinforcement through more than one perceptual strength.

How Instructional Packages Facilitate Academic Achievement

Instructional packages are multisensory, self-contained teaching units that appeal to students who learn slowly or whose learning style characteristics respond to this method. All packages have certain basic elements in common:

1. *Each package focuses on a single concept.*

Whether the package deals with learning how to tell time, identifying adverbs and using them correctly, the division of fractions, or war as a human atrocity, students know precisely what the focus is and can decide if it is appealing as a new topic or useful in reinforcing a previously learned skill. The cover and title always reveal what the package contains.

2. *At least four senses are used to learn the contents.*

A typewritten script that is repeated by the taped voice of the teacher gives clear directions to students to construct, manipulate, piece together, write, draw, complete, play, and in several ways use their sense of touch and their entire bodies in kinesthetic activities related to the package's objectives.

3. *Feedback and evaluation are built in.*

Tests are included in the package, and students may respond by writing, taping, or showing results. Correct answers and responses may be checked as the items to be learned are completed. The directions allow for immediate feedback and self-evaluation. Mistakes can be corrected through repetition of the taped and printed directions and by comparing the students' answers with ones prepared for the games and activities.

4. *Learning is private and aimed at individual learning styles.*

Only the teacher and student know how well the youngster is doing. Self-image and success are enhanced as progress increases without peer competition for the slower students. The multisensory approach; colorful materials and packaging; working alone; motivating choices; selection of when, where, and how; and the ability to move about and to eat if necessary make the instructional package an effective teaching aid for many students.

A Step-by-step Guide to Designing an Instructional Package

Step 1   Identify the topic. For example, you may want your students to understand concepts or acquire skills related to parts of speech, a specific country, pollution, writing business letters, or solving math problems.

Step 2   List the things you want the student to learn about the topic.

Step 3   Plan to tape-record simple learning objectives for your students. Use such words as *explain, describe, list,* and *identify.* For example, if you were constructing a package on nouns, the taped objective might be: "By the time you finish this package, you will be able to explain what a noun is and to recognize one in a sentence." (For specific instructions, see the section of this chapter on "How to Tape Directions for Instructional Packages.")

Step 4   Pretend you are teaching your class the most important aspects of the selected topic. Write out exactly what you would say to them. Plan to tape-record this explanation.

Step 5   Develop a visual, a tactual, and a kinesthetic activity that emphasizes these aspects in different ways. Write the directions for each of the activities as they will be taped.

Step 6   Make up a short test that will reveal whether the student has learned the skills and concepts after using the package. This may be recorded as well as written.[2]

Step 7   Use a colorful cardboard box with a design that reveals the topic and contents. Cover the entire box, including the typewritten topic and contents, with clear Con-tact, or laminate them to ensure longevity.

Examples of Appropriate Instructional Packages

LANGUAGE ARTS: Parts of speech, correct grammar, selected skills such as:

Recognizing and using adjectives	How to write a business letter
What does an adverb do?	How to develop complete sentences
Knowing nouns	When to use the possessive form
When to use capital letters	How to follow directions
How to solve problems	The_____word family
How to write an original ending	Quotation marks: Where do they go?

SOCIAL STUDIES: Map skills, geographical locations, community workers, common interests, such as:

East and West	A different kind of "key"
Locating capital cities	A visit to Paris
Estimating mileage	The Third World nations
Games children play	Customs of the Algonquins
How climate affects industrial growth	Say "hello!" in many languages
What is a family?	The energy crisis: How does it affect you?

The Canadian pipeline   How to cope with divorce in the family

MATHEMATICS: Telling time, counting, explaining money, sets, shapes, or signs:

Can you tell time by the hour?   How much is a "quarter?"

Telling time by the half hour   Counting by 5

What is your time worth?   A "pair" is never lonesome

All about triangles   Stop and Go!

Going in circles   A set of three "anythings"

How many ways can you form a group of   Recognizing DANGER signs
_____?

SCIENCE: Explaining sources of power, food, growth, and health:

What can a magnet do for you?   How wind works for us

Making a bulb light   Would you like to make a bell ring?

What Is a good breakfast?   How many ways does a tree grow?

Let's have a party!   How to plant seeds

Static electricity   Are your teeth falling out? They will!

Who is taller than whom?   Which drugs can kill you?

Are YOU a mammal?   You can have beautiful skin

What can marijuana do to you?

How to Tape Directions for Instructional Packages

The cassette tape is, perhaps, the most important part of a multisensory package. To be effective, the tape must provide simple, concise directions and explanations so that students can use the package without your assistance. The following suggestions can help you develop a good tape:

1. State the objectives clearly and simply.

2. Speak slowly and vary your speech pattern, tone, and inflection to add listening interest. Be dramatic, but not overly so.

3. Avoid picking up background noises or taping where electrical appliances can cause interference.

4. Use explicit directions for each action that the child must do. For example, request that the package's cover be placed on the table, that items be taken out carefully, that each envelope be returned to the box, and so on.

5. Pause after giving directions so that the listener has time to consider them and carry them out. Or, to allow longer periods of time, you could say, "Turn off the tape recorder while you are putting these materials away. But remember to turn the recorder back on when you are ready to continue."

6. Don't ask questions that require only "yes" or "no" responses. Avoid saying, "Are you ready to begin the next activity?" or "Did you know the answer to that riddle?" Instead say, "I hope you are ready for the next activity! Please take out the blue box with the cotton cloud on it." Or, "I hope you knew that the answer to that riddle was 'a clock.' A clock has 'hands' but never washes them!"

7. Be certain that the tape is completely self-instructional. Put yourself in the student's place and see if you can work alone without assistance or additional resources and without having to leave the area.[3]

8. Repeat important directions or difficult passages in a slightly different way to reinforce in an interesting manner.

9. Use good grammar and appropriate vocabulary.

10. Be certain that the tape and the materials are self-corrective. If you ask questions, pause sufficiently and then provide answers.

11. Use supplementary sounds (music, bells, animals, other people's voices).

12. Use a good tape recorder and fresh batteries; place the microphone in a comfortable position for you; place a "Taping" sign on your door to avoid bells and other intrusions; take the telephone off the hook; leave enough footage at the beginning of the tape so that your introduction is recorded in its entirety; watch that the tape does not run out while you are still speaking; check the volume; and test as you are recording to be certain the pickup is clear.

13. For primary level children, color-code the tape recorder's buttons.

Sample Instructional Packages

Primary Level: Transportation[4]

The following package includes a book that is read to the child on tape. If you have a commercially produced tape or filmstrip related to your topic, you may include it in any package that you design for your class.

TRANSPORTATION

Directions On Tape and Script

Hi! I'm happy that you chose this package to work with today. This box is filled with many interesting things for you to do. The things that you do will teach you about different kinds of TRANSPORTATION. You will be able to explain what the word TRANSPORTATION means, and you will also be able to name different kinds of TRANSPORTATION.

I think that you are going to enjoy learning through this package, but if you get tired and want to stop or take a rest, just turn off the tape and relax. When you finish this package—or want to stop for today—please turn off the tape, rewind it, and carefully return it and the other materials to the box.

I am ready to begin: I hope that you are too! Open the box and place the cover carefully on the top of the table. Give yourself room to work—so place the cover away from you.

Look into the box and find a booklet that is shaped like a wheel. (See Exhibit 6-2.) A wheel is a round object that rolls and is used to support different types of ground and air TRANSPORTATION. Go ahead; I'll wait for you! (Pause) I hope you've found it! It has green and blue and red letters on the cover. It is called *The Wheel Book.* I hope that you like the cover, because I made it! Let's read *The Wheel Book* together.

Visual-Auditory Activity

Open the book to the first page. See the picture of the wheel? The words say, "You will see that the wheel is very important to TRANSPOR-TATION because it *rolls.* By rolling, a wheel helps to move very big things—things that would be too heavy to push. Wheels help big things such as a car, a bus, a train, and a plane to move from place to place."

Turn the page. At the top of the next page you see a picture of a car and a bus and a train and a plane. See how big they are! We have already read that wheels help these big things to move. They help by *rolling.*

The words on this page say, "Things that help move people from place to place are called a kind of TRANSPORTATION. A car is a kind of TRANS-PORTATION, because a car takes people from their homes to their jobs or from their jobs back to their homes. A bus moves many people at one time. A train moves many people too, and a train also carries food and furniture and many other things that people want to buy. Cars and trains are a kind of TRANSPORTATION too. So is a plane.

TRANSPORTATION means, 'to carry from place to place.' Anything that carries either people or things from place to place is a kind of TRANS-PORTATION."

Do you think that a wagon is a kind of TRANSPORTATION? I hope you think it is—because a wagon carries things from place to place. So do skates! Skates carry people from one place to another, so even skates are a kind of TRANSPORTATION.

Let's turn to the next page. This new page has a picture of trains on it. The words say, "Many people depend on trains to get to work. A train can carry more people than a bus can, and it can move faster.

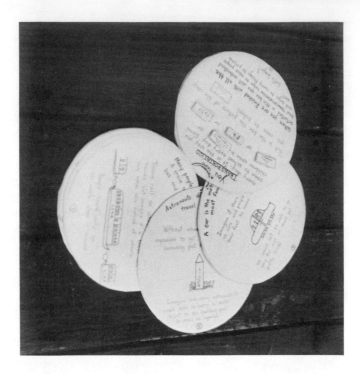

Exhibit 6-2.   This is the visual-auditory activity of Janet Perrin's instructional package for primary youngsters. Accompanied by a tape that reads the text to interested students, *The Wheel Book* is in the shape of the item it describes. (Photograph courtesy of the Department of Curriculum and Teaching, St. John's University, Grand Central Parkway, Queens, New York.)

    Trains roll on wheels that fit onto tracks, but imagine what it would be like if a train had only skis instead of wheels!

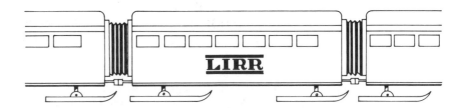

People could go to work only when it snowed!"
    On the next page there is a picture of a school bus. At the top, the

words say, "Buses are very important because they can carry many people to a place at one time. Suppose buses had no wheels, and horses had to pull them.

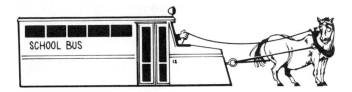

That would lead to many problems. Who would feed and take care of all the horses that would be needed? What would the bus slide on? Would it wear out at the bottom? I think wheels are better than flat bottoms for moving different kinds of TRANSPORTATION."

Let's turn the page again. The first word is "Astronauts."

ASTRONAUTS DEPEND UPON
ROCKETS TO TRAVEL INTO SPACE.
Without wheels it would be impossible to get
the rocket to the launching pad for a takeoff.

Imagine how many astronauts it would take to
carry a HUGE rocket to the launching pad!
It would be very difficult!

Turn to the next page—the one with the airplane flying. The words are,

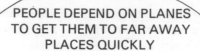

**PEOPLE DEPEND ON PLANES
TO GET THEM TO FAR AWAY
PLACES QUICKLY**

Without wheels, planes would not be able to take off and land on the ground. Wheels are part of a plane's landing gear.

If planes could not land at airports,
we could not fly to faraway places.

The next page has a picture of a familiar kind of TRANSPORTATION—a car. Let's read:

**A CAR IS THE KIND OF TRANS-
PORTATION MOST FAMILIES DEPEND
UPON.**

Imagine if there were no wheels
on cars and people had to use their
feet to move them!

We would not be able to go very far,
and we would get very tired!

Turn to the next page, please.

"You use TRANSPORTATION every day! It is the way you come to school. Some children come by

 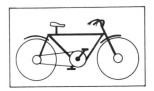

 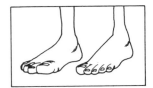

If we did not have wheels, you could not ride to school on a bicycle, or in a car, or in a bus. You could only walk! That might make things difficult for you. It would for me!

In this box draw a picture of the way you come to school.

Let's turn the page again. On this page is a poem that I wrote for you. I'll read it to you if you like.

"Cars and buses on the road, trains that pull a heavy load,
Rockets speeding past a star, planes that fly us very far,
Sleds that slide us on the snow, taxis to where we need to go,
Carriages rolling and wagons too, bikes to pedal and a horse to shoe,
Boats that sail, helicopters that fly—all kinds of TRANSPORTA-TION, but, oh my!
I almost forgot a way that's slow! Your own two feet can transport you, you know!"

Let's look at the poem again. Count the many kinds of TRANSPORTA-TION that the poem mentioned. (Pause) How many did you count? (Pause) If you counted four (4) or five (5) kinds, you are very smart! If you counted more than nine (9), you are super-smart!—And if you counted all fourteen (14) kinds that were in the poem, you have learned a great deal already!

What do you think makes it easy for most kinds of TRANSPORTATION to move very big things from one place to another? (Pause) Did you remember that the wheels help to move big things? Wheels help to move cars, and buses, and trains, and planes, because they *roll.*

I am certain that by the time you finish this package, you will be able to explain how wheels help to move very big things. You will also be able to name many different kinds of TRANSPORTATION.

Now close *The Wheel Book* and set it aside on the table.

Tactual Activity

At the top of the scramble board (see Exhibit 6–3) it says, "Below are sentences about TRANSPORTATION. The beginnings and ends of the sentences do not match. You can unscramble them by stretching the rubber bands between the two parts of the sentence that match."

For example, next to number 1 is the word TRANSPORTATION.

TRANSPORTATION is printed in blue letters. Now look at the ends of the sentences that are on the right side of the board (the side with the twin yellow circles on it).

The end of the sentence at the top, in green letters, says, ". . . is the means of TRANSPORTATION for most families."

If we put the word TRANSPORTATION together with the end of the sentence that we just read," . . . is the means of TRANSPORTATION for most families," it just wouldn't make sense.

What you have to do is to read all the sentence ends on the right side of the scramble board and find the ends that match the beginnings. I'll help you to read the beginnings and the ends, and you try to match the beginnings to the correct ends.

The first beginning, as we said before, is TRANSPORTATION. Look at the right side of the board, and I'll read the endings to you while you try to match one of the endings with the word TRANSPORTATION. We know that the first ending in green does not match, so let's move to the ending just below the green one—the one that is in red.

The red ending says, ". . . needs wheels, as part of its landing gear to take off." Does TRANSPORTATION need wheels as part of its landing gear to take off? (Pause) I don't think so. What needs wheels as part of its landing gear? (Pause) Did you remember that a plane needs wheels as part of its landing gear? (Pause) I hope you remembered. Can you find the words "A plane" on the left side of the scramble board?—that's the side away from

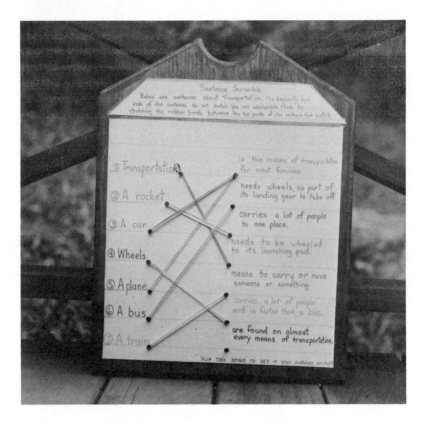

Exhibit 6-3. This is the tactual activity of Janet Perrin's instructional package "Transportation." It is a Scramble Board on which youngsters can stretch rubber bands to connect either correctly matching questions and answers, or, as in this example, the beginnings and ends of sentences. (Photograph courtesy of the Department of Curriculum and Teaching, St. John's University, Grand Central Parkway, Queens, New York.)

the yellow dots. Look down the list of beginning sentences, and see if you can recognize which words say "A plane." (Pause) I'll read the beginning words to you. The first, as you know, is TRANSPORTAION.

Below that are the words "A rocket." Does a rocket need wheels as part of its landing gear?

Below "A rocket" are the words "A car"; they are printed in green. Does a car need wheels as part of its landing gear?

Number 4 is "Wheels." Do wheels need wheels as part of its landing gear? (Pause) I guess we can count that one out!

Number 5 says "A plane." Does a plane need wheels as part of its landing gear? (Pause) I think that's it! A plane does need wheels as part of its landing gear!

Do you see the rubber band on the nail next to the words "A plane"? Leave the beginning of the rubber band near the words "A plane," but stretch the end of that rubber band to the end of the sentence that makes sense—the words printed in red: ". . . needs wheels as part of its landing gear to take off." When you do that, you have one complete sentence matched. (Pause)

Below the words "A plane," which are in red, are the words "A bus" in purple. Underneath "A bus" are the words "A train."

I am going to read all the beginning words again, starting at the top and going all the way down to "A train." I hope you are ready.

TRANSPORTATION
A rocket
A car
Wheels
A plane (That's the one we've already used.)
A bus, and
A train

Now I'm going to read the endings on the right side. The first is:
"is the means of TRANSPORTATION for most families." Next is:
"needs wheels, as part of its landing gear to take off." Then comes:
"carries a lot of people to one place." Then comes:
"needs to be wheeled to its launching pad." Below that is:
"means to carry or move someone or something." Below that is:
"carries a lot of people and is faster than a bus." Below that is:
"are found on almost every means of TRANSPORTATION."

You may play this section of the tape over and over if you wish, until you match all the beginning words with the correct ending words. When you are finished, turn the scramble board over and see whether you matched the beginnings and ends correctly. If you prefer, you may turn off the tape recorder until you have finished. After you have corrected your answers, turn the tape on again. (Pause)

Hello again! How did you do? Did you notice that the beginnings and the ends of the sentences matched in color? Look at your board. If you matched them all, color-to-color, you are correct! Let's read our TRANS-PORTATION sentences together!

(Read the entire scramble board series of sentences with the correct beginnings and ends.)

Now please unhook the rubber bands that you stretched and put the scramble board aside next to *The Wheel Book* and the top of this package on the table.

Auditory Activity

You do not have to look into the box for our next activity because it's right here on the tape. All you have to do is sit back, close your eyes, and listen. You are about to hear some sounds of TRANSPORTATION. See how many you can recognize. I hope you're ready! Close your eyes and listen.

Imagine you are standing on a pier and a huge ship has just raised its gangplank. You might hear this sound of TRANSPORTATION:

(Boat whistle)

Did you know what that was? It was an ocean liner leaving the harbor and carrying many people on a cruise across the water. That was the ocean liner's whistle!

(Jet taking off)

How about that? I wonder if you guessed it! If you said it was a "jet taking off," you are right! Can you imagine yourself, as you listen to these sounds of TRANSPORTATION, at the airport watching a jet take off?

Get ready for the next one—

(Long train)

What do you think that was? Well, it was a train going through a station. It was a long train. Perhaps it was a freight train carrying things to people all over the country.

Get ready for the next one!

(Short train)

That was a train too—but it wasn't as long as our first train. Perhaps that train was carrying people to work.

See how you do on this TRANSPORTATION sound.

(Car starting)

Did you say that was a car starting? If you did, you were right! That's a sound most of us hear very often.

Visual and Tactual Activity

Let's go back to our box now. Look into the box and find a booklet that is shaped like a rectangle. It has orange lettering on it. I'll wait for you to find it. (Pause)

If you have it, let's read it together.

(Read the booklet together)

Our Wheel Book showed us how important TRANS-
PORTATION is in helping PEOPLE to move from one
place to another.

Now we are about to discover how TRANSPORTA-
TION helps people to get all the things they need. Everything you own or use or eat came to you by one or many
ways of TRANSPORTATION.

Open this book and you will see and hear a story of a
little orange and how it traveled to your refrigerator at
home.

Please turn the page.

"Hi! I am *Little Orange,* and I want you to help me tell my
story. Peel me off this page and place me on the orange
circle on each page as you follow along with my story.
Please do not forget to put me back on this page when
we are all finished. O.K.—Peel me off and let's begin."

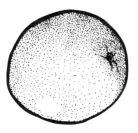

Turn the page, please.

"I had to use
many means of TRANSPORTATION
to get to your refrigerator
because I was grown on
a tree in Florida. You see—we

oranges only grow where it is warm all year. Florida is
a long distance away from New York,
and my trip to you took more than
one whole day.''

Next page!

"It was a bright sunny day when
I was picked from my tree in
the Orange Grove."

Then I was put into a truck with a lot
of other oranges to go to the FRUIT INSPECTION
STATION.

"It sure was a
bumpy ride!"

Let's look at the next page.

"At the FRUIT INSPECTION STATION, I rode on a con-
veyor belt so that the inspectors could look me over to
be certain I would be just right when I got to you."

Turn the page.

"Then I was carefully packed into a crate and loaded into a truck and carried off to the train station. Someone mentioned that we were headed for New York."

Let's turn the page.

"At the train station, I was loaded onto a freight train car that had Refrigerator Car written on it. It was cold inside the car—just like a refrigerator—brrr!"

"It was important to keep me cold so that I wouldn't spoil on my long trip."

Turn to the next page, please.

"I travelled for fifteen hours on the train, in my refrigerated car. We went 'Clickety-clack' over the train tracks until we finally reached New York—our destination."

Turn again!

"I barely had time to look around New York, when I was taken off the freight train and loaded into another big truck headed for a supermarket. In the truck with me was a lot of other foods, including cheese and lettuce and eggs and yogurt."

This truck was refrigerated too—so that all the foods in it wouldn't spoil."

Turn!

"My ride to the supermarket took about one hour. After I was unloaded from the big truck, I was placed into a fruit bin in the supermarket."

"It wasn't long before a lady put me into a shopping cart and pushed me around the store." Guess where the lady was taking Little Orange?

Turn the page!

"Soon after, I was packed into a paper bag with a lot of other food—

and then

was taken for a ride in the lady's car.

"The lady must have been your mom. I think she was bringing me home for you!"

Look at the last page.

"Finally, I was unpacked and put into the refrigerator.

  I had a long journey and used many different kinds of transportation to get to your refrigerator. Brrr—it's cold in here— just like the train and the supermarket truck."

I hope you enjoyed helping Little Orange tell his TRANSPORTATION story. Did you remember to put him back on page 2 of the booklet? If you didn't, I'll wait a few seconds while you replace the orange. (Pause) Thank you. Let's go on.

Look into the box again, and you will find a wagon, a plastic cloth, an orange and picture cards about TRANSPORTATION. Take these things out and spread the cloth on the floor. (pause) Take off your shoes and place the picture cards on the red square in the middle of the cloth. Then place the orange into the wagon. I'll wait for you while your shoes come off. (pause) Then place the picture cards on the red square.

Now put the wagon at the place that says, "Start". You are about to take Little Orange on his journey from Florida to your refrigerator (see attached directions on Maze).

Kinesthetic Activity

Maze Directions

Look at the eight picture cards that you put on the red square in the middle of the cloth. You may step onto the cloth.

You are about to take Little Orange on its journey. You can make the little TRANSPORTATION wagon any means of TRANSPORTATION you want by putting one of the cards that you placed into the red square inside the wagon.

At each STOP sign, you must change Little Orange's way of TRANS-PORTATION. You can do this by putting the correct card inside the wagon. You will recognize the correct card by looking at the picture card on the cloth next to each STOP sign.

By the time you get to FINISH, you will have used all the cards and will have changed the TRANSPORTATION wagon seven times.

Ready? Is Little Orange inside the wagon?

Go! Begin to pull him on his journey!

See which TRANSPORTATION your wagon will become next!

Exhibit 6-5 shows replicas of the eight picture cards that may be placed inside the TRANSPORTATION wagon at the various STOP signs.

Tactual Activity

Now we are going to see if you can tell the difference between kinds of TRANSPORTATION and things that are not TRANSPORTATION. Remember that TRANSPORTATION moves things from place to place.

Look into the box again. Find a blue envelope with the word TRANS-PORTATION printed on it. Take the envelope out of the box. (Pause) Open the envelope and take out all the pictures that are inside. (Pause) Spread

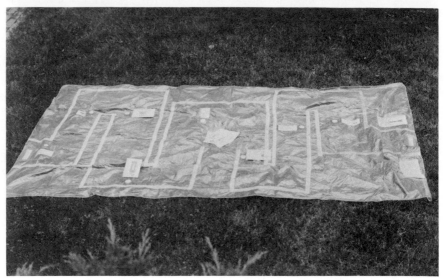

Exhibit 6-4.   The wagon and large plastic sheet are two of the items that comprise the kinesthetic activity of this instructional package. Janet Perrin designed the task so that primary children could review and evidence what they had learned about how an orange is transported from a Florida grove to a New York youngster's refrigerator. Illustrated cards representing different means of transportation are placed inside the wagon, which is then hand-pulled along the route. At each stage of the journey another card must be deposited in proper sequence. (Photographs courtesy of the Department of Curriculum and Teaching, St. John's University, Grand Central Parkway, Queens, New York.)

Exhibit 6–5.   The eight picture cards for the transportation maze wagon.

the pictures on the table so that you can see them all.

Look at the pictures carefully. Some of them are pictures of different kinds of TRANSPORTATION. Some of the pictures have nothing to do with TRANSPORTATION.

You choose the ones that you think are pictures of TRANSPORTATION. Put all the TRANSPORTATION pictures into one pile. Leave all the pictures that are NOT of TRANSPORTATION on the desk. Turn off the tape recorder while you do this task, but remember to turn it on again when you are finished. (Exhibit 6-6 shows sample pictures.)

Exhibit 6–6.   Sample Transportation and Non-Transportation pictures.

Thank you for turning the tape recorder on again. I hope you found all the pictures of different kinds of TRANSPORTATION. You can tell if you found all the pictures by comparing what you found with the list I am going to read to you.

Look at the pictures in your pile.

I hope you included the picture of the *car* . . . and the *bus* . . . and the *train* . . . and the *elephant* . . . Oh yes! An elephant carries people and things from place to place!   Did you include the boy? A boy can carry things from place to place, too! You should also have the pictures of the circus cage with wheels. See the lion that it carries from place to place? You should have the *plane* . . . and the *rocket* . . . *bicycle* . . . and the *truck.*

If you had all those pictures of different kinds of TRANSPORTATION, you did very well! You should not have included any of the other pictures, for they are not kinds of TRANSPORTATION. Put the pictures back into the blue envelope. Be careful with them, please.

Testing Activity

Please look into the box again. Find the red folder. Take the red folder out of the box. (Pause) Open it. You should see a sheet with ten questions on it. You should also see a black crayon.

Pick up the black crayon and read the sentences on the sheet with me. At the end of each sentence you will see a big "T" and a big "F." The "T" stands for "True" and the "F" stand for "False"—which means not true.

After you read—or hear me read—each sentence, you decide if the sentence is true or false. Then circle either the T or the F—depending on which answer is correct.

Let's try one together.

Sentence 1 says "TRANSPORTATION is a way of moving people and things from one place to another." If that sentence is true, circle the T. If that sentence is not true—if it is false—circle the F. Which will you circle? (Pause) Do it! (Pause)

I will read the remaining sentences with you—or you may read them by yourself, and you circle either the T or the F after each sentence. Let's continue.

(The tape then reads each of the sentences, pausing in between to provide time for the student to circle one of the letters.)

QUIZ

Answer "true" by circling the "T" and "false" by circling the "F" at the end of each sentence.

1.   TRANSPORTATION is a way of moving people and things from one place to another.

                         T   F

2.   Wheels are very important because they help to move big things.

                         T   F

3.   Cars, buses, trains, planes, and rockets all are kinds of TRANS-PORTATION.

                         T   F

4.   Wagons, skates, carriages, and bicycles all are kinds of TRANS-PORTATION.

                         T   F

5.   People depend on TRANSPORTATION to get them to different places.

                         T   F

6.   Your feet are a kind of TRANSPORTATION.

                         T   F

7.   TRANSPORTATION brings our food and clothing to us from other places.

                         T   F

8.   Animals, such as horses and camels and elephants, are a kind of transportation too.

                         T   F

9.   Wheels are helpful because they roll.

                         T   F

10.   A rocket does not have wheels, but it is a kind of TRANSPOR-TATION.

                         T   F

After the Test

Now that you have circled as many letters as you could, please bring your paper to my desk and put it into my "mailbox." I will read it as soon as

I can, and then you and I will talk about what you learned from this package.

Would you please be kind and put each of the things that you took out of the big box back into it? Remember to put back the red folder, the big plastic cloth with the word START on it, the booklet that is shaped like a rectangle, the scramble board, and the book called *The Wheel Book.* Then rewind this tape and place it, too, back into its pocket on the top of the cover.

When you have done all that, put the cover back on top of the box. Then put the box back into its place in the interest center.

I hope that you enjoyed this package, because I enjoyed making it for you!

Remember to put your Quiz sheet into my mailbox and to put the package back. Thank you, and good-bye for now!

The End

Elementary Level: Subtraction[5]

The following package (Exhibit 6–7), although designed for elementary youngsters, would be equally appropriate for other students in need of mastering the concept of subtraction. The tape; the visual, tactual, and kinesthetic activities; and the privacy in which the students may develop this skill all serve to enhance their potential for achievement and to diminish their self-consciousness about learning slowly when others appear to succeed easily. The materials for this package are housed in a gift box covered with bright red plastic and three dimensional letters that read: SUBTRACTION.

Exhibit 6-7.   Sample elementary level instructional package: Subtraction.

Tape And Script

Hello!

I'm very glad you chose this package on SUBTRACTION.

I hope you enjoy working with it.

By the time you finish this package, you will be able to explain what is meant by SUBTRACTION, and when and how to use it. Please look into the box and take out the pretty red booklet that has SUBTRACTION across its top. Open the booklet and let's read it together.

To SUBTRACT means to *take away*.

The sign that represents SUBTRACTION is called a "minus" sign.

A MINUS sign looks like this: —

When you see this example, it means:

$$4 \quad - \quad 1$$

Four   minus   One

Four minus One, 4 — 1, means that you have four (4) things and are now going to SUBTRACT (or take away) one (1).

Whenever you SUBTRACT, you always have less than you started with.

What is this sign called?   —

A minus sign. It looks like this   —

If I SUBTRACTED, (or took away), three (3) apples from five (5) apples, how many apples would I have left?

Two (2) apples

Above you will see five (5) apples, each one numbered. Point to each apple. Now, if you subtract three (3) apples, you can plainly see that you have two (2) left.

5	apples		If you have	5	apples
− 3	apples	OR	and take away	3	apples
2	apples		You then have	2	apples

Let's try to work together on another SUBTRACTION problem. If you are lucky enough to have three (3) candy bars, and you decide to give one to your friend, how many would you have left?

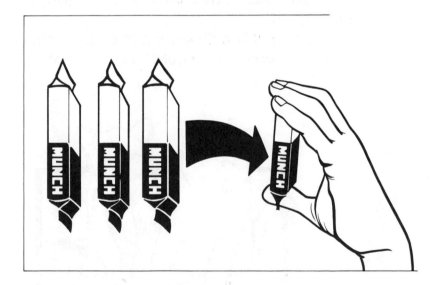

You would have 2 candy bars left.

If you had three (3) candy bars to begin with and you SUBTRACTED one (1) candy bar, you would have two (2) candy bars left.

I hope you are beginning to see from these examples that when we SUBTRACT, we are really taking away. When we take away, we have less than we started with.

Another way to say SUBTRACT is: DEDUCT

You can SUBTRACT three (3) apples from five (5) <u>or</u>

You can DEDUCT three (3) apples from five (5).

The two words mean the same thing. You can also TAKE AWAY three (3) apples if you have five (5) apples.

I have another problem I would like you to work on.

If I had two (2) kittens and gave them both away, how many kittens would I have left?

(Here is a hint for you. If you <u>give them away</u>, you are really SUBTRACTING.)

Zero (0)

If you subtracted all that you have, you will have nothing left.

If you had two (2) kittens to begin with, and you gave them both away, you would have none left.

Now, if I were to ask you, "What is meant by SUB-TRACTION?" What would you say?

When you speak of SUBTRACTION, you are talking about taking away a part of the original amount you started with. When you <u>take away</u>, your answer is always <u>less</u> than the amount you first started with. Whenever you SUBTRACT you will have less.

The End

Task Cards

Please put the book that we have been reading aside and look into the big box once more. You will see a yellow envelope with the words TASK CARDS on it. Please take the envelope out of the box and open it.

Take out the cards that are inside the envelope. Place them in front of you. (Exhibit 6-8 shows sample task cards.) These task cards are a game that will help you to remember the things that we just read.

There should be eight (8) different cards in front of you. Spread them out. You really have eight (8) halves of task cards because the parts you see must fit together to form a question part and an answer part. (See Exhibit 6-9.)

The question parts say: When you subtract you are

When you subtract you always

A minus sign looks like this

and

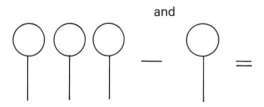

You need to find the answers to the question parts and join the answers and the questions together into whole task cards. See if you can correctly match

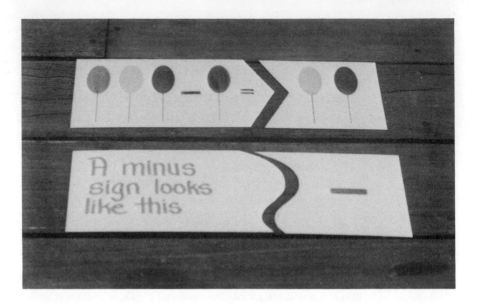

Exhibit 6-8.   These task cards are from a set that comprises the tactual activity of
Denise D'Acunto Johnert's instructional package "Subtraction." Students are given separated
cards and are invited to match the problems (or questions) with their self-correcting answers.
(Photograph courtesy of the Department of Curriculum and Teaching, St. John's University,
Grand Central Parkway, Queens, New York.)

each question part with its correct answer part. Turn off the tape recorder
while you are trying. (Pause)

    Since you've turned the tape on again, I guess you've matched the
task card parts. When did you realize that you could only match the
correct question with the correct answer? Of course! The cards are "shape-
coded" and only will fit together when they are right for each other!

Exhibit 6-9.   The eight task cards for the "Subtraction" Instructional Package.

A minus sign
looks like this

—

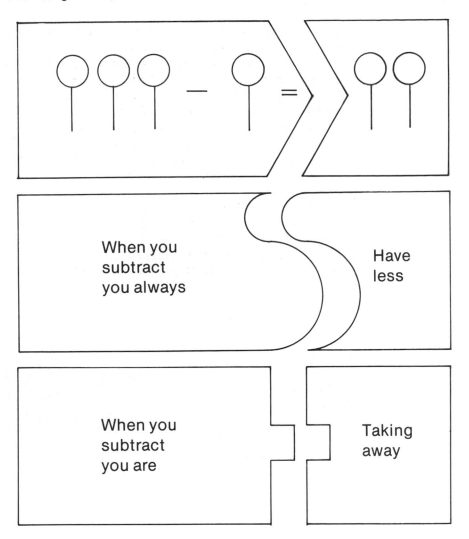

When you subtract you always

Have less

When you subtract you are

Taking away

Kinesthetic Activity

    Now you are ready for the last activity in this package. Put the task cards back into their envelope and then put the envelope on the table near you. (Pause)

    Next, find the large plastic sheet that is inside the box and take it out carefully. Spread the large plastic sheet on the floor. You will see Mickey Mouse on the sheet, but he is divided into four (4) SUBTRACTION problems. (See Exhibit 6-10.) If you can SUBTRACT correctly and find the right answers to the problems on him, the pieces of the puzzle will fit exactly onto the picture of Mickey. You may turn the tape recorder off until after you have completed the puzzle. Remember to turn it back on! (Pause)

I'm glad you came back to this tape!

If you were able to piece Mickey Mouse together, you were able to find the answers to the SUBTRACTION problems. Tomorrow we will try a different set of problems, and we'll see how much you remember about SUBTRACTION. I think you'll remember a lot!

For now, please take the large plastic sheet and fold it carefully so that it can fit back into the box. (Pause) Then place all the SUBTRACTION puzzle pieces of Mickey Mouse back into their envelope. When you have done that, put the envelope into the box on top of the large plastic sheet.

Put the task cards into the box, too. Now place the book about SUB-TRACTION on top. The last thing that you will need to do is to rewind this tape and then put it, too, into the box. Then you are finished with this package and need only carry it back to the learning station where it belongs.

You must feel proud of yourself today. After all, you learned something new about SUBTRACTION: You should feel proud. I am proud of you, too!

Good-bye!

Exhibit 6-10.   Denise D'Acunto Johnert designed this kinesthetic activity in such a way that in order to place Mickey Mouse's face together, students need to know the answers to the subtraction problems that are written on the large plastic sheet. (Photograph courtesy of the Department of Curriculum and Teaching, St. John's University, Grand Central Parkway, Queens, New York.)

High School Level: Alexander the Great[6]

High school students may prefer an instructional package to a textbook because of the illustrations and tactual and kinesthetic reinforcements that they provide. For example, this highly detailed saga of Alexander the Great's battles would be far less appealing to many if it were taught through the standard books rather than through the games included in the following instructional package (Exhibit 6–11).

Exhibit 6-11.   Sample high school level instructional package: Alexander the Great.

Alexander the Great

ALEXANDER THE GREAT

Script and Tape

By the time you finish this package, you will be able to:

1. Describe and explain Alexander's unusual ability for leadership.

2. Describe Alexander's character.

3. List the most important things that happened during Alexander's twelve years as a king.

Alexander was *born in 356* B.C.*;* he was the son of *King Philip II* of Macedonia.

Philip II had made Macedonia strong. He gathered an army and marched south against the Greeks and defeated them. Philip II died shortly after the final victory, and his son Alexander became king at the age of 20 in *336* B.C.

Alexander Becomes King

Alexander's Education

Aristotle

When he was a boy, Alexander learned much about Greek culture. His father had invited the great teacher *Aristotle* to teach his son. Alexander loved the Greek way of life and loved Greek art. He admired the Greek heroes and the ancient Greek poet *Homer.*

The other part of Alexander's education was with the successful Macedonian army. In the army Alexander learned the art of war. Although the Macedonians and Greeks were strong, the Persians were the greatest military power at that time. The Persians had burned many Greek cities, and Alexander wanted more than anything else to lead an army against their king.

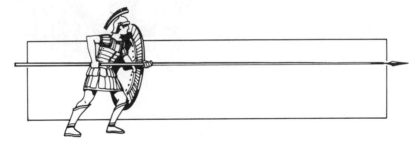

A Macedonian with Sarissa, or long spear.

Alexander became king of Macedonia in *336 B.C.* at the age of twenty. He immediately put himself at the head of the army of Macedonians and Greeks and dealt with the barbarians in the north.

NOTE: Barbarians at that time were foreigners. Anyone who was not Greek was considered a "barbarian."

By 334 B.C., Alexander's kingdom of Macedonia was so strong that he was able to leave it. He collected a Macedonian and Greek army of 35,000 men and crossed the Hellespont into Asia. He took with him a copy of Homer's *Iliad,* and he visited Troy, the scene of great events in that story.

1. Alexander (stamp)

2. Achilles (a main character in Homer's *Iliad*).

Alexander was very ambitious. He wanted to conquer an empire. His army was well-trained and drilled. It was almost impossible to defeat Alexander's army.

A Macedonian hypaspist with pike and shield.

First Battle

Alexander went to Asia for revenge—not for pleasure. A very large Persian army was waiting for him at the river *Granicus.* There, Alexander won his first great victory in Asia. The Persians were completely defeated.

A Persian Chariot.

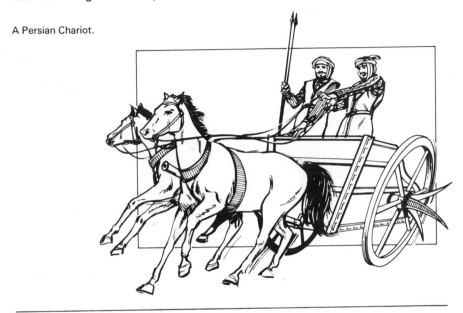

Alexander's Strategy

Alexander had taught his men to move into battle in a special way that won them a victory. A special way of planning is called a "strategy."

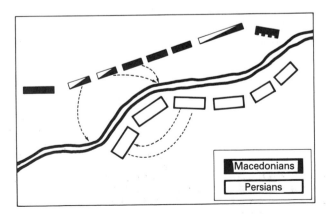

This illustration shows how the Macedonian and Persion armies faced each other shortly before the battle of Granicus began.

Second Battle

Alexander led his army through Asia Minor, and most of its cities opened their gates to him. At the *Issus* River, King Darius of Persia was waiting for Alexander with a huge Persian army. Again, the Persians were defeated because of Alexander's strategy.

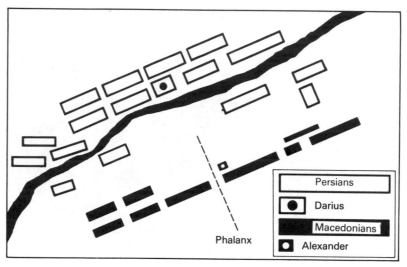

Battle of Issus

The Macedonians' particular strength was in their heavy infantry (foot) soldiers, who wore armor and used shields, swords, and spears. Alexander's heavy infantry stood and moved in a *phalanx.* A "phalanx" in ancient Greece was a body of heavily armed infantry formed in close, deep ranks and files with joined shields.

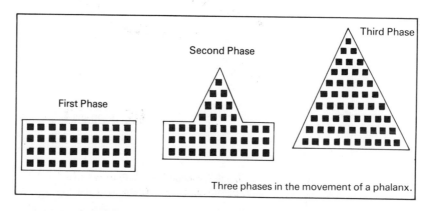

Three phases in the movement of a phalanx.

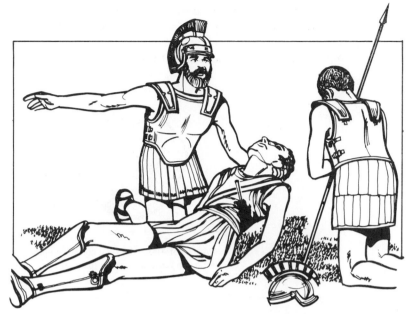

After battle, Alexander buried his dead soldiers with honor.

Alexander treated his enemies well after their defeat. After the Battle of Issus, he captured the family of the Persian king, Darius, but he treated the king's family with great kindness.

Alexander was not only clever during battle, but after each battle he had the Greek and Macedonian soldiers buried with honor. The families of the dead men in Greece and Macedonia were excused from paying taxes, and he took no more sons from those families to fight in battles.

Portrait of Alexander on a coin that was struck in Egypt soon after his death.

From Issus, Alexander led his army south. He took *Tyre* after a hard battle. The Tyrians fought bravely, but when it became obvious that all was lost, they broke in despair and threw down their arms.

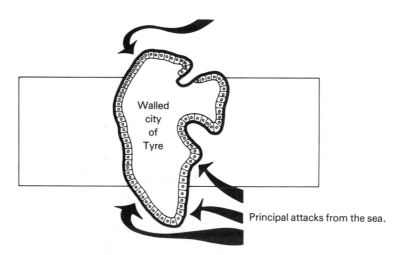

Principal attacks from the sea.

Alexander continued his march into Egypt. The Egyptians were tired of Persian rule and welcomed him. In Egypt, Alexander started a new city. It was to be at the mouth of the Nile River. The city was named *Alexandria.* Alexandria became a great center of Greek learning.

332 B.C.

Conquest of Egypt

The Battle of Arbela (Gaugamela)

From Egypt, Alexander marched north and then east through Mesopotamia. Darius had collected another army—the greatest army that the world had ever seen. With a million men, he waited for Alexander at Gaugamela. With fewer than 50,000 men, Alexander defeated Darius and went on to take Babylon. Then he took the Persian king's own beautiful city, Persepolis. Darius escaped from the battle, but one of his own men killed him.

331 B.C.

Battle of Gaugamela

Alexander fighting the Persians at the Battle of Gaugamela.

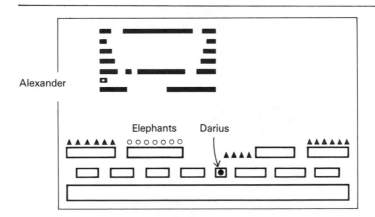

Alexander

Elephants   Darius

The Battle of Arbela (Gaugamela)

The Battle of the Jhelum River or Hydaspes

Now Alexander was ruler of the great Persian Empire. Many men would have stopped there, but Alexander planned an empire that would reach from Greece to India. For seven more years he continued to march and fight. His army went to Samarkand, to Afghanistan, and to India. They were never defeated although they had to fight some terrible battles, such as the battle against the huge army of King Porus at the Jhelum River of Hydaspes.

Battle of Jhelum

327 B.C.

War elephant

Battle of the Jhelum River or Hydaspes

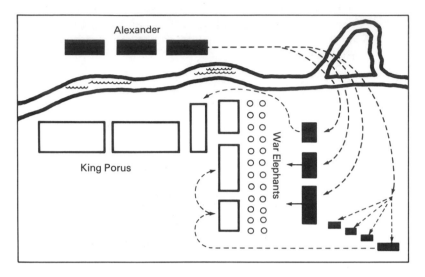

Alexander's men grew tired; they wanted to go home and see their families again. Alexander fought his way to the sea. There he sent a part of his army in ships to the Persian Gulf. The rest of his men marched west with him. The march was over difficult country, and many of the soldiers died. One of every four of the men who had crossed the Hellespont in 334 B.C. reached Susa in Persia in 325 B.C. They rested there.

Alexander's Death

Alexander went to Babylon to plan for an even greater empire. The plans were never made. A sudden illness struck him, and he died in Babylon at the age of 33 in 323 B.C.

Death of Alexander

323 B.C.

Statue of Alexander the Great in Pella.

During his twelve years as King, Alexander brought a kind of peace to Macedonia and Greece. He destroyed some cities and built others. He marched and won victories of which no other general had ever dreamed. Alexander had created an empire.

Alexander had once said:
"To my parents I owe my life, and to my teachers I owe my good life."

Quiz

Write the answer in the space provided

1._____What city was created by Alexander?

2._____Who was Alexander's father?

3._____What famous Greek teacher taught Alexander?

4._____At what age did Alexander become king?

5._____How old was Alexander when he died?

6._____What was the greatest power at the time of Alexander?

7._____Which ancient Greek poet did Alexander admire?

8._____Who did the Greeks call barbarians?

9._____At what river did Alexander win his first great victory in Asia?

10._____What was the name of the shape that Alexander's infantry used in battle?

There is a square for every year. In each square write what happened in the year given.

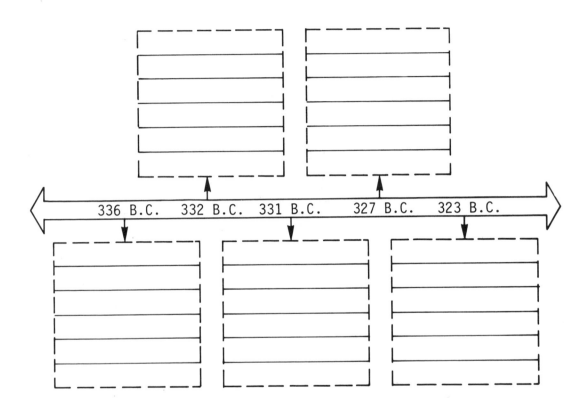

(See Most Important Fact Cards on page 314.)

According to its chronological age, place each picture into the appropriate square. If you cannot recall the date, look at the back of the picture to see to which frame you should refer.

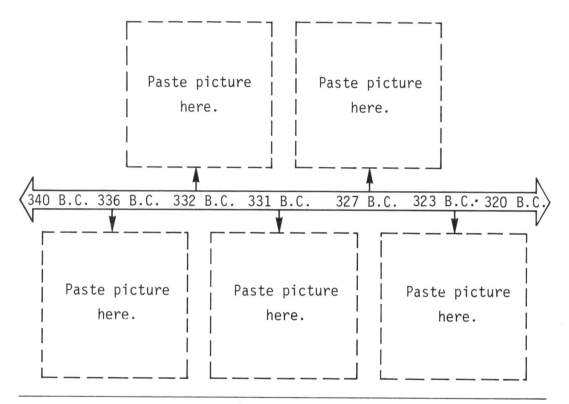

The Empire of Alexander the Great

It was Alexander's wish to carry out his father's dream of conquering the ancient world. He conquered Egypt, the Middle East, and India. To the people he conquered he brought the treasures of Greek literature, art, and learning. To the conquered lands he sent Greek artists, poets, builders, and traders. For many centuries Greek ideas and customs had an important influence on the people living in the vast area.

Kinesthetic Activity

Directions

Now that you have completed the reading, take out the large plastic map and lay it carefully on the floor. Then take out the plastic-laminated map illustration and the eight plastic-laminated cards that illustrate the most important facts. (See Exhibit 6-12.) Then take off your shoes and walk over Alexander's route on the plastic map you placed on the floor, following the map illustration. When you reach each place marked with a darkened circle, place the appropriate large card on top of it. When you finish this activity, fold the map carefully and place it in the box along with the cards and the map illustration.

Exhibit 6-12.   The kinesthetic activity for the instructional package *Alexander the Great* requires that a student demonstrate knowledge of the life of that historic figure by walking along the route that Alexander forged and placing illustrated cards depicting a sequence of events in their correct chronological order. John Papanikolaou included taped directions for youngsters who might be auditory or in need of structure. (Photograph courtesy of the Department of Curriculum and Teaching, St. John's University, Grand Central Parkway, Queens, New York.)

MOST IMPORTANT FACT CARDS

(On the reverse of each of these cards is written the appropriate reference to where it appears in the text.)

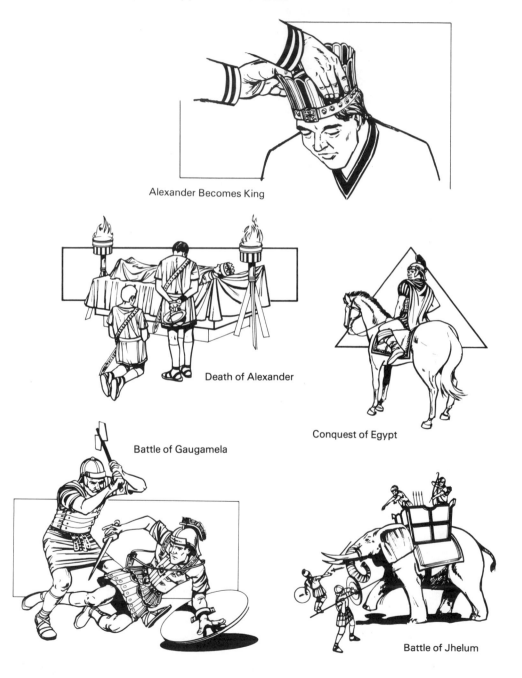

Alexander Becomes King

Death of Alexander

Conquest of Egypt

Battle of Gaugamela

Battle of Jhelum

ALEXANDER'S EMPIRE

The Map Illustration

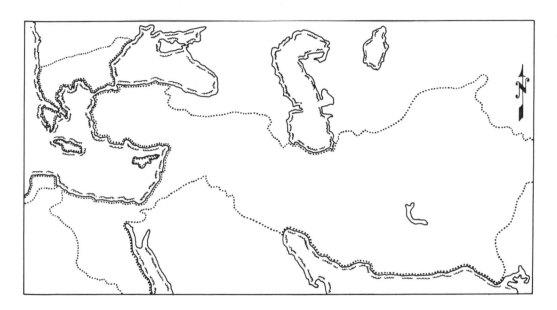

Alexander's Route of Conquest

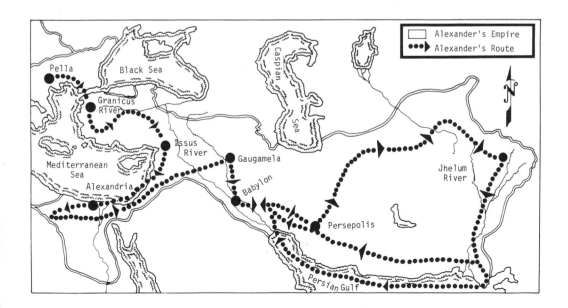

A Final Word on Instructional Packages

Teachers often do not have the time or patience to teach and reteach each student who needs individualized attention. Instructional packages can do both and offer a variety of other benefits, too. They develop listening skills, encourage independent work, and teach students to follow directions. They provide a new teaching method when all else has failed. They make youngsters aware of their own academic growth and thus build positive self-image. They are private; no one except the learner and the teacher knows who is learning what and how. They eliminate direct interaction between teacher and child when a poor or negative relationship exists. And, of course, they are fun!

7
Designing Tactual and Kinesthetic Resources to Respond to Individual Learning Styles

Students who do well in school tend to be the ones who learn either by listening in class or by reading. Because of this, most of us believe that the brighter students are auditory and/or visual learners. In reality however, we usually teach by telling (auditory) and by assigning readings (visual) or by explaining and writing on a chalkboard (auditory and visual). Therefore, youngsters who are able to absorb through these two senses are, of course, the ones that retain what they have been taught, and, thus, respond well on our tests, which also are usually auditory (teacher dictates) or visual (written or printed).

Our own research during the past decade verifies that many students who do not do well in school are tactual or kinesthetic learners;[1] their strongest perceptual strengths are neither auditory nor visual. These boys and girls tend to acquire and retain information or skills when they are involved either with handling manipulative materials or by participating in concrete "real-life" activities. Because so little of what happens instructionally in most classes responds to the tactual and kinesthetic senses, these students are, in a very real sense, handicapped. What's more, once they begin to fall behind scholastically, they lose confidence in themselves and either feel defeated and withdraw (physically or emotionally) or begin to resent school because of repeated failure.

Many young children appear to be essentially tactual or kinesthetic learners. As they grow older, some youngsters begin to combine their tactual inclinations with a visual leaning; for these, the resources suggested in this chapter will be helpful. Eventually, some youngsters develop auditory strengths and are able to function easily in a traditional class where much of the instruction is through discussion or lecture; this group, however, does not represent the majority.

Although we have found some parallels between age and perceptual strengths among students, many high schoolers continue to be unable to learn well by either listening in class or by reading. Sensory strengths appear to be so individualized that it is vital to test each student and then to recommend resources that complement their strengths rather than their weaknesses. When you recognize that selected students are not learning either through their readings or from class discussions or lectures, experiment with several of the following resources to provide tactual or kinesthetic instruction that should prove to be helpful.

Learning Style Characteristics Responsive to Tactual And Kinesthetic Resources

Because tactual and kinesthetic materials tend to be gamelike, they usually are naturally motivating, particularly for young children. Where they are perceived as being babyish however, they can cause embarrassment and turn off many youngsters. It is important that the students to whom these resources are assigned are positive about them and are therefore willing to follow directions for their use, care, and replacement. If they enjoy learning this way, they will become persistent and will continue using the materials until they have achieved the goals or objectives that have been outlined for them. All the materials are self-corrective, so that should youngsters experience difficulty while using them, they are able to manipulate them to find the correct answers. Nevertheless, the motivation for using these materials is necessary if the students are to be responsible for them—for the parts or sections of each set need to be kept intact, returned to holders or boxes, and generally maintained in good condition. However, as we have observed previously, apathetic children may become highly motivated because of their interest in and enjoyment with learning circles, task cards, electroboards, and games.

Other than the directions for using the resources, little structure is provided through these materials; students using them may, therefore, need some structure—but not too much. Beyond the need for motivation, persistence, responsibility, and structure, these resources respond to students who have visual-tactual, tactual-kinesthetic, or visual-kinesthetic inclinations and who do not learn easily either by listening or by reading.

Learning Style Characteristics to Which Tactual and Kinesthetic Resources Can Be Accommodated

Because these resources may be used in a classroom, in a library, in a corridor, or in an instructional resource center as well as at home, they can accommodate each student's environmental and physical preferences. Because they may be used independently, in pairs, with a small group, or with an adult, they also respond to each student's sociological needs.

Step-by-step Guide to Designing Tactual Resources

Developing tactual resources is easy. Once you have designed one or two samples, older students and parents can duplicate and create additional samples for you. Although many of these materials are available in primary and elementary schools, they often are used indiscriminately rather than with those youngsters whose perceptual inclinations would complement them, and they usually are commercially produced and do not respond directly to either the topics that you teach or the objectives on which you focus. After you have made a few samples for experimentation and observed the progress that certain students make through their use, you will become committed to their availability as an instructional resource for your classroom. Another advantage is that they save labor by being adaptable to different levels, questions, and even subject areas, for example, a learning circle with interchangeable parts.

Designing Learning Circles[2]

A learning circle is an interesting way for children to review many worthwhile skills. For example, you can teach the formation or recognition of new words, mathematics concepts, historical data, and almost any kind of skill development through them. Why not try making one or two learning circles to see whether your slow achievers respond favorably to them? If they do, let them assist you in creating more. You also will find that auditory or visual achievers will enjoy them—even though they do not need them.

Let us assume that you have been teaching students to add. Begin with a learning circle that provides them with opportunities to practice completing different number fact problems. You will need the following items:

Materials

- Two pieces of colored oaktag, heavy construction paper, or poster board
- One wire coat hanger

- Black thin-line felt pens
- Eight clip-on clothespins (the colored plastic type are pretty and do not break easily)
- Masking tape or strong glue
- Clear or lightly colored transparent Con-tact paper
- Old magazines that may be cut up to either color-code or picture-code the mathematics examples and their answers (optional)

Directions

(Exhibit 7–1 illustrates the steps for making the learning circle.)

1. Cut two circles, eighteen inches in diameter, for each learning circle.

2. Divide each circle into eight sections.

3. In each of the eight sections, print (using a black felt pen) an addition problem that is simple enough to compute by the students for whom it is intended.

4. Print the answer to one of the math problems on the tip-end (rather than the squeeze-end) of a clothespin. Follow suit for each of the seven remaining problems and clothespins.

5. Turn the second circle so that its eight sections become its back. Place the front of the second circle against the back of the first circle (spoon-in-spoon fashion).

6. Either color-code or picture-code each correct answer the same as its problem. Do this by placing an identically shaped and colored symbol underneath the clothespin that matches the problem and inside the section of the second circle (bottom one) that will be pasted directly beneath the problem.

7. Cover both circles with clear Con-tact paper.

8. Glue the two circles together with a wire hanger securely fastened between them. The learning circle will remain in excellent condition when covered with the clear Con-tact paper despite extensive use, and it may be stored easily by hanging on a doorknob, a hook, or a hardware arm (see Exhibit 7–2).

Store the learning circle in a convenient place in the classroom—preferably in or near an instructional area where the students may use this resource when they are free to do so. Remove the clothespins from their storage niche—either on the lower half of the wire hanger or in an oaktag pocket attached to the back of the learning circle. Have the student mix the clothespins and then try to match the answer on each to the related question or problem on the chart.

Exhibit 7-1. Constructing a Learning Circle.[3]

Exhibit 7-2.   Joan Aberman designed this learning circle to teach her primary young-sters to recognize and begin to spell words concerned with transportation. After the children clip the clothespin with the word that they believe says or spells the name of the picture on the front of the learning circle, they turn the circle over and check their answers against the self-correcting back side. (Photographs courtesy of the Department of Curriculum and Teaching, St. John's University, Grand Central Parkway, Queens, New York.)

When the clothespins have been matched to what the student believes is the correct section of the chart, show him or her how to turn the entire chart over (onto its back) to see whether the color-coded or picture-coded symbols match. The design of the underside of the clothespin should be identical to and directly above the same design on the back of the second circle to permit self-correcting. When the two symbols match, the answer is correct; when they do not, the matching answer may be found by comparing the paired colors or pictures.

Variation on the Design of Learning Circles

1. Cut four circles, eighteen inches in diameter, for each learning circle; make two from poster board or heavy oaktag, the third from clear Con-tact and the last from colored construction paper.

2. Divide each circle into eight sections.

3. Place the clear Con-tact circle directly on top of one poster board circle so that the eight sections match exactly.

4. Sew the diagonal lines of the two circles together across the top from side to side, leaving the outer edge open to form eight separate pockets.

5. Using pinking shears (scissors that cut a serrated edge), cut the colored construction paper circle into eight equal sections.

6. In each of the eight colored construction paper sections print (using a black felt pen) a problem that is simple enough for the students for whom it is intended. (See Exhibit 7–3.)

7. Print the answer to one of the problems on the tip-end (rather than the squeeze-end) of a clothespin. Follow suit for each of the seven remaining problems and clothespins.

8. Turn the second poster board or heavy oaktag circle so that its eight sections become its back. Place the front of this circle against the back of the first poster board or oaktag circle (spoon-in-spoon fashion).

Either color-code or picture-code each correct answer the same as its problem. Again, do this by placing an identically shaped and colored symbol underneath the clothespin that matches the problem and inside the section of the second circle (bottom one) that will be pasted directly beneath the problem.

10. Glue the two circles together with a wire hanger securely fastened between them.

11. Cut a large envelope-shaped piece of colored oaktag, and paste it onto the back of the two joined together circles to form a pocket.

12. Insert the construction paper sections into the front triangular-shaped pockets on the top of the two joined together circles with the problems facing up.

Exhibit 7-3.   These are the front and back views of a CAP learning circle developed by Helen Pozdniakoff to accompany the Contract Activity Package on Shakespearian Plays in Chapter 4. Students are directed to match correctly the quotations with the plays from which they emanated. (Photographs courtesy of the Department of Curriculum and Teaching, St. John's University, Grand Central Parkway, Queens, New York.)

You now have a learning circle with exchangeable construction paper problems so that the same resource can be used for several different sets of problems. For example, one day you can insert math problems, another day you can insert language problems, and so on. The pocket on the back of the learning circle can be used to hold alternative sets of problems so that either you or your students may use different materials as they are needed.

Designing Learning Strips

A similar tactual resource is the learning strip, an elongated version of the learning circle (see Exhibit 7–4). It can be made by dividing a long piece of oaktag, construction paper, or poster board into eight or ten sections and printing a different number (or problem) in each box. Tape the wire hanger to the top of the back of the board. Place different numbers (within the student's range of addition facts) on each of the clothespins.

If the students for whom you are designing these resources are learning to recognize numbers, a simple match will do. If they are practicing the addition of numbers, then on the back of each section neatly print the number combinations that complement the addition of all the numbers on each clothespin that may be added to the number on the front. For example, if the number 3 is placed in the first section on the front of the learning strip, and if the numbers 1, 2, 3, 4, 5, 6, 7, or 8 each appear on a different clothespin, then on the back of the section of the learning strip that has number 3 on top, print the following:

$$3 + 1 = 4 \qquad 3 + 5 = 8$$
$$3 + 2 = 5 \qquad 3 + 6 = 9$$
$$3 + 3 = 6 \qquad 3 + 7 = 10$$
$$3 + 4 = 7 \qquad 3 + 8 = 11$$

Follow suit for each of the strips, providing the correct answer by printing all the correct number combinations added to the number on the front of the chart. In this case, you would not need to color or picture code the answers, for they will be evident.

Learning circles or strips are excellent resources for either introducing or reinforcing an endless number of facts or skills that your students may be required to learn. For example:

1.   In each of the sections on the front of the resource, place the letters: an, and, at, ear, en, end, in, and on. (Any word roots may be substituted.) Place a different letter on the top of each clothespin. By placing one clothespin at a time in front of each of the sections on the circle, your students may be able to form new words and read them. If they are just beginning first grade, they may need you to work with them to be certain

Exhibit 7-4.   A Learning Strip.

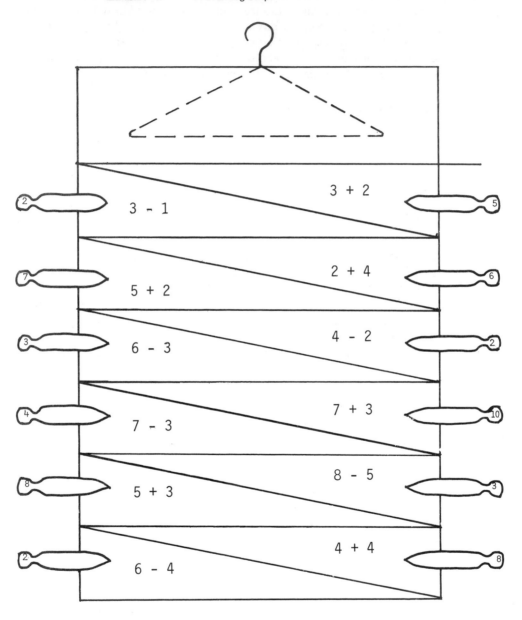

that the words they form are correct. When they are able, perhaps toward
the end of that year, write all the possible words that may be made by adding
a single letter or group of letters to the basic letters on the chart. Do this

on three-by-five-inch index cards, which you can store in a pocket on the back of the chart.

2.   Print the names of each of eight different geometric shapes on the chart and paste pictures of the shapes onto the clothespins. Your students will learn to *recognize, spell* and *write* the names before most of their grade-level peers.

3.   Print new vocabulary on the chart and paste pictures of the words onto the clothespins. By matching the pictures to the words, students will become familiar with the formation and letter combinations and will begin to read them—first on the chart and then in a text.

By using tactual, self-instructional, and self-corrective materials, your students will gradually become increasingly independent. By using learning circles or learning strips, you will be introducing them without direct assistance from others, to the facts and skills they need to know. This activity will increase their independence, and if they learn well, it will facilitate their academic achievement in later years when they will be expected to learn on their own.

Teaching Reading and Spelling through a Variety of Tactual Resources

As described in the review of the eighteen elements of learning style in Chapter 1, youngsters learn through different senses determined by their individual perceptual preferences or strengths. When teaching your tactually inclined students important skills such as language concepts, word recognition, reading, spelling, or writing, use more than one sense to help them to internalize what they learn.

When we teach by telling (either personally or on tape) we are appealing to a child's *auditory* (or listening) ability; when we teach by showing, we concentrate on the *visual* (or seeing) sense; when we teach through touching methods, we appeal to the *tactual* sense; and when we teach by doing (providing real experiences, such as teaching inches and feet by building a wagon) we are emphasizing a kinesthetic (whole body involvement) approach.

Materials that facilitate a tactual approach include clay; sandpaper; fabrics of varied consistency such as felt, velvet, or buckram (you can cut up old clothing that will no longer be worn); sand, water, fingerpaints, or uncooked macaroni. For example, if you wished to help your students to learn to spell a very difficult word, you might use any or all of the following activities, depending upon their preferences and how long it would take for them to master the word.

1.   Say the word. Explain its meaning. Give them an example of how it might be used in a sentence. Ask them to say the word and to use it in a sentence. When each student can do that, spell the word for them.

2.   Print the word in black on a white sheet of paper, then print it in white on a black piece of paper. Repeat the spelling and point to each of the letters as you say them. Ask the students to look at the spelling and try to memorize the letters in correct sequence. Ask them to try to spell the word without looking at it.

3.   Ask the youngsters to write the word by copying the letters that you wrote. If they can copy the letters accurately, ask them to spell the word again without looking. When they are correct, praise them. If they are not correct, show them the word written by you and point out their errors.

4.   Empty the contents of a small bag of sand into an aluminum pan. Encourage your students to trace the letters of the word in the sand. Permit them to look at the printed word as they "write" the letters. Then see if they can write the letters without looking at the word. If they can, ask them to spell the word without looking and without writing.

5.   Ask each youngster to dip one finger into a plastic cup of water and to write the word on the chalkboard without looking.

6.   Cut the small letters of the alphabet out of heavy sandpaper. Make duplicates of letters that are used often. Place all the letters into an empty shoe box and ask your students to find the letters in the spelling word without looking (strictly by feeling each of the letters and discarding those that are not in the word). When they have found all the letters, ask them to place them into the correct sequence so that the word is spelled correctly.

7.   Cut the small letters of the alphabet out of old fabric. Place them into an unused shoe box. Follow the procedure suggested for using sandpaper letters.

8.   Press different colored strips of clay into a pan. Ask your youngsters to write the word in the clay with a toothpick.

9.   Keep a jar of uncooked macaroni available for spelling. If you have "alphabet macaroni," ask each student to find each of the letters in the word and to glue them onto a cardboard. They will then have a three-dimensional spelling list. If you have the more common forms of macaroni, print the word in large letters on an eight-and-a-half by eleven-inch sheet of writing paper or shirt cardboard, and let them paste the food bits into the letters so that they, too, form the word.

10.   They can also trace the word in salt, colored or white sugar, or use fingerpaints to write it.

All these activities will not be necessary at one time. Nor will all your students require so many tactual experiences. The variety was suggested to provide you with alternatives so that you approach teaching through varied—and thus interesting—techniques for youngsters who profit from more than an auditory-visual method. When your students learn to read or spell a word merely by hearing it, seeing it, writing it once or twice, or by concentrating on or memorizing its letters, you need not introduce the tactual materials described here. But if learning does not occur through a phonics or word-recognition approach, offer them a choice of these activities and continue experimenting with the options until their task has been mastered. Unless your students indicate special preferences, use different activities for different words so that they do not become bored.

These suggestions may be used to teach numbers, letters, mathematical computations, geometric shapes, and other items in addition to reading and spelling words.

Understanding Task Cards

Task cards are easy-to-make, multisensory resources that respond to a youngster's need to see and to touch simultaneously. Often designed in sets or groups, each series teaches related concepts or facts. This resource tends to be effective with students who cannot remember easily by listening or by reading. They are used both to introduce new material and to reinforce something to which the student has been exposed but did not learn.

The most effective task cards are the ones that are self-corrective. These (1) permit students to recognize whether they understand and can remember the material; (2) allow no one other than the youngster using the cards to see errors made—thus preserving the student's dignity and self-image; (3) enable students who do make mistakes in their responses to find the correct answers; and (4) free the teacher to work with other students.

Task cards can be made self-corrective through any one of several methods: color-coding, picture-coding, shape-coding, or through the provision of answers. Task cards for young childen are usually simple and easy to manipulate; for high school students they become complex, exacting, and challenging at many different levels. They may be used by individuals, pairs, or a small group. They permit self-pacing. Students may continue to use them until they feel secure about their knowledge of the topic; they can be reused as a means of reinforcement if specific data has been forgotten. They are gamelike in character and often win and sustain youngsters' attention. They appeal to young people who cannot learn through other available resources, and, therefore, they are important for those whom they do teach.

Students who select or are assigned task cards may work with them at their desks, in an instructional area such as a learning station or interest center, in the library, on carpeting, or anywhere in either the school or home environment that they prefer.

Designing Task Cards

Task Cards are easy-to-make and extremely effective resources for tactual students at all levels. Begin by listing exactly what you want your students to learn about a specific topic, concept, or skill. Then translate your list into either questions and answers concerning what they should learn or samples of the answers—some true and others false. For example, if you were concerned about teaching the derivation of commonly used American words, you would list the words and the people who coined them.

Example

WORDS	DERIVATION
Prairie	French
Oasis	Greek
Shanty	French
Pretzel	German
Piano	Italian
Sputnik	Russian
Canoe	American Indian
Algebra	Arabic
Vanilla	Spanish
Cereal	Latin

Materials

- Colored oaktag or cardboard
- Black thin-line felt pens
- Colored thin-line felt pens (optional)

Directions

1.   Cut the colored oaktag or cardboard into three-by-twelve-inch rectangles.

2.   On the left side of each of the rectangles, in large easy-to-read letters, print one of the words on your list. On the right side of the rectangle, print the corresponding derivation of the word. Be certain to leave space between the word and its derivation.

3.   Either laminate or cover each rectangle with clear Con-tact.

4.   Cut each rectangle into two parts by using a different linear separation for each (to code them according to shape). For examples see Exhibit 7–5.

5.   Package the set in an attractive box and place a title on top that

describes the task cards inside. For the set we just discussed, appropriate titles might include:

How Did You Learn the Foreign Words You Use?

or

The Background of Words We Use Every Day

or

Foreign Words in Our Everyday Vocabulary

Exhibit 7-5. Sample task cards on word derivations.

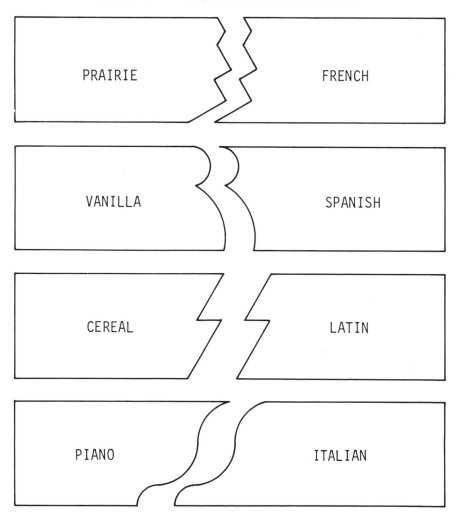

6. Either laminate or cover the box in clear Con-tact so that it remains sturdy and can be wiped clean whenever necessary.

7. If the box top is not very tight, use a couple of strong rubber bands to hold the lid down and the cards inside.

One teacher, interested in getting her students to understand the concept of analogies, worked backward. She folded a large yellow envelope, and on the back flap she printed:

What Is an Analogy?

Below the title she also printed:

An analogy expresses a likeness between things that are otherwise unlike.

Exhibit 7-6.   Sample task cards on analogies.

Track is to train
as highway is to   car.

Lunch is to noon
as breakfast is to   morning.

Then she thought of several analogies and printed one on each of half a dozen cards. She cut each card into two sections and shape-coded them in the process. The end product was an interesting way to teach (or reinforce) the concept of analogies (see Exhibit 7–6).

Exhibit 7-6. Continued.

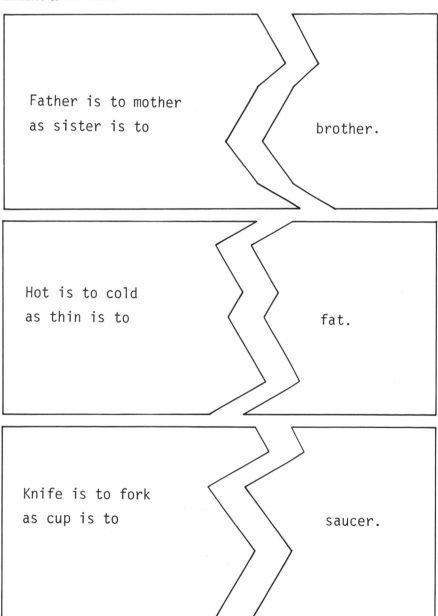

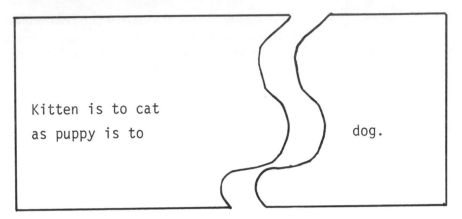

Kitten is to cat
as puppy is to   dog.

Exhibit 7-6. Continued.

Task cards that were designed to supplement the Contract Activity Package on "Ants" in Chapter 4 are shown in Exhibit 7-7. The task is to match the description on one set of cards to the type of ants on the other set.[4]

Exhibit 7-7.   Sample task cards on ants.

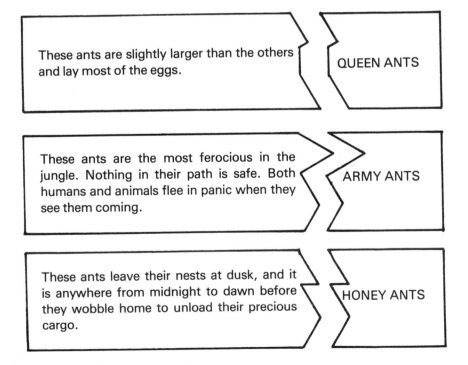

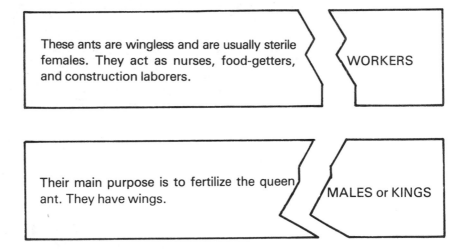

These ants are wingless and are usually sterile females. They act as nurses, food-getters, and construction laborers.

WORKERS

Their main purpose is to fertilize the queen ant. They have wings.

MALES or KINGS

(Answers on back of card)

When designing task cards for young children, you might consider number facts and their answers as comprising one set (see Exhibit 7–8), word blends and possible letter combinations to form new words as another task, initial letters that can be combined with "letter families" to form new words as another alternative, and so on.

For older and advanced students, you might consider

1. Outlining the shape of each of the original states; adding their official state nicknames, their capital cities, and the rank order in which they became a state; then having the youngsters piece the facts together (see Exhibits 7–9 and 7–10).[5]

2. Identifying famous buildings through illustrations (see Exhibit 7–11).[5]

3. Placing the name of a state, the person who founded it, and the year in which it was founded all on one task card that is divided into three sections; then having students piece together an entire set—perhaps entitled "Who Founded What and When?"

4. Completing a puzzle that combines all the parts of the eye into a single task card (see Exhibit 7–12).[6]

There is no limit to the intricacy and complexity that task cards may reach when subdivided into many parts. They are an effective introductory and reinforcement device for tactually and visually inclined students and often are successful in motivating students toward achievement after many previous methods have failed.

Exhibit 7-8.   These self-corrective task cards are a series of rectangular shapes, each with a printed numeral and a number of picture objects that are equivalent to it. Each rectangle is divided into two pieces separated by a differently shaped dividing line. Little children can piece together the task cards and learn to recognize the shape of each numeral and then to identify it with the correct number of objects that it represents. (Photograph courtesy of the Westorchard Elementary School, Chappaqua, New York.)

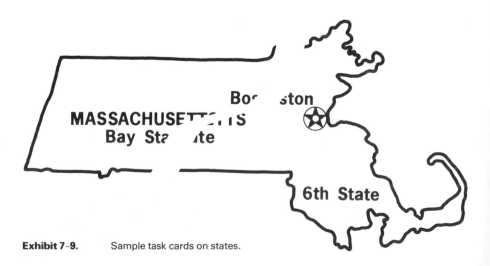

MASSACHUSETTS
Bay State

Bo   ston

6th State

Exhibit 7-9.   Sample task cards on states.

Exhibit 7-9. Continued.

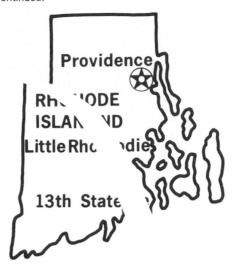

Providence

Rh ODE
ISLA ND
Little Rh die

13th State

Exhibit 7-10. This student is using a set of task cards designed by Jeanne Pizzo to memorize the order in which the first thirteen states entered the Union, their capital cities, and their nicknames. (Photo courtesy of the Department of Curriculum and Teaching, St. John's University, Grand Central Parkway, Queens, New York.)

The Supreme Court Building

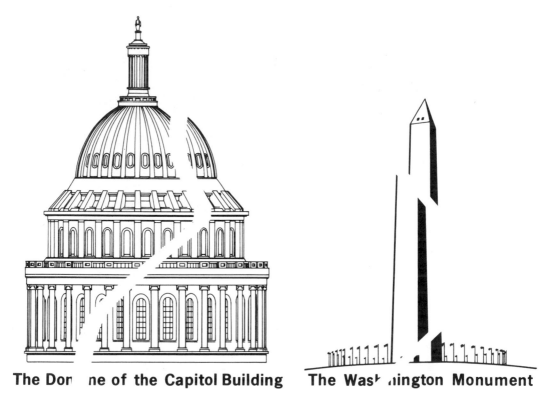

The Dome of the Capitol Building   The Washington Monument

Exhibit 7-11.   Sample task cards on famous buildings and monuments in Washington, D.C.

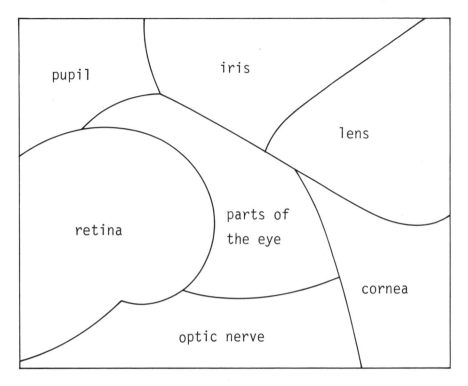

Exhibit 7-12.　　Sample task card puzzle on the parts of the eyes.

Designing an Electroboard

Another effective instructional device for tactually and visually oriented students is the electroboard. This is a gamelike board or cardboard box that teaches and reinforces information through an interesting approach.

Materials

- One large, flat cardboard box that is at least three inches deep
- Attractive construction paper to cover the cardboard box
- Clear Con-tact to cover and preserve the construction paper
- White labels or other paper that can be cut into strips
- Black thin-line felt pens
- Plastic tape
- Twenty brass paper fasteners
- A dry cell

- A lamp socket and bulb
- Approximately twenty feet of covered wire
- Rubber bands

Directions

1.   Cover the cardboard box and its cover separately with construction paper.

2.   Cover the box and its cover with clear Con-tact.

3.   Mark ten evenly spaced holes about two inches in from both the left and the right side of the cardboard box cover. Punch out the twenty holes (ten on each side).

4.   From above, push one paper fastener down into each of the ten holes on both sides of the face of the cover—as if each fastener were a swimmer jumping feet first into a pool.

5.   Cut ten pieces of wire that are long enough to stretch easily across the surface of the cover and to be wound around two fasteners—one at each side of the cardboard.

6.   From the underside of the cover, attach one end of a piece of wire to the first fastener at the top on the right side. Wind the other side of that wire around any fastener on the left side of the cover. Wind the ends tightly.

7.   Bend the ends of the two fasteners apart and flatten them against the cover.

8.   In the same way, attach a wire between the second fastener on the right side with any fastener on the left side. Make ten such connections until each fastener on the right side is connected to another fastener on the left side. Be certain to wind all the ends tightly, to bend all the fastener points apart, and to flatten them all against the cover.

9.   Make twenty paper strips and attach them next to the fasteners with plastic tape.

10.   Fasten the lamp socket to the cover. Connect the wires as illustrated in Exhibit 7–13. Notice the two long wires. Use one as the question wire and the other as the answer wire.

11.   Develop ten questions related to a topic that your students are studying. Print one question on each strip on the left side of the cover next to each fastener. Print ten answers, one to each of the ten questions. Attach these to the right side of the cover, next to the paper fastener that is wired to the fastener on the left side that has the question that matches that answer.

12.   Outline the strips with the black felt pen and illustrate the cover to increase its attractiveness. You can illustrate it with figures or letters that

can be attached for the present set of questions but removed and changed for another set at another time.

13. Print the directions for usage on the side of the box. Observe a student use it for the first time to be certain your directions are clear and easy to follow.

Your directions might read like this:

Directions for Using This Electroboard:

Touch the end of the question wire on the left to the fastener next to the question you want to answer. Touch the end of the answer wire on the right to the fastener that has the answer you think is correct. When the answer is correct, the lamp should light.

By printing new strips with different questions and answers, your electroboard can be used repeatedly for any curriculum. The light often delights youngsters and causes them to focus on the questions and their answers with an intensity that is not often rivaled by other approaches.

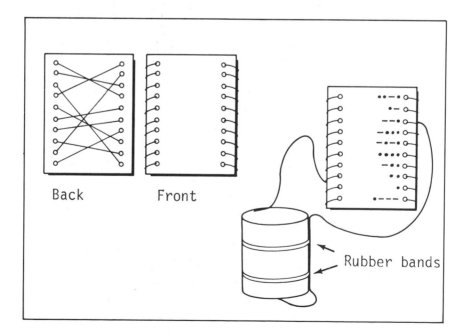

Back   Front

Rubber bands

Exhibit 7-13.   Electroboard.

Designing a Touch-Compute Can[7]

Although many teachers have been using a compute-can to facilitate addition and multiplication processes for youngsters who need assistance, the added touch of letting the students *feel* the answers may help younger or slower students to commit number facts to memory much faster than they could without the aid of this clever device.

Materials:

- 2 sheets of different-colored construction paper
- 1 Pringle's Potato Chips can or a similarly-shaped product.
- Clear Con-tact paper
- Black, thin-line felt pens
- Scotch Tape
- Dennison Glue-Stic
- Elmer's Glue

Directions:

1. Cut sheet #1, which is to be permanently attached to the can, as follows: 9¼ inches × 8¼ inches. (See Exhibits 7–14 and 7–15.)

2. Cover sheet #1 with Con-tact on its top side and attach to the can. Cut the clear Con-tact 10¾ inches long and 8¼ inches wide to fully cover sheet #1 (addition or multiplication), which is 9¼ inches high and 8¼ inches wide. The additional ¾ inch at the top and ¾ inch at the bottom are used to attach sheet #1 to the can permanently. Use either glue or Scotch Tape as you wrap sheet #1 around the can.

3. Outline the numerals with Elmers Glue so that the children can feel the shape of the number as well as see them.

4. Cut sheet #2, which will rotate around the can, 9 ³/₈ inches long and 7 ³/₈ inches wide. Cut out and remove all the boxes marked with an "X". (See Exhibit 7–16.) Cut Con-tact the same size (9 ³/₈ inches long and 7³/₈ inches wide). Place the Con-tact over the front of sheet #2 even with the top so that the additional 1 inch of length is at the bottom. When curling sheet #2 around the can, this additional inch will attach to the top forming a sleeve that can rotate around sheet #1, which is attached to the can. Sheet #2 may be used for addition and multiplication.

5. Place sheet #2 "sleeve" over sheet #1. The correct answers will appear in the cut-out boxes.

6. Label the Touch-Compute Can, adding the phrase (perhaps at the bottom), "Give me a turn!"

Demonstrate how to use this device for youngsters who need help with their number facts and then permit them to try it. Be certain to emphasize that, when they turn to the correct answer in the "boxed" cut-out, they also touch the numbers.

0+		0	1	2	3	4	5	6	7	8	9
9+		9	10	11	12	13	14	15	16	17	18
8+		8	9	10	11	12	13	14	15	16	17
7+		7	8	9	10	11	12	13	14	15	16
6+		6	7	8	9	10	11	12	13	14	15
5+		5	6	7	8	9	10	11	12	13	14
4+		4	5	6	7	8	9	10	11	12	13
3+		3	4	5	6	7	8	9	10	11	12
2+		2	3	4	5	6	7	8	9	10	11
1+		1	2	3	4	5	6	7	8	9	10

Exhibit 7-14. Sheet #1 to be used for addition.

0x		0	0	0	0	0	0	0	0	0	0
9x		0	9	18	27	36	45	54	63	72	81
8x		0	8	16	24	32	40	48	56	64	72
7x		0	7	14	21	28	35	42	49	56	63
6x		0	6	12	18	24	30	36	42	48	54
5x		0	5	10	15	20	25	30	35	40	45
4x		0	4	8	12	16	20	24	28	32	36
3x		0	3	6	9	12	15	18	21	24	27
2x		0	2	4	6	8	10	12	14	16	18
1x		0	1	2	3	4	5	6	7	8	9

Exhibit 7-15. Sheet #1 to be used for multiplication.

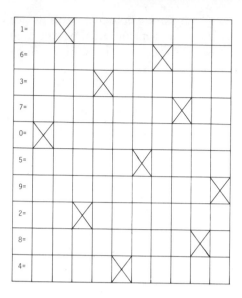

Exhibit 7-16.   Sheet #2 to be used for either addition or multiplication.

Creating and Using Tactually Oriented Activity Cards

Writing and drawing are, in themselves, tactual activities, but students often enjoy these tasks most when they encompass varied, short, interesting, and creative assignments. Activity cards are just that, when they are effective: (1) varied, (2) short, (3) interesting, and (4) creative.

Activity cards can be colored with water-soluble marking pens and then laminated. If laminated, students may work directly on them with either grease pencils (which wipe clean with a tissue) or with water-soluble pens (which wipe clean with a damp sponge).

On the primary level, activity cards provide an outlet for a young child's accumulating knowledge so that it is reinforced and, simultaneously, praised. Beginning with what the child actually knows (see Exhibits 7–17, 7–18, and 7–19), skillful cards gently prod the youngster to move into areas with which he or she is still groping (see Exhibits 7–20, 7–21, and 7–22); they stimulate imagination (see Exhibits 7–23 and 7–24) and also begin to build positive self-image (see Exhibit 7–25).[8]

As children move into advanced levels of understanding, activity cards should continue to challenge them. For a more able primary youngster, cards that utilize existing knowledge might be like those in Exhibits 7–26 and 7–27; ones that encourage new skills might be similar to those in Exhibits 7–28 and 7–29; and those that begin to make young people aware of their own feelings and values might reflect the insights in the card in Exhibit 7–30.[9]

In the intermediate grades, activity cards can become the vehicle for sparking creative ventures (see Exhibits 7–31 and 7–32) and for developing insight into one's own emotions (see Exhibits 7–33 and 7–34).[10]

To increase your ability to manage the volume of productivity that activity cards generate, either make them self-corrective by printing alternative answers on their backs or include them as part of the activity and reporting alternatives of a Contract Activity Package so that classmates share their completed activities with peers as you observe and spot-check.

Draw 5 foods that you like.

Name each one.

Exhibit 7-17.

Draw your favorite toy.

Exhibit 7-18.

Write the names of 5 stores that you like.

Exhibit 7-19.

Draw your hands

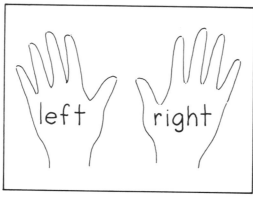

1. Put each hand on paper.
2. Trace around each hand with a pencil.

Exhibit 7-20.

Write the names of 5 children in your class.

Exhibit 7-21.

Write the names
of 5 people
who make you happy.

Exhibit 7-22.

Draw an animal
that you would
like to be.

Exhibit 7-23.

MAGIC

SLIPPERS

Magic slippers can
take you anywhere

Write about where you
would want to go.

Exhibit 7-24.

You are special.
Write about yourself.

Exhibit 7-25.

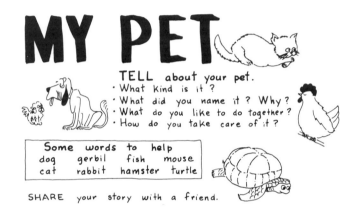

MY PET

TELL about your pet.
· What kind is it?
· What did you name it? Why?
· What do you like to do together?
· How do you take care of it?

Some words to help
dog   gerbil   fish   mouse
cat   rabbit   hamster   turtle

SHARE your story with a friend.

Exhibit 7-26.

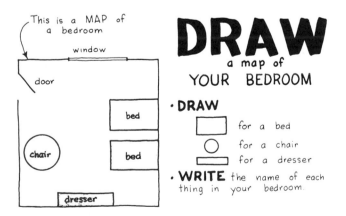

This is a MAP of a bedroom

window

door

bed

chair

bed

dresser

DRAW
a map of
YOUR BEDROOM

· **DRAW**

☐ for a bed
○ for a chair
▭ for a dresser

· **WRITE** the name of each thing in your bedroom.

Exhibit 7-27.

FIND OUT
about YOUR GRANDPARENT

QUESTIONS TO ASK

1. Where were you born?
2. When were you born?
3. What language did you speak as a child?
4. What did you like to do when you were my age?
5. What do you like to do now?

WHAT TO DO

1. Use your information to write a story.
2. Add drawings and photographs if you can.

Exhibit 7–28.

CAN YOU SAY
Some words in another language?

There are more than **3000** languages. It's fun to know many languages.

FIND OUT how to say some words in different languages. **Ask** your family, your teacher, and your friends to help.

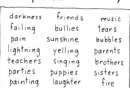

Some Words to learn	
mother	friend
house	hello
father	love
thanks	toy

Some Languages
Spanish
French
German
Italian

merci   gracias   grazie

- **LEARN** more words in another language.
- **TEACH** your friends what each word means, and how to say it.

Exhibit 7–29.

Feelings

FIND words that could answer each question.

1. What makes you feel happy?
2. What makes you feel sad?
3. What makes you feel scared?
4. What makes you feel angry?
5. What makes you feel excited?

ASK a friend his answers.

darkness	friends	music
failing	bullies	tears
pain	sunshine	bubbles
lightning	yelling	parents
teachers	singing	brothers
parties	puppies	sisters
painting	laughter	fire

TRY to add more words.

Exhibit 7–30.

Dr. Quackenbush has just completed his new invention. It is a secret X-Ray machine. He thinks it can make a person invisible for one day. He hasn't tried it out **yet**.

It is time for your annual check-up during your summer vacation. As you walk into Dr. Quackenbush's office, you notice a strange grin on his face. **YOU** are the perfect subject for his experiment. Not knowing the doctor's plan, you have your X-Ray taken.

The machine works! You are invisible.

WRITE about your adventures while you are invisible.

I'M INVISIBLE!

Exhibit 7-31.

YOU CAN SPEAK

to any animal. Each animal has a special language. You are able to understand and speak each one. Choose one animal.

WRITE a conversation you might have together.

MAKE A LIST of the real sounds made by the animal. Tell what the sounds might mean.

Exhibit 7-32.

WHAT DAY
DO YOU REMEMBER ?

Some days seem wonderful, while others seem terrible.

LOOK AT these story titles
CHOOSE ONE to write about.

My Happiest Day
My Funniest Day
My Saddest Day
My Scariest Day
My Most Exciting Day
My Worst Day
My Loneliest Day
My Most Interesting Day

TELL
- **WHO** was with you
- **WHAT** happened
- **HOW** you felt

SHARE your story with a friend.

Exhibit 7-33.

GIVE ADVICE
TO YOUR FRIENDS

Many newspapers have an expert who helps people with their problems.

• **ASK** your friends to write about their problems.

• **THINK** about each problem and write down your suggestions for its solution. Post your answers on a bulletin board.

Exhibit 7–34.

Other Tactual-Visual Games That Are Easy to Make

Any games that students play by both seeing and moving them with their hands are, in a sense, tactual-visual; they are not always as tactual as are task cards or the compute can, but they often facilitate learning for youngsters who require some tactual involvement with the learning materials.

"The Mystery Animal"[11] (see Exhibit 7–35) is one such device and is easy to duplicate at any level. In fact, given an example to study and the following directions, many upper elementary students can make new samples for you.

Materials

• A photograph or illustration of something connected with the theme that your students are studying

• A piece of colored construction paper the same size as the illustration you select. Light colors are preferable.

• Black thin-line felt pens

• Clear Con-tact to cover the front and back of the illustration

• Glue (Glue-Stic or Super Stik adhesive seems to work best)

Directions

1. Back the illustration by gluing the construction paper to it.

2. On the construction side, print questions all over the paper at varying angles. Turn each question upside down, and beneath it print the answer to it.

THE MYSTERY ANIMAL

Cut out the pieces. Put them together by matching the numbers that add up to the same totals. If you piece them together correctly, you will see a mystery animal.

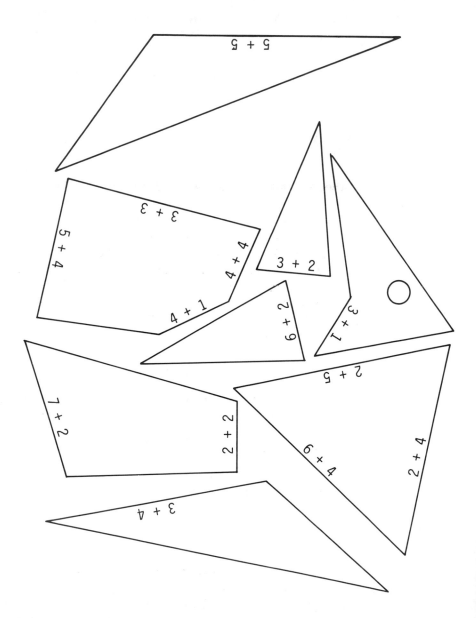

Exhibit 7-35.

3. Glue clear Con-tact to both the illustration side and the construction side of the game.

4. Cut the illustration into several pieces—each question separated from its answer.

5. Cover a box or envelope that can hold the questions and answers with construction paper. Label it to explain the contents and directions for usage. If the box cover is large enough, suggest that the students piece together the question and answer sections inside the top of the box. When the puzzle has been completed, it can be turned upside down and the original illustration should be intact.

6. Cover the box or envelope with Con-tact.

Scramble Word Games

Most of us have, from time to time, used word games in which we scramble letters in an answer and ask students to decode them. To make such a device tactual, merely cut out the letters that comprise the answers and place all the letters together into one envelope or box. Again, place a title and directions on the box, and cover both the letters and the box with clear Con-tact. Voila! A tactual-visual game that will both introduce new ideas and reinforce old ones.

Example

TOPIC: WOMEN OF THE PAST AND PRESENT[12]

Directions

Inside this box are 120 alphabet letters. When placed together correctly, they will form the names of nine outstanding women that you should know about.

Inside the box, the letters would include:

14	A's	7	N's
5	B's	4	O's
5	C's	12	R's
5	D's	3	S's
14	E's	5	T's
1	F	1	U
2	G's	2	W's
7	H's	3	Y's
7	I's	1	Z

2   K's

16   L's

4   M's

You might also add a hint to help them decode the names.

Example

One of the women founded the nursing profession; another overcame multiple handicaps; one was the first woman attorney in the United States, another the first physician; one was the printer of the Declaration of Independence; another was the first instructor of sanitary chemistry, appointed to the faculty of the Massachusetts Institute of Technology, and eventually became the first president of the American Home Economics Association; another organized the American Red Cross after nursing soldiers on battlefields throughout the Civil War.

Step-by-step Guide to Designing Kinesthetic Activities

Some youngsters can learn only by doing; for them, real-life experiences are the most effective way of absorbing and retaining knowledge. It is easy to teach students to convert pints to quarts and quarts to gallons through baking and cooking or to teach them inches and feet by helping them to build a scooter or antique doll house, but it is not simple to teach all the skills and information that must be achieved through reality oriented activities. To begin with, such activities are time consuming; secondly, many activities require supervision; finally, we are not used to teaching that way and to do so requires an endless source of creative suggestions.[13] There is, however, a new kind of kinesthetic (whole body) game that you can design for classroom use, reuse, and ever-continuing learning by your slower charges.

Designing Body-action Games

Many teachers save old things and then use them creatively to instruct their students. Now is the time to locate all the large plastic tablecloths, shower curtains, carpet and furniture coverings, and sails that may be hidden away in basements, attics, garages, and wherever else too-good-to-throw-away things are placed. Old sheets and bath towels may also be pressed into service, but they are not as durable as plastic, and when they are washed, the printed matter on them often fades and occasionally disappears altogether. If you are not a collector of old valuables, you may need to either solicit cast-off materials from others or purchase a large sheet of plastic from your neighborhood bargain store.

Materials

- One large sheet of plastic, approximately four-by-five, five-by-five, or five-by-six feet or another material within that size range
- Smaller pieces of multicolored plastic that can be cut into decorations and illustrations and then glued or sewn onto the larger sheet
- Black thin-line permanent ink pens
- Black and brightly colored permanent ink felt pens
- Glue that will adhere plastic to plastic
- Assorted discarded items that, depending on your imagination and creativity, you use as part of the game you design
- Pad and pencil for sketching ideas

Directions

1. Identify the information or skills that you want your students to learn.

2. Consider ways in which you can either introduce that information or reinforce it through a body-action game in which selected students can hop or jump or merely move from one part of the large sheet to another as they are exposed to the major (or finer) points of the topic.

3. Sketch a design on a sheet of paper to work it out before you begin cutting, pasting, or sewing.

4. When you are satisfied with your conceptualization of the game, plan a layout of the various sections on the plastic sheet that you will use; consider the placement of articles, and list the additional items that you can use, noting the ways in which you can use them.

5. In pencil, lightly sketch on the large sheet where you will paste each item, the dimensions that you must plan for, and where you will place key directions.

6. Cut the smaller plastic pieces into appropriate shapes or figures and glue them onto the larger sheet.

7. With a felt pen that will not wash off, trace over those penciled lines that you wish to keep.

8. Develop a set of questions and answers or tasks that students may complete as they use the body-action game. Then either develop an answer card so that students may correct themselves or color-code or picture-code the questions and answers so that the game is self-corrective.

9. If you teach either very young children or poor readers, develop a tape that will tell them how to play the game, what the game will teach them,

and how they can recognize that they have learned whatever it is the game is designed to teach.

10.   If your students are capable of reading and following printed directions, print or type a set of directions for them and attach it to the sheet (perhaps in a pocket that you cut out and glue or sew onto its underside).

Examples

For an instructional package on "Perimeters,"[14] several activities were designed that taught students to find the perimeter of a series of different shapes (see Exhibit 7–36). As the culminating exercise, a body-action game was created with the following directions:

To play this game, you must find the perimeter of each shape as you come to it. Travel along the path according to the direction on the answer side of each card.

1.   START AT THE CENTER OF THE GAME. (See Figure 7–37.) What is the perimeter of the blue square if its sides measure 12 inches each?

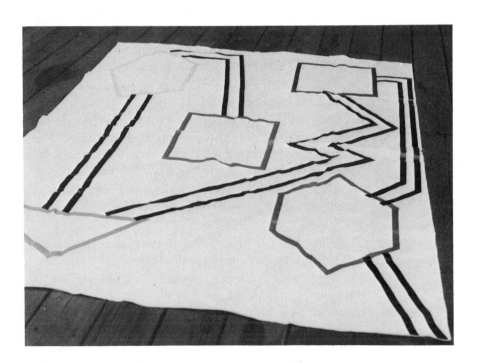

Exhibit 7-36.   As part of an instructional package on "Perimeters," Miriam K. Landau designed a body-action game that required students to find the perimeter of a series of different shapes. (Photograph courtesy of the Department of Curriculum and Teaching, St. John's University, Grand Central Parkway, Queens, New York.)

2. Look at Answer Card 1 in the pocket on the underside of the game. If your answer was correct, hop on one foot to the next shape. If you were *not* correct, take "baby steps" to the next shape.

3. You now should be standing on the yellow shape. It has five sides. Three of its sides measure 12 inches each, and two of its sides are 10 inches each. What is the perimeter of the yellow shape?

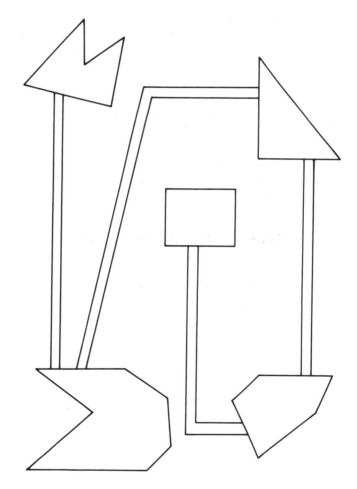

Exhibit 7-37.

The directions guided students through a series of varied geometric shapes, permitting them to check their answers, and if they had computed incorrectly, to learn why they were wrong. When the body game was completed, a duplicated sheet attached to the larger package tested them on their ability to determine the perimeter of a variety of shapes. The teacher then checked their final assessment responses.

For a social studies unit on "The Battle of Manila Bay: May 1, 1898," a body-action game was designed that duplicated the geographical maps of the South China Sea, the Philippines, and Manila Bay.[15] Students were asked to reenact the first and second battles in sequence using toy ships and other replicas.

For a unit on westward expansion, a map of the entire United States, including many geographical representations and divisions representing the acquisition of territories was recreated on an eight-by-ten-foot plastic sheet.[16] Students were directed to play a game in which they identified which territories were added and when, what their contribution to the country ultimately was, and the value of those contributions to present-day students.

Granted, the time and effort devoted to the development of body-action games is extensive. However, if you find that students who rarely achieved before they were exposed to this method suddenly begin to learn and to enjoy learning, won't you agree that the outcomes are well worth the input? Besides, the sheets can be used over and over again for different sets of facts and skills by merely changing the directions and the cards that are given to the students.

A Final Word on Tactual And Kinesthetic Resources

Try them! The tactually and kinesthetically oriented students will love them and learn through them, and you will feel like the epitome of the professional teacher!

8

Matching Individual Learning Style Characteristics with Instructional Programs, Methods, and Resources

Throughout this book we have emphasized the need to identify the learning style characteristics of students and then to assign them to methods and resources with which they are most likely to achieve. The final consideration that should be brought to your attention is the one concerning overall programs—the ways in which, ostensibly, we group students together in order to facilitate their academic progress.

The four most familiar types of programs in existence today are the traditional, individualized, open, and alternative. Each responds to different learning styles, and each attracts teachers with fairly definitive teaching styles (see Exhibits 8-1 through 8-4).[1] Each is an excellent program for students whose learning style characteristics are complemented by the philosophy and practices that it represents.

One problem that often accompanies student placement is that when a teacher becomes interested in experimenting with a specific program, the youngsters who have been assigned to that teacher are automatically also in the new program, whether or not it is a good choice for them. Of course the opposite is true, too; unless a teacher is interested in trying varied approaches, all students are automatically in a traditional classroom. Neither extreme used exclusively is a good one unless the program's characteristics match all the students' learning styles.

The descriptions of the four program types are, of course, "book definitions," defined to show clearly the differences that exist among them. In reality, however, we recognize that individual teachers have incorporated some aspects of perhaps several programs into their own unique styles.

Exhibit 8-1.   Traditional classroom.

INSTRUCTIONAL PROGRAM: TRADITIONAL CLASSROOM

Philosophy

The teacher is responsible for helping students to achieve (minimally) grade-level standards. Children are expected to pay attention, try, work, take their work seriously, and be good—all of which presuppose that they are each able to achieve through the methods selected by the teacher. Most of the instruction is through lecture and questioning occasionally supplemented by media. Lesson plans are written by the teacher for the principal as indications of what the class will be taught. Grades are determined by the student's achievement on group tests. All students learn sequential blocks of subject matter at the same time. A few students are permitted some enrichment if it does not interfere with the curriculum to be covered. For all, self-selection of subject content and method of learning are rare.

Required Student Skills

1. To pay attention for consecutive intervals of 20 to 50 minutes each.

2. To sit still for consecutive intervals of one to three hours.

3. To refrain from needing a drink, a break, or using a lavatory except during specified times (recess, lunch, etc.).

   To raise one's hand, interrupt the teacher, and publicly request permission to do any of the above during instructional time.

4. To concentrate on studies for several hours during the school day and while engaged in homework after school.

5. To retain information by listening.

6. To learn at a table and chair or desk.

7. To learn at his or her desk wherever it has been placed.

Learning Style Characteristics

Is motivated.

Does not require mobility.

Does not require intake, except at correct times.

Is not embarrassed by being different from peers.

Is persistent.

Is an auditory learner.

Requires a structured environment.

Sound, light, and temperature are not factors.

8. To accept that what is taught is necessary, valuable, and interesting.	Is authority-oriented.
9. To conform to externally established standards and rules.	Is authority-oriented.
10. To accept being marked on a competitive basis regardless of inherited ability or environmental background.	Is authority-oriented.
11. To learn whenever a subject is being taught.	Time is not a factor.
12. To keep working at an item until it is mastered.	Is persistent.
13. To maintain a positive self-image and creativity while following directions, controlling normal body needs, learning in a way that prohibits use of personal learning style, studying what may be irrelevant and uninteresting, and avoiding conflict.	Is authority-oriented.

Exhibit 8-2.   Individualized classroom.

INSTRUCTIONAL PROGRAM: INDIVIDUALIZED CLASSROOM

Philosophy

The teacher is responsible for diagnosing, prescribing for, and guiding each student through the learning process. Recognizing the different elements of learning style, he or she permits students to work anywhere in the environment, in any sociological pattern that they choose. When students evidence ability to follow objectives that have been assigned to them, they are permitted to continue working as they prefer and are gradually permitted more and more options in objectives, resources, activities, and evaluation. When students do not appear to be able to work independently, structure is added to their prescriptions so that they work to varying degrees under the direct supervision of the teacher. Multimedia, multisensory resources are available to students, who may select from among them. Objectives are written on an individual basis and may be contributed to or be developed by the student. When progress is not satisfactory, the teacher becomes increasingly directive. Grades are determined as a result of criterion referenced testing related to each youngster's enumerated objectives.

Required Student Skills

Learning Style Characteristics

1. To identify those objectives, resources, activities, and assessment devices that need to be fulfilled. This will be done by

Varied levels of responsibility.

students who can function independently, and with the teacher for students who need guidance.

2. To identify the resources through which the objectives may be achieved. These will be itemized by the student. When student progress is not apparent or appropriate, resources will be prescribed by the teacher.

    Varied perceptual strengths.

3. To complete individual prescriptions. When this is not done, the instruction will become formalized and traditional. As the student shows achievement, options in the mode of instruction will become available. As options increase with evidenced achievement, achievement continues to increase.

    Varied levels of motivation.

4. To assess one's own progress. Students who are able to evaluate objectively their academic growth are permitted to continue doing so. Students who are unable to do so are evaluated by the teacher frequently.

    Varied degrees of self-and authority-orientation.

Exhibit 8–3.   Open classroom.

INSTRUCTIONAL PROGRAM: OPEN CLASSROOM*

Philosophy

Children are permitted to select their own curriculum, resources, schedule, and pace of learning. Students may remain with a topic as long as it interests them and may study alone, with a friend or two, or in a small group. Since youngsters learn in very individual ways, the teacher is responsible for providing an environment rich in multimedia resources and for encouraging student involvement with the materials. Objectives, if used, are determined by the child and may vary from student to student and on a continuously changing basis. Grades are not given, but evaluations are made in terms of each child's demonstrated growth. A positive and "happy" attitude is considered very important for student progress.

---

*Because of the wide variety of multimedia and manipulative resources available to students involved in open classroom approaches, less motivated youngsters are often intrigued into active participation. In addition, the deemphasis on grades permits an immature child to explore materials and experiences without penalty. These procedures afford such a student additional time in which to adjust to an academic environment. Children must be carefully watched, however, in the event continued exploration without substantial academic achievement over a two to four month period may become habit forming.

Required Student Skills	Learning Style Characteristics
1. To learn without continual direction and supervision.	Is motivated.
2. To avoid an essentially social, rather than academic, experience.	Is responsible.
3. To discipline oneself to concentrate and to learn self-selected ideas, data, and values.	Is motivated and responsible.
4. To study in the midst of movement, discussion, and varied activities.	Sound, structure, and the mobility of others are not factors.
5. To interact positively with other children.	Is peer-oriented.
6. To retain information without drill reinforcement.	Is not in need of imposed structure.

Exhibit 8-4.   Alternative programs.

INSTRUCTIONAL PROGRAM: ALTERNATIVE PROGRAMS**

Philosophy

Students are given curriculum choices, freedom, and objectives, and they are expected to gather and retain information independently. Students are usually permitted a voice in their program development. Since alternative programs differ widely, the degree to which options are provided concerning objectives, resources, activities, and evaluations is dependent on the individual program, not the student.

Required Student Skills	Learning Style Characteristics
1. To learn without continual direction and supervision.	Is motivated.
2. To determine the scope, sequence, and depth of undertaken studies.	Is responsible.
3. To assess one's own progress and potential accurately.	Is self-oriented.
4. To discipline oneself to study and achieve.	Is motivated and responsible.
5. To retain information without drill reinforcement.	Is not in need of imposed structure.

**Because of diversification, it is assumed that such a program permits students to achieve in ways different from those of the traditional classroom. If an open campus approach is used, students need not be present at all times and may be scheduled into programs of less than 5.5 hours of formal instruction. Student learning is partially self-directed and may occur out of the school building. Usually, this approach is used only with secondary students.

Furthermore, the explanations cited here are not intended to promote one program over another. Rather, they are intended to provide you with a clear understanding of why each program is preferable for certain students and inappropriate for others. Because each student learns in ways that often are extremely different from those of his or her classmates, each program is advantageous to some students. Of greater importance is the reality that no program can respond sensitively to every learning style and that should youngsters be placed into the wrong program for them, their ability to progress academically will be severely hampered.

Case Studies to Test Your Growing Knowledge of Learning Styles and Complementary Methods, Resources, and Programs

You undoubtedly have made some intuitive and observational judgments about your own students. You may not, however, feel very confident about your ability to diagnose learning styles and then to prescribe some of the methods and resources detailed in previous chapters. The following case studies will provide you with an opportunity to test your developing diagnostic skills and to compare your responses with ours, so that you can assess how well you are doing. You will be gaining accuracy and insight. You will also become sufficiently confident so that you will implement some of the suggested techniques in your classroom.

When you have completed the case studies, compare your answers with the ones we have prepared for you. Where there are differences in opinion, please examine the reasons we present for our choices. If you disagree with the rationale, try it your way when planning for your students; if you are successful—continue; if you are not pleased with the results, try it as suggested and see if the results are better. At the very least, you will have experimented with a variety of alternatives for a youngster with whose progress you have not been satisfied and you will have made every possible effort to assist that student to achieve.

Guidelines for Analyzing the Case Studies

When analyzing the students in each of the following case studies, use these checklists:

Learning Style Elements Refer To

- Sound
- Light
- Temperature
- Design (formal or informal)

- Pair-Oriented learning
- Peer-Oriented learning
- Team-Oriented learning
- Authority-oriented (teacher or other adult or authority) learning

- Motivation

- Persistence

- Responsibility

- Structure

- Self-Oriented learning

- Varied orientation (includes several socio-logical possibilities) learning

- Perceptual strengths (auditory, visual, tactual, kinesthetic)

- Time of day

- Need for intake

- Need for mobility

Instructional Methods Refer To

- Contract Activity Packages
- Programmed learning sequences
- Multisensory instructional packages
- Task cards, learning circles or strips, compute-cans, and other tactual resources
- Lectures, discussions, tapes, films, and other auditory resources
- Body-action games and other kinesthetic resources
- Books, films, filmstrips, transparencies, study prints, and other visual resources

Programs Refer To

- Traditional
- Individualized
- Open
- Alternative

Use the Learning Style Profile form as a guide for beginning your diagnosis for each student (see Exhibit 8–5),[2] and then compare your findings with ours.

Primary Case Study: Willie

Complete the assignment below, and then compare your answers with the ones we prepared for you at the end of this chapter.

1. List the learning style elements that the case study reveals about Willie.

Exhibit 8-5.

LEARNING STYLE PROFILE

Name_____Teacher_____School_____

Grade_____Counselor_____Date_____

Comments based on highest ratios noted on questionnaire:

I.   Environmental   Sound_____

                                 Light_____

                                 Temperature_____

                                 Design_____

II.   Emotional   Motivation_____

                                 Persistence_____

                                 Responsibility_____

                                 Structure_____

III.   Sociological   Appears to work best: (alone, with peer(s), with adult(s), in a variety of ways).

                                 1._____

                                 2._____

                                 3._____

IV.   Physical   Perceptual Preferences_____

                                 Intake_____

                                 Time_____

                                 Mobility_____

                                            Checked by_____

2.   List the learning style elements that the case study did not clarify or about which you have doubts.

3.   Name the methods that you would suggest for Willie's use.

4.   Based on the Learning Style Profile form that you completed for Willie, which program might be most appropriate for him?

5.   Explain any special considerations that you see in this case.

Willie had grown up in a family comprised of four children, a working mother, and an ill father who suffered from constant headaches. Because of his dad's condition, the children were required to be quiet in a small four-room flat in the poorest section of the city. Willie's naturally outgoing nature may have suffered because of his father's daily demands for solitude and privacy.

Willie was constantly up and down the stairs that led to his parents' fifth floor apartment. He would go down to search for fun, find that he did not like the other children on the block, and return to the apartment where his father would admonish him to "Go out and play!" He felt comfortable in the apartment because of the cool, softly lit rooms and the fact that he could nibble constantly at bits and pieces of leftovers, but dad's continuing pleas for "Quiet!" drove him, reluctantly, to the streets—for a little while at least.

The happiest time of Willie's day was when his mother returned from work. She would greet him with wide open arms and strong hugs and kisses and ask whether he had had enough to eat during the day, whether he had found some friends with whom to play, and whether the other "kids treated you right?" Willie never told her that he did not like the other boys or girls, although he wished he could tell her; but he felt that she would be disappointed in him. He also was afraid to ask why his father did not want him around, for although he did not want to bother his father, he did not like the hot, noisy streets that were filled with loud, screaming, aggressive kids who made lots and lots of noise.

Since he was scheduled to start school in September, Willie wondered whether it would be a nice place to be while Mom was working and what his father would do all alone in the apartment during the day when Willie's older sister and brothers were away. He hoped there would be lots of things he could do in school.

Elementary Case Study: Kathy Hightower[3]

Complete the assignment below, and then compare your answers with ours at the end of this chapter.

1.   List the learning style elements that the case study reveals about Kathy.

2.   List the learning style elements that the case study did not clarify or about which you have doubts.

3.   Name the methods that you would suggest for Kathy's use.

4.   Based on the Learning Style Profile form that you completed for Kathy, which program might be most appropriate for her?

5.   Explain any special considerations that you see in this case.

Kathy shook her head in a continuing expression of frustration. Her negative body language had become apparent at home as well as in school.

Her fifth-grade peers were just as upset with her wandering curiosity as she was with her teacher's repeated commands to sit still.

The teacher's voice began to rise as he fought to control his composure—and Kathy. "Return to your seat at once or I'll have to send you to the principal."

Kathy looked up from her friend's desk. She liked the principal; they often compared their opinions on the underlying symbolism in recent movies they had seen. For an instant she toyed with the notion of saying something fresh so that she could take the long walk down to the main office. Maybe the principal has seen *Jeremiah Johnson,* mused Kathy. I'll bet he didn't notice Jeremiah preparing those tasteless Indian bread cakes toward the end of the movie after his Indian bride had been killed.

She shook her head again. No, she really didn't want to get her teacher even more upset. Kathy went back to her seat.

Kathy strained to see the print. It was comparatively dark in her far corner, and she had difficulty reading the work assigned to the class. She stopped and shook her head again. She knew her answers were right; she had completed the vocabulary words and used them in sentences in one-fourth the time that was needed by most of the others. She smiled as she looked at her last math test; her sixth straight 100!

She felt restless and tried to bring her work to the teacher, but he was talking to another youngster, and there were three more lined up waiting.

Kathy felt the urge to eat again and sneaked a health food bar out of her desk. She also attached a tiny earplug under her long brown hair and switched from an analysis of Beethoven's Fifth by Leonard Bernstein to "News of the Day" to catch the latest weather report. She felt a glow of achievement as the forecast from the hidden radio matched hers. She wondered if she should sneak home at lunchtime to check her rain gauge.

She was deeply into her homemade weather charts and maps (while munching and listening to *Aida*) when her name was called by the teacher in exasperation. He was ready to move the class onto the next topic and was irritated that Kathy apparently had tuned him out once again. She had not heard his crisp command, "Put all other materials away now and turn to page 97 of your science book," and "Kathy, please stay with us this time!"

She shook her head. She already knew the material being presented on rocks. As a matter of fact, she had collected those rocks and compared them to samples in the high school science room last fall.

Junior High or Middle School Case Study: Jose Martinez

Complete the assignment below, and then compare your answers with ours at the end of this chapter.

1.   List the learning style elements that the case study reveals about Jose.

2.   List the learning style elements that the case study did not clarify or about which you have doubts.

3.   Name the methods that you would suggest for Jose's use.

4.   Based on the Learning Style Profile form that you completed for Jose, which program might be most appropriate for him?

5.   Explain any special considerations that you see in this case.

Jose, a tall, intelligent youngster of Puerto Rican background, cut classes and was frequently absent from the 6,000-student building in the inner city junior high school he attended. When the attendance officer questioned Jose, he candidly responded, "No one here comes every day, not even the teachers! Nobody cares about anybody! When I was knifed two years ago, the kids in the corridor walked away, and the teachers pretended not to see! In this place it's each guy for himself!"

The dean of students' report of several meetings with Jose included the following phrases:

> He is obviously lacking in respect, for he does not know how to sit in this office! He is always throwing his legs up and over the arms of the chair. He never stops chewing; when I told him to throw the gum into the wastepaper basket, he did so, but within a few minutes, he had the end of his pencil in his mouth and was actively biting on it. When told to wait outside my office, he obeyed; before long my secretary was chastizing him for putting his feet onto the table in front of the couch.

You study Jose's official records and are surprised to find that, at fifteen, he is reading on a ninth-grade level. His mathematics scores are also on grade level, and his achievement throughout the grades has always been good. His anecdotal record reveals an unusual series of remarks from former teachers:

Miss Price, Kindergarten Teacher:

> Jose is such a serious little boy. He tries so hard! He loses patience with the other children when it takes them a long time to do the things that he does so easily. He is reading! (How remarkable for this neighborhood!)

Mrs. Shapiro, First-grade Teacher:

> This child does not belong in this school! He is too bright for the class and too good to be exposed to the kind of antics to which these children are subjected in the yards, in the halls, and in the streets. I feel sorry for him. . . .

Mrs. Sunshine, Second-grade Teacher:

> Jose is really reading! I never would have known but while I was talking to one of the mothers, he picked up a book from the back shelf and apparently became absorbed in it. When I noticed, I praised him for "reading," but actually thought that he had only been looking at the pictures. He surprised me by explaining the story with enthusiasm and in detail! He must have learned all by himself because these children have had little formal instruction. The others are just beginning to manage their primers.

Mr. Ryan, Fifth-grade Teacher:

> I can't seem to get Jose interested in the sports the boys engage in during recess; he is obviously a loner. Not at all athletically inclined, he brings his texts down with him and insists on sitting someplace close to wherever one of the teachers is and just reads. He is often teased by the other kids because he won't join in their games. Too bad the kid can't cut the mustard with his peers. Another thing, the kid never stops eating! He ought to weigh 140 with his appetite. Wonder how he stays so stringbeany?

Mrs. Rodriguez, Sixth-grade Teacher:

> I wish I could take Jose home with me. He is so pitiful! He does not belong in this group! He is an able child who is being stultified by the lack of opportunity. He could learn anything in the sixth-grade curriculum if only I could teach him, but the other children absorb so much of my time with their poor behavior and need for remediation that I cannot really spend time on this one child who needs special attention.

April 7th . . . I discussed Jose's case with the principal. He said that we are doing the best we can for him, "under the circumstances." He said that, next year, when Jose goes into the Junior High School he will be in classes with students who can achieve more easily than the ones we have here, and then Jose will catch up. I certainly hope so! Somehow I feel we should be doing more for this boy. His parents are concerned about him. His mother has called several times saying Jose does not like to come to school. The guidance counselor talked with him, but said that he could not see what the problem was.

Mr. Wright: Seventh-grade Teacher:

Jose said that he was attacked by a gang of five boys in the corridor this morning. He said that he did not recognize them. They wanted his money and, according to Jose, "cut" his arm when he refused to give it to them. No one in the school has admitted seeing the assault. Mrs. Deckado was on duty but did not notice anything. There is something wrong with this boy! He may have brought on the assault himself in a way, because he is always pulling away from the other kids, acting as if he'd rather not know them. Of course, part of the problem might be that he is ahead of his peers academically, but we would not recommend advancing him a grade because he is obviously not as mature socially as he might be.

High School Case Study: Patrice

Complete the assignment below, and then compare your answers with ours at the end of this chapter.

1. List the learning style elements that the case study reveals about Patrice.

2. List the learning style elements that the case study did not clarify or about which you have doubts.

3. Name the methods that you would suggest for Patrice's use.

4. Based on the Learning Style Profile form that you completed for Patrice, which program might be most appropriate for her?

Patrice is a sixteen-year-old student attending the Orchard Hill High School in affluent suburban Philadelphia. She writes beautifully and creates poetry and songs. She spends hours (usually in the quiet of the night) composing skits and plays that include musical adaptations of her social and political science studies. She enjoys the development of these activities but prefers to submit them to her teachers and have others perform in them; she also refuses to direct the productions, claiming that she would rather limit her contributions to authorship.

Her teachers consider Patty antisocial, essentially because she does not demonstrate any particular interest in or liking for either her classmates (in any class) or her teachers. Her attitude, though politely disguised, is, "Tell me what to do and I'll do it to the best of my ability . . . but please let me do it my way—and at home, if possible." Students envy her ability but dislike her "snobbishness." Teachers also dislike her, although few will admit it. She makes some of them feel inferior and others ineffective because they cannot reach her. She is attractive—even pretty—but she is not interested in either boys or girls. When approached, she is proper, friendly, and polite, but she will not engage in extended conversations or in activities of a social nature with classmates. She does have some interactions with her older sister's friends, but these young college students are several years her senior. She sometimes accompanies her parents to the theater and opera and often paints in the loft of a group of aspiring artists who are students and teachers from the Philadelphia School of Art, although she believes her artwork to be crude and undeveloped.

Patty is an A student and achieves easily. She likes writing, painting, English, languages, social studies, political science, and philosophy best, although she does well in all subjects. She rarely takes time to eat lunch, preferring the language lab or music room to eating. She works wherever she can find a quiet corner, a place where people are not there to interrupt her train of thought. Her guidance counselor has recommended that she seek private counseling because of her inability to socialize with other youngsters.

High School Case Study: Mike Hughes

Complete the assignment below, and then compare your answers with ours at the end of this chapter.

1.   List the learning style elements that the case study reveals about Mike.

2.   List the learning style elements that the case study did not clarify or about which you have doubts.

3.   Name the methods that you would suggest for Mike's use.

4.   Based on the Learning Style Profile form that you completed for Mike, which program might be most appropriate for him?

Mike Hughes leaned against the corridor wall, disgruntled and ill at ease. He was waiting for Mrs. Carr, the guidance counselor, to discuss his chances of being graduated in June. He anticipated the worst, for his grades throughout his high school career had been marginal at best, and he knew he was failing physics and bio—and possibly social science, too.

Mrs. Carr's door opened and another senior emerged from the inner sanctum. Mike had been inside the guidance offices only once before, when he was a freshman and had trouble fitting his courses into a program where he could be free after the ninth mod each day so that he could work after school. At that time he'd seen another counselor who had urged him to give up his after-school job so that he could spend more time on his homework and, perhaps, do better. The counselor never thought to ask Mike why he worked or whether he could give up his job. At the time Mike had considered the suggestion, but only for a minute or two. He knew intuitively that the only place he'd ever excelled was in the machine shop where he'd worked since he was eleven or twelve. He'd been big for his age and had lied to Joe, the owner, when he first applied. Joe surmised that Mike might have been younger than the sixteen years required by law, but he was desperate. Two men had quit and his father-in-law (who usually filled in) was ill. Joe had given him a chance to work at the shop and had been delighted with the ease with which Mike had learned and the skill he had demonstrated in repairing motors and parts. Joe called him "a natural" and overlooked the working papers he had not gotten around to getting. Now that Mike was close to graduation, Joe had offered him a full-time salary and a semi-partnership—5 percent of the profits. To Mike, this was success.

Mrs. Carr's voice called out, "Whoever's next—come in!" Mike walked through the door and faced several small cubicles, each with a different plaque across its top. He searched for the one that read "Mrs. Carr" and found it. He walked toward the entrance.

"Sit down," the woman directed. "What is your name?" "Mike Hughes." "What can I do for you?" she asked. "You sent for me," Mike responded. "I guess it was about graduation." For a moment her face went blank, and then Mrs. Carr remembered. "Oh, yes!" she recalled, "I did want to discuss something with you." She searched for a file and found it beneath a series of other folders. She opened it and read through several pages slowly. Mike became more concerned. His feet shuffled and suddenly he couldn't sit. He stood up.

"Where are you going?" Mrs. Carr asked. "Nowhere," Mike answered. "I just can't sit." "Well, you'd better sit!" she snapped. "I haven't even begun with you!" Mike sat down again. "Your record has been very poor," Mrs. Carr stated. "It's been bad throughout school. To what do you attribute this?"

Mike stared at her. He was a graduating senior (he hoped) and now, for the first time in four years, someone was asking him why he had not been doing well in school. He did not know the answer.

"Well?" Mrs. Carr snapped again. "What have you to say for yourself?" "What do you mean?" Mike queried. "What do you want to know?"

"Young man," Mrs. Carr barked. "I asked a simple question! If you don't understand, I'll ask it another way. Why have you been such a poor student in high school?"

Mike shuffled his feet and shifted his position. He really wanted to get up again and get away from this lady. He didn't know what to say. Spontaneously he blurted out, "I guess I'm just dumb."

"Perhaps." Mrs. Carr seemed satisfied with the response. "Well, you are at the end of your school career," she answered, "and you have not filled out all the necessary forms for graduation."

"What forms?" Mike asked.

"Young man," she said in exasperation, "students have been told repeatedly about the forms that must be completed before any diploma can be issued. Whey didn't you fill them out?"

Mike sat quietly in his chair. Anger was beginning to well up inside him. "When were we told about the forms?" he asked.

"Many times!" Mrs. Carr responded.

"When?" Mike asked again.

"In assemblies, in home rooms, in letters sent from the guidance office," she answered.

"There have been no assemblies since April," Mike responded. "I don't remember hearing about graduation forms in home room, and I never received a letter from the guidance office—except for this one (he held it up) telling me to be here today."

Mrs. Carr's face contorted slightly. "Don't challenge me, young man! I tell you that other students heard the messages and received the letters and that you are irresponsible and unthinking. That is why I had to send for you today! You cannot be graduated unless you fill in those forms!"

Mike looked at her in astonishment. "Does that mean that I have passed physics . . . and bio . . . and social science?" he asked.

Mrs. Carr looked at her records. "It seems to me that your teachers have agreed to permit you to be graduated because you probably wouldn't do any better if they made you repeat the work."

Mike shifted his position again, but he sat quietly.

"Does that surprise you?" Mrs. Carr asked.

"Does what surprise me?"

"Can't you understand a simple question?" Mrs. Carr asked in desperation. "Are you surprised that your teachers have agreed to pass you so that you may be graduated?"

Mike began to perspire. The anger that had been welling up in him increased in intensity. He looked at her piqued face and retorted, "No, ma'am. I am not surprised. That is what teachers have been doing to me since the fourth grade."

"Doing to you?" Mrs. Carr almost shouted. "You mean 'doing for you,' don't you?"

"No," Mike responded. "They didn't do anything for me, except make it harder to understand the next term's work and the next term's work, and so on. They made it easy for themselves—because they got rid of me and didn't have to get me to learn."

Mrs. Carr's face grimaced. "You are so ungrateful!" she shouted. "Everyone has been trying to help you all along. You don't deserve a high school diploma! Your teachers have been helping you get through so that you might get a job and earn a living! You don't appreciate even that!"

"Mrs. Carr, nobody's been helping me. All the way through school I had trouble learning what my teachers taught. Nobody ever tried to teach me so that I could learn. I learn many things! I am the best mechanic in this county, people all the way from Pond Ridge and Middle Neck bring their cars into Joe's garage to have me work on them. I learned how to fix motors all by myself, and when I had problems, I got help from the mechanics at Cadillac and Pontiac and all the other dealers around. That was six or seven years ago, and now they send their worst problems to me! I can learn, but I can't learn how my teachers teach—and NOBODY'S tried to teach me any differently. How did the mechanics teach me? How did Joe teach me? What made them good teachers and my teachers in school such rotton ones?!"

Mrs. Carr's mouth fell open. She stared at Mike with unmasked fury. She finally responded, "You are the most ungrateful fool I have ever met! I think this matter should be referred to the principal. You are not worthy of a high school diploma." She viewed Mike's squirming figure and said, with all the dignity she could muster, "This meeting is ended. Please leave."

Mike entered the machine shop in a despondent frame of mind. Joe, without glancing up, called out, "Glad you're in, Mike. The Senator's car is here, and he needs it by 4:00 today. He said that only you could get it ready for him by then! Wanna' get to it as soon as you can?"

Mike sat down at Joe's feet. "Joe," he said, "I think I blew graduation."

Joe stopped what he was doing. "Physics?" he asked.

"No, my big mouth," Mike said. He then told Joe what had happened in Mrs. Carr's office that morning.

"Well, you know Mike, you've been saying things like that for years. You often say, 'If I can learn this, why can't I learn in school?' Maybe you were right; maybe you should have told her what's been on your mind."

Mike did not answer. He merely stretched his long legs and frowned. "I blew graduation," he said sadly. "I should not have told her how I felt."

"It's too late to think about that," Joe answered. "Get to work on the Senator's car so that he can have it by 4:00."

"I don't know how to handle this," Mike said. "I want to get the diploma, but I feel I don't deserve it. What's more, although it's probably my fault, it's their fault, too. It's all mixed up in my mind."

"You know what?" Joe asked. "Get the Senator's car ready, and when he comes in, ask him what to do. He's a smart man! He'll know how to advise you. Besides, I don't think they can keep you from graduating because you didn't fill out a form, or for blowing your stack at that cold lady. After all, they kept passing you!''

Elementary Case Study: Ruth M.

Now let's try to prescribe a program based on an existing Learning Style Profile form for Ruth M. Examine the data provided, answer the following questions, and then compare your answers with the ones at the end of this chapter.

1. Which methods would you suggest for Ruth?
2. Which program would be most suitable for her?
3. Are there any special considerations in this case?

LEARNING STYLE PROFILE

Name   Ruth M.   Teacher   B. Gold   School Howard Elementary
Grade   Nongraded, 4-6   Counselor   L.T.P.   Date   October 16

Comments based on highest ratios noted on questionnaire:

I.	Environmental	Sound: Sound does not seem to be a factor although she tends to speak loudly. Light: She is sensitive to excessive light and avoids it. Temperature: She dislikes heat. Design: She can't seem to sit at her desk; prefers sprawling.
II.	Emotional	Motivation: She works well when interested. Persistence: She is persistent when she is interested. Responsibility: She is confident that she is able to do her work well and does to the best of her ability. She can be given long-term assignments when she likes what she is doing. She feels pressured when she knows completion is expected of her, and she is not interested or motivated.
III.	Sociological	Works well alone when interested; requires another classmate to work with in order to complete assignments that don't motivate her. Rarely needs teacher, except for assistance with difficult problems.

IV. Physical

Perceptual Preferences: Visually oriented; does not retain well through listening; tactual (touching) is her secondary perceptual strength.

Intake: She could eat all day; nibbles constantly—particularly when working on required tasks that are not of major interest to her; she calms down when involved with studies that motivate her.

Time: Interest, rather than time of day, is the factor of importance.

Mobility: Cannot sit still; moves constantly; works everywhere.

Answers to the Primary Case Study: Willie

If we were to list all the data that relates directly to Willie's learning style, we would note the following:

- He is in need of *mobility* (is constantly up and down the stairs).
- He prefers *cool,* rather than warm, temperatures.
- He appears to prefer being *alone* to being with the children downstairs.
- He prefers *soft light* rather than the brightly lit outdoors.
- He needs *intake* (is constantly nibbling).
- He is *adult* (mother) oriented (doesn't tell her that he did not like the other boys or girls—believing that it will disappoint or displease her; also leaves the apartment to please his father).
- He does *not like noise* (may prefer silence or quiet).
- He is *responsible* (wonders what his father will do when he is alone).
- He is *motivated* (hoped there would be lots of things he could do in school).
- He may be *persistent* (going up and down the stairs) or he may be authority-oriented (his father's admonitions to "Go out and play!").

2.   When considering what the case study does not tell us about Willie's learning style, we should find out whether he:

- Prefers a formal or informal design.
- Will be as persistent in schoolwork as he is going up and down the stairs to his apartment.
- Needs structure or will be self-structured in school.
- Will like the children he meets in school (he may just not have liked "loud, screaming, aggressive kinds who made a lot of noise";

- Has perceptual preferences;
- Functions best at specific times during the day.

3.   Willie could be exposed to any and all of the methods described in this book because we do not really know enough about his learning style at this time to limit him to a single technique. His need for mobility, coolness, soft lighting, and intake, and his self- and adult-orientation can be accommodated with each of the methods. If he needs extensive structure, programmed learning would be appropriate. If he requires a multisensory approach, instructional packages would be effective. If he would profit from interacting with some nice, quiet youngsters in his class, a Contract Activity Package would be a good choice.

We would suggest beginning with a programmed instruction sequence and then alternating with the other two approaches to permit you to observe him functioning with all. Then, depending on his achievement and attitudes, you could determine whether one is preferred over the others or whether a combination of two or three might be best for him.

4.   Willie's need for mobility would rule out a traditional program at an entry level. His lack of rapport with the youngsters in his neighborhood might also eliminate an open classroom as an initial assignment. His youth prohibits an alternative program (which is used at the junior and middle school and high school levels). An individualized program that uses a variety of methods and permits self-pacing (to allow him some mobility and occasional breaks) might be the way to begin.

5.   Special considerations in Willie's case might include the fact that his father's illness and need for quiet might have made him feel rejected. Willie would thus need a teacher who is caring and outwardly responsive to him. His need for mobility and intake requires another form of consideration, and certainly a teacher who will use methods other than those that require strict conformity and docility would be more likely to provide him with a positive first-year school experience.

Willie might respond nicely to less aggressive, quiet youngsters, and he should be given opportunities to interact with such children. Because of his close relationship with his mother, it would be good to have her visit the school occasionally and become involved (even through a personal note or two) in his activities and achievements.

A curriculum for Willie should include each of the following:

a.   Introduction to quiet, leisure-type games that he can play at home by himself to occupy him in the afternoons, on holidays, and on weekends.

b.   Knowledge of how illness affects people, so that he understands that his father's characteristics are not a rejection of him.

    c.   A focus on the foods that are nutritious; since he snacks so much, he should become aware of those that are healthful.

    d.   Use of small-group techniques to permit him positive interaction with classmates in ways that are controlled and place them on teams with common interests. If he continues to resist peer-group interactions, he should not be required to continue.

Answers to the Elementary Case Study: Kathy Hightower

1.   If we were to list all the data that relates directly to Kathy's learning style, we would note the following:

- She is unaffected by *sound* and is able to listen while reading or completing other activities (listening to radio and working on weather forecasts).
- She seems to be *uncomfortable* in a *low-light* area (dark in her corner, has difficulty reading).
- She is highly *motivated* (pleased with good grades, has success in activities).
- She is *persistent* (stays with all tasks to completion).
- She is *responsible* (listens to requests despite frustrations; wants to be part of class).
- She is *self-structured* when interested.
- She likes to work with *peers* and *adults* (goes to their desks, likes to talk to the principal).
- She appears to have *multiple perceptual abilities* (listens; sees; and is kinesthetic, for example, radio, films, weather station).
- She likes *intake* (urge to eat again).
- She appears to require *mobility* (went to friend's desk, felt restless, wanted to bring her work to teacher, thought about walking to principal's office and going home).
- She is *authority-oriented* (wants to please the teacher).

2.   When considering what the case study does not tell us about Kathy's learning style, we would need to note that we do not know:

- The time of day in which she functions best.
- The degree of temperature she prefers.
- The types of resources and instructional materials required to produce the most effective use of her ability to work alone and with her peers.

- The amount of structure, if any, that she might need if not interested in a particular topic or subject.
  - Whether she learns best alone, with one or more peers, with adults, or in a designed combination.
  - Whether she would be in need of mobility if she were challenged by appropriate studies.
  - Whether she would learn better in a formal or informal design.
  - Whether she could function independently on advanced studies in which she was not interested.
  - Whether she can use the senses of touch or smell effectively.

3. Kathy needs neither the structure of programmed instruction nor the multisensory aspects of instructional packages. She learns easily and well; therefore a Contract Activity Package would be ideal for her. The curriculum for such Packages, however, should be challenging and not repetitious as suggested by the vignette. She easily could tackle advanced studies, and were she permitted to work with brighter or older students, she would undoubtedly be happier in her school activities.

4. Kathy's learning style characteristics that might respond to a traditional program include these: she is motivated, persistent, authority-oriented, an auditory learner, and time does not seem to be a factor for her. Those characteristics that would not respond to a traditional program include her apparent requirement for mobility and need for intake. Since traditional programs concentrate on grade-level studies and standards, and since Kathy can function far above normal grade levels, she either would need to be advanced to a higher (older) grade or her program would need to be varied extensively.

Because of Kathy's learning style characteristics, she would probably respond well to an open classroom program, which would permit her to select her own curriculum. However, there are two factors about Kathy that we don't yet know and that we should investigate before making a final decision: (1) we do not know if she is really peer-oriented, for she has had no opportunities to work directly with real peers, and (2) we do not know whether she would need structure if required to learn mandatory subjects.

An individualized instructional program would certainly respond to Kathy's learning style, for it permits wide flexibility for those students who require variations in the environment and the curriculum, and, simultaneously, it provides structure for those who are not self-directive. In this case however, given the wide range of Kathy's abilities, her high degree of motivation, persistence, responsibility, and her high academic achievement, an open classroom would be our primary choice.

5. Kathy's problems center about the fact that she is far brighter

than her classmates and that her teacher does not design advanced studies for her. By requiring that all students participate in the identical curriculum, the teacher is ignoring Kathy's intellectual giftedness. Because she must listen to and repeat studies that she has already mastered, Kathy is bored, frustrated, and irritated. The other students in her class are not really peers, for they are not able to function on her academic level. The teacher's disparagement (" . . . please stay with us this time!") is causing the students to react to her negatively, too—("her peers were upset with her . . ."). Had Kathy been able to work with actual peers, she might have developed an excellent relationship with some of them.

Answers to the Junior High or Middle School Case Study: Jose Martinez

1.   The learning style elements that the case study reveals about Jose include the following:

- He needs an *informal design* ("He is always throwing his legs up and over the arms of the chair." He put "his feet onto the table. . . .").
- He needs *intake* ("He never stops chewing"; he "had the end of his pencil in his mouth and was actively biting on it"; he "never stops eating!")
- He is undoubtedly *visual* for, without being formally taught by his teachers, he learned to read and to compute enough to be on grade level in an environment that was not at all conducive to achievement.
- He is *motivated* (taught himself and continued in spite of difficult class and school factors).
- He is *persistent* (continued teaching himself throughout the grades despite negative conditions).
- He is *responsible* (read while teacher was talking to parent and did what he was directed to do by dean of students and dean's secretary. His absenteeism, under the circumstances of the assault, is understandable).
- He provides his *own structure* (teaches himself, studies whenever time or the occasion permits).
- He is *self-oriented* and, under certain circumstances, is (or was) authority-oriented until he was assaulted and the teacher on duty ignored the incident.
- He does *not prefer* to be among *students* who are different from himself. Because his classmates were very different from him in intellect, behavior, attitude, and values, they were not really his

peers. We are not justified, therefore, in stating that he is not "peer-oriented."

- Sound probably is not an element that affects him (reads while others are talking, teaches self despite disturbances).

2.   The learning style elements that the case study did not reveal include:

- How light, temperature, time of day, or mobility affect him.
- Whether he might have been positive toward them, had he been able to interact with real peers.

3.   Jose learned easily; he therefore does not require a multisensory instructional package. He provides his own structure and does not need programmed materials. Since he does well at teaching himself, a Contract Activity Package would be perfect for him.

4.   If Jose were in an academically oriented class, a traditional program would suit him well. Since the schools that he has attended do not have classes that enhance his achievement, he could have progressed more rapidly had the program been individualized, and had he been permitted to pace himself. Because of the student population in his school, Jose would profit from being entirely removed from that situation. He is motivated, responsible, persistent, and achieving and would, therefore, do well in an alternative program. Such a program would enumerate objectives; provide him a CAP to follow; and permit him to study anywhere that resources were available, such as in a local library, museum, or resource center; or provide him with an apprenticeship in industry. Removing him from that junior high school environment would have been a positive step.

5.   The special considerations in this case center around the fact that Jose is more able and motivated than his classmates and that his teachers are unable to provide for an academically achieving youngster while having to cope with students who have learning and behavior problems.

Other concerns are that (1) the dean of students does not know the difference between lack of respect and learning style differences, (2) his kindergarten teacher did not try to accelerate Jose's achievement although she recognized his readiness and ability, (3) his second-grade teacher never pretested him to determine his reading level and was surprised to learn accidentally that he was able to read, (4) his fifth-grade teacher was unable to differentiate between athletically and academically inclined individuals and unable to analyze boys that were not interested in sports, (5) his sixth-grade teacher did not have the professional courage to insist on a different placement for the youngster, (6) the elementary school guidance counselor was insensitive to Jose's needs, and (7) the seventh-grade teacher was inclined to believe the students who did not admit to seeing anything and the teacher who did not notice the assault. The reality of the situation was that Jose was assaulted and was knifed; that others refused to serve as witness is testimony to the atmosphere permeating the school.

That the entire system required revamping is obvious; that Jose was one of its victims is equally apparent.

Answers to the High School Case Study: Patrice

1.   The case study reveals the following information concerning Patrice's learning style:

- She is *self-structured* (creates poetry and songs, composes skits and plays, and so forth).
- She is *persistent* (spends hours doing the things she enjoys).
- She may prefer night, but does well at all times.
- She prefers *quiet* and does not appreciate interruptions.
- She does not require *intake* (rarely takes time to eat).
- She probably has many *perceptual strengths,* since she achieves easily and excels in many subjects.
- *Design* may not be important—she works anywhere, as long as it is quiet.
- She is, to some degree, *authority-oriented* since she learns from teachers and is willing to take directions from them; she is definitely *self-oriented.*
- She is *motivated* (an A student).
- She is *responsible* (does homework and extra assignments, and agrees to follow directions).

2.   The learning style elements that the case study does not clarify include the following:

- Whether light or temperature affect her at all.
- Whether, when working with real peers, she might not be more social. Extremely bright students have little in common with their age-level classmates and often prefer older or more talented students. Patty's peers were people who shared her interests and were of a similar artistic bent—which excluded her teachers and the other students in the class.
- Whether she required mobility.

3.   Programmed instruction has too much structure for a creative person such as Patrice. Instructional packages are unnecessary for an extremely bright student. A Contract Activity Package would have been ideal

for her—telling her what to do and, thus, enabling her to complete assignments without necessitating classmate interaction.

4.   Although Patrice achieved academically in a traditional class, she was viewed negatively by her teachers and classmates, whose social expectations for her were identical with the ones they had for everyone else. Patrice is not everyone else; she is a highly intellectual, artistic, achieving young lady who cannot interact with less able people and enjoy it. Although her standoffishness may offend some people, they should be sufficiently secure to ignore her; her behavior is normal for superior people.

An open classroom would have necessitated much more interaction with classmates, although the selection of a curriculum based around her major interests would have been positive. An individualized program might have met her needs, but even that would have added the unnecessary constraints of attendance in formal classes requiring some social interaction with students of the same age and also with teachers.

The most appropriate program for Patrice would have been an alternative one in which she might have studied in theaters and art studios for part of the day and then participated in classes at the high school at other times. In that way, her own enjoyment would have increased, her social interactions might have occurred with authentic peers, and the socialization expected of her by the teachers and students at the high school would not have developed. In effect, she would have been present only part-time, and they would not have seen enough of her to require more interaction than she was capable of providing.

Of greater importance, participation in activities in "the real world" in which she was so interested, would have been a better source of education and growth for Patrice than engaging in isolated creativity, which was an "extra" to her regular work, rather than the nucleus of it.

5.   A special consideration in this case was that Patrice was different from the students we teach each day. Most of us operate under an outdated theory that suggests that people must be able to get along with their classmates or they are immature. If anything, Patrice was more mature than her classmates; she had nothing in common with them. Since most adults select their friends on the basis of common interests, she was behaving in a most adult way.

Another incorrect assumption that many of us still subscribe to is that people should be well-rounded. No one can do everything well, and the few who can do many things well are talented (and fortunate) indeed. Patrice excelled in the academic subjects and in the arts. Is it also necessary for her to be a social butterfly if she is happy with her work and the few people who share her interests? We think not, but we acknowledge that old concepts die slowly and that many teachers will sympathize with the guidance counselor's recommendation that Patrice seek counseling. To the contrary, we suggest that the guidance counselor read *Your Erroneous Zones*[4] and permit Patty to be her own person.

Answers to the High School Case Study: Mike Hughes

1.   The learning style elements revealed by this case study suggest the following:

- Mike needs *mobility* (his feet shuffle, he cannot remain seated, and he shifts position).
- He is *not auditory*. Initially, he had done poorly academically, and most achieving students in a traditional school do learn by listening. Secondly, he requires repetition of verbalized statements and does not appear to understand questions that are posed to him. He is probably *not visual* to the extent that he can read well or enjoy reading, or he would have achieved through that medium. Since he is so successful at the repair shop, it is fairly safe to assume that he is *tactual* (learns by working with his hands), or *tactual-visual* (learns by seeing and doing) or *kinesthetic* (learns by being engaged in the activity).
- He is *motivated* to do things that he enjoys. He did well at the repair shop in spite of his youth and inexperience. He also *wants* to graduate and has tried to conform.
- He is *persistent* when involved with things that he enjoys.
- He is *responsible*. He did see Mrs. Carr and tried to find out what ought to have been done. He also assumed a great deal of responsibility at the repair shop and was admired by his real peers (the other repairmen), Joe, and the customers.
- He is *self-oriented* (when motivated), *peer-oriented* (at the shop with the other repairmen), and *authority-oriented* (with Joe and his customers). He could not do better in school and was therefore in a situation that he could not control—thus the evident frustration.

2.   The learning style elements that the case study did not clarify include:

- Whether he is affected by sound (although he learned to repair cars in a machine shop, which may be noisy).
- Whether he is affected by light or temperature.
- Whether his constant movement is a result of his need for mobility or a need for an informal design.
- The extent to which he is capable of structuring his time and learn-

ing tasks. Apparently he can do so at the shop but may be unable to do so at school.

- Whether he is in need of intake.
- Whether the time of day affects him at all.

3.   Since Mike is a poor student academically, he probably would have profited from multisensory instructional packages supplemented by task cards, activity cards, electroboards, touch-compute cans, and body-action games.

4.   Although either a traditional or an individualized program that utilized instructional packages and the supplementary tactual-visual-kinesthetic resources would have been far more productive for Mike than the program in which he had been registered, the best solution for him would have been an alternative program where he could have worked in the repair shop part-time and engaged in regular studies at other times. In that way, he would not have been required to have competing interests and might have been able to blend the two better so that his school work might have improved.

Another consideration, of course, is that had Mike's teachers diagnosed his learning style and recognized that he needed different methods and resources in order to be successful academically, he might have been an excellent student; and rather than becoming a partner in the repair shop, he might have gone on to invent special motors that use fuels other than gasoline, cars that cost less to operate, parts that do not wear easily; or to pursue another possibility, he might have used his skillful hands to become an outstanding designer, artist, or computer technologist.

5.   A special consideration in this case is that no one did anything to alter Mike's course during his school career. Had he been tested, had alternative methods been used, had someone worked with him to develop study skills and an ability to use alternative resources, his high school life might have been more rewarding and gratifying than it was.

Answers to the Elementary Case Study: Ruth M.

1.   Since Ruth requires visual and tactual resources, she might do well with either a programmed learning sequence or an instructional package. Try both—one at a time—and observe her attitude and progress. When she needs peer interaction to complete assignments in which she is not interested, use the small-group techniques.

2.   If her class is either individualized or an open classroom, she will be permitted the mobility she needs at certain times. If it is traditional, the teacher may permit Ruth to work in the rear of the room in a learning station or interest center so that she may move but not disturb her peers.

3.   In your analysis, note that Ruth (a) speaks loudly, (b) is sensitive to excessive light, (c) dislikes heat, (d) "can't . . . sit," (e) does not retain well through listening, and (f) eats continually. There are perfectly healthy children who share these same characteristics, but, as a concerned teacher, you might want to have Ruth checked by a physician just to be certain that the loud speech and inability to learn through listening does not reflect poor hearing. You certainly would have her eyes checked to determine whether sunglasses would make her feel more comfortable on sunny days.

If Ruth were your student, you would set aside a softly lit, cool, carpeted area where she could lie on the floor or lean against cushions when she studies or reads. You might have a bowl of sliced carrots or celery available for her as snacks. Understanding her need for mobility, you would permit her several breaks wherein she could relax or move to another area during or between the studying periods.

Since Ruth works well and will be persistent when interested, the school work that she is required to complete will be no problem when it is something that she wants to learn. When she is not interested in the topic or assignment, you might suggest that she invite a classmate to work with her. Ruth's profile indicates that she is usually responsible; therefore, when she seeks your assistance, give it willingly until she understands what needs to be done.

Ruth's seat should be placed away from the light and heat and should be near a classmate with whom she get along so that the two may work together on tasks that are not motivating to her. She should be encouraged to learn through books, transparencies, filmstrips, films, pictures, and other visual resources. Since her secondary perceptual strength is tactual—games, task cards, and manipulative materials would also benefit her. Ideally, new knowledges and skills should be introduced to her through visual resources and reinforced through tactual ones.

In Conclusion

The systematic identification of individual learning styles, although new, is not a fad and is not a process that will be embraced for a time and then discarded. Legal challenges to the quality of programs that have produced disparate academic progress among students have been brought into our judiciary system across the nation, and some of the decisions that have been rendered to date imply that the courts are willing (or would be) to overthrow school conventions if those practices are deemed to be unreasonable. The famous case of *Tinker* v. *Des Moines Community School District* (1969), which concerns itself with student rights, will undoubtedly be extended to encompass the right of a student to learn in ways that complement his ability to achieve. The case of *Griggs* v. *Duke Power Company* (U.S. Supreme Court, March 1971) manifested the inability of broad and general testing devices, as well as the infirmity of using diplomas or degrees as fixed measures of capability. In *re Held, Dkt. No (H-2-71) (H-10-71)* (Family Court, Westchester County, New York) a school district's failure to teach a "teachable" child resulted in an award of private school tuition. And finally, Public Law 94–142, which requires the identification of learning style and individualization for all handicapped children, is only one step away from mandating individualization for all.[5]

The natural outgrowth of these decisions suggests that, eventually, the courts will rule that (1) if a student does not learn the way we teach him, we must teach him the way he learns, and (2) if professionals with recognized credentials cannot teach selected students, persons with *different kinds of credentials* will be permitted to teach students with whom they can evidence success.[6]

Research Supplement: Research on Learning Style with Suggestions for Teacher Experimentation

by Dr. Gary E. Price

Summary Statement

Recent research concerned with identifying the relationship between academic achievement and learning style has provided consistent support for the following: (1) students do learn differently from each other; (2) student performances in differing subject areas are related to how individuals do, in fact, learn; (3) when students are taught through the methods each prefers, they do learn more effectively; and (4) systematic ways to identify individual preferences for learning and suggestions for teaching students with varying learning styles can be developed based on an individual diagnosis.[1]

This chapter presents a review of recent research concerned with learning style identification and effects of different learning styles. This includes a summary of how the Learning Style Inventory (LSI) (see the Appendix) was developed using a factor and content analysis, the rationale that was used to include the items described in Chapter 1, and the different components of learning style that have been identified. In addition, reliability and validity data are presented.

Reliability indicates whether an instrument measures consistently. For example, if one administered the LSI to a group of students and then tested the group again either one month or one year later and obtained essentially similar or identical results, this outcome would indicate that the LSI is a reliable instrument. Validity relates to how well an instrument measures what it is designed to measure. For example: are we in fact measuring different preferences of how people learn? Do individuals who have different preferences actually learn differently?

This chapter also examines the relationships among different preferences for learning styles. The research indicates that males and females have different preferences as groups and as individuals. Recent findings in the areas of self-concept, reading, and math achievement, and their relationship to learning style will also be presented. The last part of the chapter provides suggestions for additional research in this area.

Results of the Factor Analysis on Learning Style

The first procedure used involved the development of a pool of items designed to measure the important areas of learning style. A total of 223 items were administered to 1,000 subjects in grades one through twelve. A factor analysis technique[2] was used to identify the areas that were unique and independent of each other and to select those items that seemed to assess the areas (factors) best.

Based on the factor analysis, several areas were found to be unique and independent of each other.[3] Many of the areas had a relatively pure structure, which was consistent with the content analysis of the LSI subscales. Moreover, several factors followed an expected pattern; for example, one of the factors indicated that individuals who are teacher-motivated need structure. A second factor revealed that individuals who prefer a cool environment also require food intake, while a third demonstrated that individuals who like low light do not require food intake.

This analysis, therefore, suggests many interrelationships between how individuals prefer to learn and their achievement. The factor analysis, based on the 1,000 subjects in grades one through twelve, accounted for 68 percent of the variance on the LSI.

Of great importance was the evidence that individuals vary greatly in how they prefer to learn and that certain factors clustered together. For example, it might be expected that individuals would prefer to learn with a couple of peers, several peers, or only one peer. All these items grouped together, however, as one area on the factor analysis that we now call the peer-oriented learner scale. In addition, the items originally developed did not differentiate between those individuals who had tactual and kinesthetic preferences. Thus, these two areas were combined as they both involve the senses of touching and feeling and an "activity" sense in terms of how individuals prefer to learn.

Reliability Analysis

An instrument possesses reliability when the areas investigated can be consistently measured over a period of time. High reliability predicts that individuals who take the instrument at one time and get a certain score will get that same score or a score close to the original when they respond to the instrument again in the future. Obviously, it is necessary to have a consistent instrument from one test taking to repeated test taking in the future.

Another way of understanding reliability is to determine if the items consistently discriminate between those individuals who rate high in a given characteristic and those who rate low in a characteristic. In calculating reliability for the Learning Style Inventory, it was found that of the forty-eight reliabilities calculated separately for males and females, 80 percent were greater than .30 and of the 80 percent, 33 percent were above .70 with a maximum of seven items per subscale. The Hoyt analysis of variance procedure was used to estimate reliability for each subscale.[4] The Hoyt analysis is equivalent to the Kuder and Richardson formula (20) procedure.[5]

Correlational Analysis

Correlational analysis examines the interrelationships of the different elements of the Learning Style Inventory. Studying the various subscales on the Learning Style Inventory is important in that it helps identify different relationships among the individuals' preference of learning elements. To determine these relationships, a product moment correlation coefficient was computed for each of the areas on the LSI for males and females in grades one through twelve.

The highest correlation possible is 1.00, and the lowest correlation is −1.00. A high positive correlation reveals that a high score on one scale is related to having a high score on the other scale; and if an individual achieves a high score on one scale, it is likely that he or she will achieve a high score on the other scale. A negative correlation indicates achievement of a high score on one scale and a low score on the other scale. The closer a correlation is to .00, the more likely it is that no relationship is present between how individuals responded on the two scales compared. One must understand that these data are based on trends within groups and do not respond to specific individual preferences for learning.

A summary of the significant correlations or the significant relationships between the scales indicates that the following Learning Style Inventory areas are related for males:

- Preferring *quiet* is positively correlated with light, learning alone, tactual and kinesthetic preferences, and mobility; and is negatively correlated with being unmotivated, being a peer-oriented learner, having auditory preferences, and desiring food while learning.

- Preferring *light* is positively correlated with responsibility and is negatively correlated with preference for an informal design and being unmotivated.

- Preferring a *cool temperature* is positively correlated with being a peer-oriented learner and is negatively correlated with learning alone.

- *Informal design* is negatively correlated with being self-motivated, adult-motivated, teacher-motivated, and persistent.

- *Self-motivated* learning is positively correlated with being adult-motivated, teacher-motivated, persistent, responsible, and with learning alone and learning in the afternoon; and is negatively correlated with being unmotivated and learning with adults, and need for food intake and mobility.

- *Teacher-motivated* learning is positively correlated with persistence, responsibility, learning in several ways, auditory preferences, tactile and kinesthetic preferences, and learning in the afternoon; and is negatively correlated with being unmotivated.

- *Unmotivated* learning is positively correlated with need for food intake and mobility; and is negatively correlated with persistence, responsibility, visual preferences, and learning in the afternoon.

- *Persistence* is positively correlated with responsibility, learning alone, and learning in the afternoon; and is negatively correlated with learning with adults, food intake, learning in late morning, and mobility.

- *Responsibility* is positively correlated with learning in the afternoon and is negatively correlated with need for food intake and mobility.

- *Needing structure* is positively correlated with learning in several ways.

- *Learning alone* is negatively correlated with being peer oriented, learning with adults, learning in several ways, learning in the late morning, with visual preferences, and with need for food intake and mobility.

- *Peer-oriented learning* is positively correlated with learning with adults, learning in several ways, auditory preferences, tactile and kinesthetic preferences, need for food intake, preferring to learn in late morning, and having mobility.

- *Learning with adults* is positively correlated with learning in several ways, visual preferences, tactile and kinesthetic preferences, need for food intake, learning in the late morning and afternoon.

- *Learning in several ways* is positively correlated with auditory preferences, visual preferences, tactile and kinesthetic preferences, and learning in morning and afternoon.
- *Auditory preferences* are positively correlated with need for food intake.
- *Visual preferences* are positively correlated with tactile and kinesthetic preferences and learning in the late morning; and are negatively correlated with learning in the evening.
- *Tactile* and *kinesthetic* preferences are positively correlated with learning in the late morning and learning in the evening.
- *Food intake* is positively correlated with mobility and is negatively correlated with learning in the afternoon.
- *Learning in the morning* is positively correlated with learning in the late morning.
- *Preferring to learn in the afternoon* is negatively correlated with need for mobility.

A summary of the significant correlations indicates the following LSI areas are related for females.

- Preferring *quiet* is positively correlated with preferring light, being teacher-motivated, learning alone, learning with adults, and learning in the evening; and is negatively correlated with responsibility and need for food intake.
- Preferring *light* is positively correlated with being adult-motivated and teacher-motivated, and with auditory preferences.
- *Informal design* is negatively correlated with being peer oriented, and with need for food intake and mobility.
- *Self-motivation* is positively correlated with being adult-motivated, teacher-motivated, persistent, responsible, and with learning in the afternoon; and is negatively correlated with being unmotivated, learning with adults, and with need for food intake and mobility.
- Being *adult-motivated* is positively correlated with being teacher-motivated, persistent, responsible, and peer-oriented; and is negatively correlated with being unmotivated.
- *Learning with adults* is positively correlated with learning in several ways, visual preferences, tactile and kinesthetic preferences, and with learning in the morning, late morning, in the afternoon, and in the evening.
- *Learning in several ways* is positively correlated with tactile and kinesthetic preferences and learning in the morning and late morning.

- *Auditory preference* is positively correlated with food intake; and negatively correlated with learning in the morning.

- *Visual preference* is positively correlated with tactile and kinesthetic preferences, and learning in the late morning; and is negatively correlated with food intake, learning in the evening, and mobility.

- *Tactile* and *kinesthetic preference* is positively correlated with learning in the late morning and learning in the evening.

- Desire for *food intake* is positively correlated with mobility; and is negatively correlated with learning in the afternoon.

- *Learning in the morning* is positively correlated with learning in the late morning.

- *Learning in the afternoon* is negatively correlated with mobility.

- Being *teacher-motivated* is positively correlated with persistence, learning with adults, and tactile and kinesthetic preferences; and is negatively correlated with being unmotivated and with mobility.

- Being *unmotivated* is positively correlated with food intake and mobility; and is negatively correlated with persistence, responsibility, learning in several ways, visual preferences, and learning in the afternoon.

- *Persistent* is positively correlated with responsibility, learning alone, and learning in the afternoon; and is negatively correlated with learning with adults, food intake, learning in the late morning, and mobility.

- Being *responsible* is positively correlated with tactile and kinesthetic preferences and learning in the afternoon; and is negatively correlated with food intake and mobility.

- *Structure* is positively correlated with learning with adults and learning in several ways.

- *Learning alone* is positively correlated with visual preferences; and is negatively correlated with being peer-oriented, learning with adults, learning in several ways, food intake, and mobility.

- *Peer-oriented learning* is positively correlated with visual preferences, food intake, learning in late morning, and mobility.

Comparison of Learning Styles for Males and Females across Grades

This analysis was conducted to see how preferences for different kinds of learning styles relate to sex differences within and between grades. One-way analysis of variance procedures were used to determine where significant differences occur. Analysis of variance is a statistical procedure that determines if groups are significantly different from one another in a way other than by chance. Both the mean and variance are calculated for each group. The variance is defined as the average squared deviation from the mean for each score in the group. The groups are then compared to see if there is a significant difference in, on the average, how far apart individual scores arc from each other, and if the means are significantly different from one another.

This procedure was used to determine if males and females in grades one through twelve were different from each other in their preferred method of learning. The analysis provided the following. In general, the lower the grade of male students the more they wanted to concentrate or learn in a quiet environment; the lower the grade, the higher was the percentage of males who indicated they were teacher-motivated. There were significant differences in the area of persistence for males, but there seemed to be no pattern among grades. Males in grade one were significantly less persistent than males in grades five, six, and twelve. Male students in the lower grades preferred learning with adults significantly more than did male students in the higher grades. The longer male students are in school, the less they like to learn with adults. In addition, the higher the grade, the less males preferred to learn through the tactile and kinesthetic modality. Additionally, the earlier the grade, the more male students preferred to learn in the late morning.

The following areas were significantly different for the female students. Females preferred more warmth in grade eight than did females in grade ten. However, there was no obvious pattern across grades. Females were significantly less persistent in grade one than were females in grades two through twelve. Females preferred to learn with adults less, the higher the grade. Females in the upper grades expressed a greater preference for learning through auditory senses than did females in the lower grades. This may be due to how schools reinforce learning by teaching mainly through auditory senses. Therefore, individuals, in traditional instructional environments gradually may learn that the best way to get along is to learn through the auditory sense.

The higher the grade, the less females preferred to learn through tactile and kinesthetic senses. Both males and females start out preferring to learn through tactile and kinesthetic modalities; but this seems to decrease, the higher the grade. This may be the result of maturation or may be due to the fact that these modalities are not commonly used and reinforced in the learning environment.

In the area of food intake, females in the lower grades and in the intermediate grades want food present while learning but females in the other grades do not prefer food as much. This may be related to the growth cycle for females. Females in the higher grades preferred to study in the late morning.

These comparisons do not indicate why individuals change in their learning preferences. The change may be related to maturation or a desire to adapt to the existing educational environment. Additional longitudinal research must be conducted to determine which variables affect the development of preferences for learning. In longitudinal research an individual's progress over several years must be examined to see which changes in the fact that these modalities are not commonly used and reinforced in the learning environment.

Comparison of Learning Styles for Males and Females within Grades

For each of the areas from the Learning Style Inventory for each grade, males and females were compared to see which had the greater preferences for a given learning style. One must realize that even when statistical significance is found there may not be a meaningful or understandable difference.

A summary of the statistically significant results includes the following:

- Females desired more light in grades eight and eleven than did males, and males desired more light in grade two.
- Males liked a cooler environment in grade nine and females liked a cooler environment in grade three.
- Males preferred a more informal design than females in grades five, six, and eleven.
- Females were more self-motivated in grade eleven and more adult-motivated in grades four and six.
- Females were more teacher-motivated in grades three, four, six, and twelve.
- Males were more unmotivated in grades four, five, seven, and ten.
- Females were found to be more persistent in grades four, five, six, eleven, and twelve, and more responsible in grades two, three, five, and ten.
- Females preferred learning alone in grade five.
- Females preferred learning through the auditory sense in grades six, ten, and twelve.
- Males preferred learning through the visual sense in grades six and eleven and preferred learning using the tactile and kinesthetic senses in grades five, six, and eight.
- Males preferred learning in the morning in grade five, and in the late morning for grade six.
- Females preferred to learn in the afternoon in grades four, five, seven, and ten, and in the evening in grade one.

- Males desired mobility while learning in grades four, five, and nine and females desired mobility more than males in grade eight.

The analyses were calculated based on female and male students within each grade and many differences were found when the groups were compared. However, the most important implication is that individuals are different from each other and instruction should be designed to meet the individual's learning preferences.

Learning Style and Self-Concept

In this study, 321 subjects from grades three, six, and seven from twelve different schools took the LSI and Ira Gordon's "How I See Myself" Scale. Individuals were clustered into two groups: those having a high self-concept (mean of 159.56), and those having a low self-concept (mean of 123.27), with the overall mean of both groups at 142.30. These two groups were compared on each of the twenty-four areas of the LSI to determine if a significant relationship between self-concept and how individuals prefer to learn could be found. A discriminate analysis was used to determine which of the variables significantly discriminated between the two groups.

Overall, eight learning style variables were found that discriminated significantly between the subjects who had a high self-concept and subjects who had a low self-concept. Based on this analysis, individuals having a high self-concept preferred quiet, liked to study in a warm temperature, were adult- and teacher-motivated, were persistent, preferred to learn in several ways, namely by self or with peers, did not have auditory preferences, and did not need mobility. In general, individuals having a low self-concept preferred to study in a cool, noisy environment, were not adult- or teacher-motivated, not persistent, preferred not to learn in several ways, had auditory preferences, and showed a need for mobility.

The variables that discriminated the most between the two groups were persistence, being teacher-motivated, and needing mobility. Individuals with low self-concepts needed more mobility and required noise as well as the presence of adults. In addition, a dimension related to being unsettled, perhaps not wanting to be alone, and learning through the auditory senses, seemed to characterize individuals having a low self-concept. Individuals having a high self-concept were persistent, able to stay in one place, and liked to learn in many different ways.

Learning Style and Reading and Math Achievement

A total of eighty-five subjects in grades three and six from three different schools in the New York City area took the LSI and the New York State's Pupil Evaluation Program (PEP) in reading and math.

A discriminate analysis was used to determine which of the LSI variables differentiated the individuals having high and low reading and math achievement scores. The overall mean of the group in reading was 35.58, with the high achieving group having a mean of 43.25 (N = 51) and the low achieving group having a mean of 24.06 (N = 34). The overall mean of the group in math was 36.08, with the high achieving group mean equal to 46.41 (N = 44) and the low achieving group mean equaling 25.00 (N = 41).

There were eleven LSI variables that significantly discriminated among subjects in the high and low reading achievement group as measured by the New York State PEP test. Individuals with high reading achievement preferred low light and a formal design, were self-motivated and were not adult-motivated (unmotivated was a suppressor variable), were persistent and responsible, did not prefer to use tactile and kinesthetic senses, did not prefer food intake, did not function best in late morning, and needed mobility. Individuals with low reading achievement preferred bright light and an informal design, were not self-motivated, were adult-motivated, were unmotivated, were not persistent, and not responsible, preferred to learn using tactile and kinesthetic senses, preferred food intake, functioned best in late morning, and did not need mobility.

Persistence, functioning best in late morning, preference for an informal design, and being responsible were the variables that discriminated the most among those subjects having high and low reading achievement.

Overall, there are several factors relating students' preferences in learning style to reading achievement. Individuals who achieve in reading are generally persistent, responsible, and self-motivated, desire a formal design, and do not like bright light; whereas low achievers in reading are not self-motivated, but are adult-motivated, wish to learn using tactile and kinesthetic senses, want food present while studying, and like an informal design and bright light. It may be possible that individuals do not achieve well in reading because, in part, of our failure to meet their preferred methods of instruction.

There were eight LSI variables that significantly discriminated among subjects who scored high and low in math, as measured by the New York State PEP test. Individuals with high math achievement preferred a formal design when studying, were not adult-motivated, were persistent, were responsible, were not peer-oriented learners, did not require food when studying, did not function best in late morning, and needed mobility. Individuals with low math achievement preferred an informal design when studying, were adult-motivated, were not persistent, were not responsible, preferred to study with peers, required food when studying, functioned best in late morning, and did not need mobility.

Desire for a formal design, persistence, and functioning best in late morning were the variables that discriminated the most among those subjects having high and low math achievement.

Overall, there are several areas within student preferences for learning styles that relate to math achievement. High achievers in math are persistent and responsible, like to work independent of adults, and like a more formal design in which to study; whereas, low math achievers are not persistent or responsible, like to study with adults and peers, need food (many of these preferences may serve as distractor variables from achievement), and prefer an informal design when studying.

It is highly possible that individuals who achieve well in math are being taught in ways that best meet their learning preferences; and if math teachers would change their instructional strategies for low achievers to match their preferred learning styles, it is likely that there would be fewer low achievers in math. The research on this sample predicts that by knowing how a person prefers to learn in eight areas, one could predict correctly eight out of ten students who would do well in math and seven out of ten students who would have difficulty with math. We hope educators will become more aware of learning style and the individual differences each person brings to the instructional setting.

Suggestions for Conducting Research on Learning Style

In conducting research it is very important to carefully define the problem to be studied. For instance, do students having auditory preferences learn a given subject best by being taught through the medium of tape, lecture, or group discussion? After carefully defining the problem, it is important to gather all related data. It is also important to control for as many of the variables as one can expect for the treatment (in this case, type of instruction). Another important factor is that the content remains the same for each treatment and that each treatment—tape or lecture—is "pure," that is, not contaminated by other approaches. In addition, one needs to select a measure that assesses the effectiveness of the treatment. To test reading comprehension, a valid and reliable reading comprehension test should be used. There are many factors that must be considered in conducting research. An excellent book that provides detailed procedures in a nonmathematical language is Isaac and Michael's *Handbook in Research and Evaluation.* [6]

There are numerous areas for further research in the area of learning style. These include research aimed at the following:

1.   Does an individual's learning style change in relationship to how he or she is taught or does learning style stay the same for an individual?

2.   How early in an individual's development are the various areas of learning style formed?

3.   How much does maturation affect changes in learning style?

4.   Why do various learning style elements, such as bright light, affect achievement in reading?

5.   Do students actually learn more when they are taught in their preferred modalities?

6.   Can teachers individualize instruction through modalities that they themselves do not prefer?

7.   Will instruction improve when students' learning styles are matched with appropriate teaching styles?

8.   What is the relationship of learning style to other selected groups of students, such as those having learning disabilities, the culturally different, high and low achievers, and the gifted?

9.   Do individuals with different learning styles learn at different rates?

10.   Which subject areas are best taught through specific modalities?

11.   How can individuals be helped to learn their most effective method of learning in a given subject area?

12.   What is the relationship of personality development to the development of learning styles?

13.   Are there similarities between the learning styles of parents and siblings?

14.   What is the relationship between learning style and cognitive style?

Education is currently under the scrutiny of many people and we, as professionals, are called upon to defend our teaching methodologies. A major benefit can be derived from understanding how individuals prefer to learn and by using instructional methods that meet an individual's learning style.

We should be aware of how and why our instructional strategies do or do not work for our individual students. Additionally, when an atmosphere can be created that encourages us to examine what we do through systematic research that is carefully designed and conducted over five to ten years or more so that real effects can be assessed, we should be able to develop programs that will provide a better education for all.

Appendix

LEARNING STYLE INVENTORY

by

Rita Dunn, Ed.D.
Kenneth Dunn, Ed.D.
Gary E. Price, Ph.D.

Directions

This inventory has several statements about how people like to learn. Read each statement and decide whether you usually would agree with that statement or whether you usually would disagree with that statement. If you agree, answer "true" to that statement and if you disagree, answer "false" to that statement.

You should give your immediate or first reaction to each question. Please answer each question on the separate answer sheet. Do not write on this booklet.

Before you begin to answer the questions, be certain to write your name, your sex, and the other information called for in the space provided on the answer sheet.

Remember, try to answer every question.

Now open the booklet and start with question 1.

ORDERS	INFORMATION
AND	AND
INVENTORY ANALYSIS	WORKSHOPS

PRICE SYSTEMS
Box 3271
Lawrence, Kansas 66044

RITA DUNN AND ASSOCIATES
Educational Consultants
18 Brookdale Lane
Chappaqua, New York 10514

1. I study best when it is quiet.

2. I can block out noise when I work.

3. I like studying with lots of light.

4. I study best when the lights are dim.

5. I concentrate best when I feel warm.

6. I concentrate best when I feel cool.

7. When I study I like to sit on a soft chair or couch.

8. I feel sleepy if I do not sit on a hard chair when I study.

9. I feel good when I do well in school.

10. When I do well in school, grown-ups in my family are proud of me.

11. Things outside of school are more important to me than my school work.

12. I try to finish what I start.

13. I hardly ever finish all of my work.

14. I have to be reminded often to do something!

15. I remember to do what I am told.

16. I like to be told exactly what to do.

17. When I really have a lot of studying to do I like to work alone.

18. When I really have a lot of studying to do I like to work with a group of friends.

19. I like to study with one or two friends.

20. Sometimes I like to study alone and sometimes with friends.

21. The things I remember best are the things I read.

22. I study better when I eat while I study.

23. I like to eat, drink, or chew -- but only after I finish studying.

24. I often nibble something as I study.

25. I think best just before lunch.

26. I remember things best when I study them early in the morning.

27. I remember things best when I study them in the afternoon.

28. I hate to go to sleep at night.

29. I usually start my homework after dinner.

30. When I study I often get up to do something (like take a drink, get a cookie, etc.) and then go back to work.

31. When I study I stay with it until all of my work is finished.

32. Noise usually keeps me from concentrating.

33. I can ignore most sound when I study.

34. At home I usually study under a shaded lamp while the rest of the room is dim.

35. When I study I put on many lights.

36. I usually feel more comfortable in cool weather than I do in warm weather.

37. I usually feel more comfortable in warm weather than I do in cool weather.

38. When it's warm outside I like to go out.

39. I study best at a table or desk.

40. I like to study on carpeting or rugs.

41. I think my teacher feels good when I do well in school.

42. I like making my teacher proud of me.

43. Nobody really cares if I do well in school.

44. My mother wants me to get good grades.

GO ON TO NEXT PAGE

-2-

45. I want to get good grades for me.

46. I love to learn new things.

47. I usually finish my homework.

48. I often forget to do or finish my homework.

49. I have to be reminded often to do something.

50. I keep forgetting to do the things I've been told to do.

51. I always do what I promise to do.

52. I like to be told exactly what to do.

53. I like to be able to do things my own way.

54. I do better if I know my work is going to be checked.

55. When I really have a lot of studying to do I like to work alone.

56. When I really have a lot of studying to do I like to work with two friends.

57. I like adults nearby when I work alone or with a friend.

58. The things I like doing best in school I do with a group of friends.

59. The thing I like doing best in school I do with grown-ups.

60. If I have to learn something new, I like to learn about it by playing games.

61. The things I remember best are the things I hear.

62. I really like people to talk to me.

63. I really like to watch television.

64. I really like to mold things with my hands.

65. I really like to do experiments.

66. I like to eat or drink, or chew while I study.

67. I do not eat or drink, or chew while I study.

68. I study best near lunchtime.

69. I remember things best when I study them early in the morning.

70. I remember things best when I study them before dinner.

71. If I could go to school anytime during the day, I would choose to go in the early morning.

72. When I can, I do my homework in the afternoon.

73. I stay awake for a long time after I get into bed.

74. When I study I stay with it until all my work is finished.

75. It's hard for me to sit in one place for a long time.

76. I can sit in one place for a long time.

77. Noise bothers me when I am studying.

78. My father wants me to get good grades.

79. There are many things I like doing better than going to school.

80. I hardly ever finish all my work.

81. I often get tired of doing things and want to start something new.

82. I keep my promises most of the time.

83. I like to be given choices of how I can do things.

84. When I really have a lot of studying to do I like to work with two friends.

85. I like to study by myself.

86. The thing I like doing best in school, I do with one friend.

87. The thing I like doing best in school, I do with a grown-up.

88. If I have to learn something new, I like to learn about it by having it told to me.

GO ON TO NEXT PAGE

89. If I have to learn something new, I like to learn about it by seeing a filmstrip or film.

90. The things I remember best are the things I write about.

91. I really like to draw, color, or trace things.

92. I really like to listen to people talk.

93. I often nibble on something as I study.

94. I feel wide awake after 10:00 in the morning.

95. It's hard for me to sit in one place for a long time.

96. I can sit in one place for a long time.

97. I think my teacher wants me to get good grades.

98. I like to do things in my own way.

99. I really like to build things.

100. I can work best for short amounts of time with rest periods.

STOP

Notes

Chapter 1

1. Rita Dunn, Kenneth Dunn, and Gary E. Price, "Diagnosing Learning Styles: A Prescription for Avoiding Malpractice Suits," *Kappan,* January 1977, pp. 418–20.

2. Vincent Arnone, "An Investigation of the Effects of an Inquiry Process Instructional System of Parameters of Learner-Style," *Dissertation Abstracts International,* November-December 1971, p. 2518A.

   Darlene Atteberry, *Teachers on Individualization: The Way We Do It* (New York: McGraw-Hill, 1974), p. 34.

   John C. Banks, "An Investigation of the Interaction of Learning Style and the Type of Learning Experience in Vocational Technical Education," *Educational Resource Information Center,* June 1973.

   B.E. Bernstein, "Tailoring Teaching to Learning Styles," *Independent School Bulletin* 34 (December 1974): 50–52.

   Barbara Blitz, *The Open Classroom: Making It Work* (Boston: Allyn and Bacon, 1973), pp. 62–65.

   Christine Bennett Button, "Teaching for Individual Differences: A Necessary Interaction," *Educational Leadership,* March 1977, pp. 435–38.

   Wendy Jean Cheyney, "The Relationship between Preferred Learning Style and

Methods of Teaching Word Recognition Skills to Children with Severe Reading Disabilities,'' *Dissertation Abstracts International,* vol. 35A, October 1974, p. 2079.

Peter F. Drucker, *The Age of Discontinuity* (New York: Harper and Row, 1968).

Robert M. Gagne, ed., *Learning and Individual Differences* (Columbus, Ohio: Charles E. Merrill, 1967).

Owen A. Hagen, *Changing World/Changing Teachers* (Pacific Palisades, Calif.: Goodyear Publishing, 1973), p. 70.

David E. Hunt, ''Learning Styles and Teaching Strategies'' (Paper presented at the Fifty-Second Annual Meeting of the National Council for the Social Studies, Boston, Mass., November 21, 1972).

V. John, ''Structure of Failure: An Overview—Children's Styles of Learning and Teaching Styles of Their Teachers,'' *Urban Review* 7 (July 1974): 207–14.

Hope Jensen Leichter, ''The Concept of Educative Style,'' *Teachers College Record* 75 (December 1973): 229–50.

John M. Lembo, *Why Teachers Fail* (Columbus, Ohio: Charles E. Merrill, 1971), p. 11.

Don Mack, ''Privacy: A Child's Need to Be Alone in the Classroom,'' *Teacher,* February 1976, pp. 52–53.

Bernard H. McKenna and Martin N. Olsen, ''Class Size Revisited,'' *Today's Education* 64 (March-April 1975): 29.

Gertrude Noar, *Individualized Instruction: Every Child a Winner* (New York: John Wiley, 1972), pp. 79–81.

A. H. Passow, ed., *Nurturing Individual Potential: Papers and Reports* (Washington, D.C.: Seventh Curriculum Research Institute, Association for Supervision and Curriculum Development, 1964).

Neil Postman and Charles Weingartner, *The School Book* (New York: Delacorte Press, 1973), pp. 176–77.

Mary Ann Raywid, ''Models of the Teaching-Learning Situation,'' *Kappan,* April 1977, pp. 631–35.

Harry Reinert, ''One Picture Is Worth a Thousand Words? Not Necessarily!'' *The Modern Language Journal* 60 (April 1976): 160–68.

Marshall B. Rosenberg, *Diagnostic Teaching* (Seattle: Special Child Publications, 1968).

Jean Sanders and Linda Zalk, *Learning Styles* (Chelmsford, Mass.: Merrimack Education Center, 1972), 21 pp.

Galen Saylor and William Alexander, *Planning Curriculum for Schools* (New York: Holt, Rinehart, and Winston, 1974).

Len Sperry, ''Counselors and Learning Styles,'' *Personnel and Guidance Journal,* March 1973, pp. 478–83.

Donna Kofod Stahl and Patricia Anzalone, *Individualized Teaching in Elementary Schools* (West Nyack, N.Y.: Parker Publishing Company, 1970), pp. 21–23.

H. Levine Taba and F. F. Elzey, *Thinking in Elementary School Children* (San Francisco: San Francisco State College, 1964).

G. K. Talmadge and J. W. Shearer, "Relationship among Learning Styles, Instructional Methods, and the Nature of Learning Experiences," *Journal of Educational Psychology,* 1969, pp. 222–30.

Steven R. Wagner and John W. Wilde, "Learning Styles: Can We Grease the Cogs in Cognition?" *Claremont Reading Conference 37th Yearbook,* 1973, pp. 135–41.

Alan H. Wheeler, "Creating a Climate for Individualizing Instruction," *Young Children* 27 (October 1971): 12–13.

L. Craig Wilson, *The Open Access Curriculum* (Boston: Allyn and Bacon, 1972), pp. 39–40.

James Young, "The Effects of Knowledge of Perceived Learning Style on the Educational Development of Selected Community College Students," *Dissertation Abstracts International* 35 (January 1975): 4268.

3. Rita Dunn and Kenneth Dunn, *Educator's Self-Teaching Guide to Individualizing Instructional Programs* (West Nyack, N. Y.: Parker Publishing Co., 1975), chap. 3.

4. George Domino, "Interactive Effects of Achievement Orientation and Teaching Style on Academic Achievement," *ACT Research Report* 39 (1970): 1–9.

Beatrice J. Farr, "Individual Differences in Learning: Predicting One's More Effective Learning Modality" (Ph.D. dissertation, Catholic University of America, 1971) (Ann Arbor, Mich.: University Microfilms, July 1971), p. 1332A.

5. Rita Dunn, Kenneth Dunn, and Gary E. Price, "Summary of Research on Learning Style Based on the Learning Style Inventory" (paper presented at the Annual Meeting of the American Educational Research Association, New York, N.Y. April 1977).

6. Barbara Bond and S. S. Stevens, "Cross-Modality Matching of Brightness to Lightness by 5-year-olds," *Perception and Psychophysics* 6 (1969): 337–39.

Blitz, in *The Open Classroom* on p. 85, states that "students are judged on their ability to adjust their learning styles to those of the teacher. . . .", and on p. 196, "All of us must learn to inhibit the conscious perception of noise and/or movement within the classroom to attend to things with any depth of concentration."

Studies that verify the relationship between sound in the environment and achievement include David C. Glass, Sheldon Cohen, and Jerome E. Singer, "Urban Din Fogs the Brain," *Psychology Today,* May 1972, pp. 94–98; John J. O'Malley and Alex Poplowsky, "Noise-Induced Arousal and Breadth of Attention," *Perceptual and Motor Skills* 33 (December 1971): 887–90; and Susan J. Samtur, *Graduate Research in Education and Related Disciplines* (New York: City College of the University of New York), 4 (Spring 1969): 63–81.

7. Joan Arehart-Treichel, "School Lights and Problem Pupils," *Science News* 105 (April 1974): 258–59.

Esteban Lucan Olmeda, "Effects of Environmental Variation on Arousal and Performance of a Vigilance Task" (Ph.D. dissertation, Baylor University, 1972).

8. B. Givoni and Y. Rim, "Effect of the Thermal Environment and Psychological Factors upon Subject's Responses and Performance of Mental Work," *Ergonomics* (London) (January 1962) 99–107.

   I. D. Griffiths and R. R. Boyce, "Performance and Thermal Comfort," *Ergonomics* (London) 14 (July 1971): 457–68.

   I. Holmber and O. Wyon, "The Dependence of Performance in School on Classroom Temperature," *Educational and Psychological Interactions* 31 (1969): 1–20.

   Frederick H. Rohles, "Thermal Sensations of Sedentary Man in Moderate Temperatures, Human Factors of Children under Imposed Noise and Heat Stress," *Ergonomics* (London) 13 (July 1970): 598–612.

   John F. Wing, "A Review of the Effects of High Ambient Temperature on Mental Performance," *United States Air Force Publication from the Aerospace Medical Research Laboratory,* Wright-Patterson AFB (TR, 1965), pp. 65–102.

9. Blitz, *The Open Classroom,* pp. 95–109.

   Rita Dunn and Kenneth Dunn, *Practical Approaches to Individualizing Instruction: Contracts and Other Effective Teaching Strategies* (West Nyack, N.Y.: Parker Publishing Co., 1972), pp. 73–74.

   Herman Eugene LaForge, "Effect of the Open Space Design of an Elementary School upon Personality Characteristics of Students" (Ed. D. dissertation, University of Houston, Texas, 1972).

   Mark Phillips, "Conceptual Systems and Educational Environment Relationships between Teacher Conceptual Systems and Classroom Management as Perceived by Fifth and Sixth Grade Students" (Ed.D. dissertation, University of Massachusetts, 1972).

   Alan H. Wheeler, "Creating a Climate for Individualizing Instruction," *Young Children* 27 (October 1971): 12–13.

10. Rita Dunn and Kenneth Dunn, *Administrator's Guide to New Programs for Faculty Management and Evaluation* (West Nyack, N.Y.: Parker Publishing Co., 1977), chap. 3

    Frederick Herzberg, "Managers or Trainers?" *Management Review,* July 1971, pp. 2–15.

    Edward E. Lowler and J. Richard Hadman, "Impact of Employee Participation in the Development of Pay Incentive Plans: A Field Experiment," *Journal of Applied Psychology* 53 (1969): 467–71.

    Norman R. Maier and Ronald J. Burke, "Influence of Motivation in the Reorganization of Experience," *Psychological Reports,* vol. 23, no. 2 (1968), pp. 351–61.

    Abraham H. Maslow, *Toward a Psychology of Being* (New York: Van Nostrand Reinhold, 1968), chap. 2.

    Elton Mayo, "The Hawthorne Experiment," in *The Human Problems of an Industrial Civilization* (New York: Viking Press, 1968), pp. 53–94.

    Douglas McGregor, *The Human Side of Enterprise* (New York: McGraw-Hill, 1960).

N. Nishikawa, "A Study of Job Satisfaction: An Empirical Test of the Herzberg Theory," *Japanese Journal of Psychology* 41 (1971): 285–94.

Gertrude Noar, *Individualized Instruction: Every Child a Winner* (New York: John Wiley, 1972), pp. 79–81.

Benjamin Schneider and Olson Lorenk, "Effort as a Correlate of Organizational Reward System and Individual Values," *Personnel Psychology* 23 (1970): 313–26.

11. *Analysis of the Effectiveness of Tutorial Assistance in English: Performance and Persistence among Low Achieving Students* (Washington, D.C.: Educational Resources Center, U.S. Department of Health, Education, and Welfare) 6 (January 1971), no. ED052-819; see also Blitz, *The Open Classroom,* pp. 4, 194.

Keith Barton and James W. Barnard, "The Effects of Two Kinds of Reinforcement on the Persistence Scores of Children of Different Ability Patterns," *Journal of Psychology* 82 (September 1972): 13–19.

David Brookes Waters, "Differential Effects of Skill and Change on Persistence, Time and Attention Breaks as a Function of Locus of Control in Elementary School Children" (Ph.D. dissertation, Emory University, 1972).

12. Helen Davis Bell, *Individualizing Instruction: Materials and Classroom Procedures* (Chicago: Science Research Associates, 1972), p. 13.

See also Marshall B. Rosenberg's description of the following learning styles: (1) rigid-inhibited, (2) undisciplined, and (3) creative, in *Diagnostic Teaching* (Seattle: Special Child Publications, 1968), pp. 38–63.

13. See Chapter 3. For more detailed descriptions of these and other small-group techniques see Dunn and Dunn, *Practical Approaches to Individualizing Instruction,* chaps. 5–7.

14. See Chapter 5. See also Rita Dunn and Kenneth Dunn, "How to Design Programmed Learning Sequences, *Instructor,* February, 1978, pp. 124–128.

15. See Chapter 7. See also Rita Dunn and Kenneth Dunn, "How to Develop Multisensory Instructional Packages That You'll Want to Use Yourself," *Instructor,* April 1978, pp. 90–99.

16. George A. Morgan, "Effects of a Less Prescriptive Student-Centered College Curriculum on Satisfaction and Achievement" (Proceedings of the Annual Convention of the American Psychological Association) (Bethesda, Md.: National Institute of Child Health and Human Development, 1972), vol. 7, pt. 1, pp. 505–506.

This study examines the impact of change from a traditional liberal arts curriculum to one in which requirements were essentially eliminated; student freedom and responsibility were increased; and ungraded, value-oriented discussion courses were encouraged. After a two-year period, the students exposed to the new curriculum were compared with the group involved in the traditional curriculum, and it was revealed that the former expressed higher satisfaction with their study program, developed stronger intellectual values, had a feeling of better adjustment than previously experienced, and scored equal to or better than the latter group on academic testing measurements. On the elementary level, Blitz, in *The Open Classroom,* pp. 93, 194–96, suggests ways that the arrangement of furniture and the teacher's presence establish a degree of structure that tends to communicate the expectations of behavior and learning to the students.

17. Herbert J. Walberg, "Social Environment as a Mediator of Classroom Learning," *Journal of Educational Psychology* 60 (1969): 443–48.

Herbert J. Walberg and Andrew Ahlgren, "Predictors of the Social Environment of Learning," *American Educational Research Journal* 7 (March 1970): 135–67.

Herbert J. Walberg, "Class Size and the Social Environment of Learning," *Human Relations,* vol. 22, no. 5, 1969, pp. 465–75.

18. Gerard A. Poirier, *Students as Partners in Team Learning* (Berkeley, Calif.: Center of Team Learning, 1970), chap. 2. Poirier's thesis is verified by Blitz in *The Open Classroom,* pp. 194, 206.

Richard A. Schmuck, "Influence of the Peer Group," in G. S. Lesser, ed., *Psychology and Educational Practice* (Glenview, Ill.: Scott, Foresman, 1971).

19. Ralph James Ankenbrand, "An Investigation of the Relationship between Achievement and Self-Concept of High Risk Community College Freshman" (Ph.D. dissertation, St. Louis University, 1971).

20. Don Mack, "Privacy: A Child's Need to Be Alone in the Classroom," *Teacher,* February 1976, pp. 52–53.

Deborah H. Ashly, "Children Need To Be Treated As Individuals," *Instructor,* August 1974, p. 23.

James Victor Griesen, "Independent Study versus Group Interaction in Medical Education: A Study of Non-Cognitive Factors Relating to Curricular Preferences and Academic Achievement (Ph.D. dissertation, Ohio State University, 1971).

21. Lee Marcus, "A Comparison of Selected 9th Grade Male and Female Students' Learning Styles," *The Journal* (New York: School Administrators' Association of New York) 6 (January 1977): 27–28.

Gerald Marwell, "Types of Past Experience with Potential Work Partners: Their Effects on Partner Choice," *Human Relations,* vol. 19, no. 20, Nov., 1966, pp. 437–47.

22. Martin Fishbein, "Prediction of Interpersonal Preferences and Group Member Satisfaction from Estimated Attitudes," *Journal of Personality and Social Psychology* 6 (1965): 666–67.

Paul DeHart Hurd and Mary Budd Rowe, "A Study of Small-Group Dynamics and Productivity in the BSCS Laboratory Block Program," *Journal of Research in Science Teaching* 4 (1966): 67–73.

Albert Lott and Bernice E. Lott, "Group Cohesiveness and Individual Learning," in Albert H. Yee, ed., *Social Interaction in Educational Settings* (Englewood Cliffs, N.J.: Prentice-Hall, 1971), pp. 215–28.

Richard A. Schmuck, "Some Relationships of Peer Liking to Patterns in the Classroom to Pupil Attitudes and Achievement," *School Review* 71 (1963): 337–59.

John W. Solocum, Jr., "Group Cohesiveness: A Salient Factor Affecting

Students' Academic Achievement in a Collegiate Environment," *Journal of Educational Science* 2 (September 1968): 151-57.

William M. Weist, Lyman W. Porter, and Edwin E. Chiselli, "Relationships between Individual Proficiency and Team Performance and Efficiency," *Journal of Applied Psychology* 45 (December 1961): 435-40.

23. When a teacher believes that a student is capable of achieving, the relationship between student input and output variables is frequently exaggerated through expectation. Thus students whom teachers expect to do well will do so in part as a result of the teacher's faith and inevitable encouragement. The following sources discuss this idea:

J. E. Brophy and T. L. Good, *Teacher-Student Relationships: Causes and Consequences* (New York: Holt, Rinehart and Winston, 1974).

J. D. Elashoff and R. E. Snow, *Pygmalion Revisited* (Belmont, Calif.: Wadsworth, 1971).

R. Rosenthal and L. Jacobson, *Pygmalion in the Classroom* (New York: Holt, Rinehart and Winston, 1968).

R. Rosenthal, "Teacher Expectations and Their Effects upon Children," in G. S. Lesser, ed., *Psychology and Educational Practice* (Glenview, Ill.: Scott, Foresman, 1971).

24. Rita Dunn, Kenneth Dunn, and Gary E. Price, "Identifying Individual Learning Styles and the Instructional Methods and/or Resources to Which They Respond," Paper presented at the Annual Conference of the American Educational Research Association, New York, New York, April, 1977, p. 9.

Also see Rita Dunn and Kenneth Dunn, "Educational Accountability in Our Schools," *Momentum* (Washington, D.C.: National Catholic Education Association, October 1977, p. 14; Sonia Hudes, Antoinette Saladino, and Donnal Siegler Meibach, "Learning Style Sub-Scales and Self-Concept among High Achievement Third Graders," *The Journal* (New York: School Administrators' Association of New York State, Fall 1977), pp. 7-10.

25. H. Munsterberg and J. Bingham, "Memory," *Psychological Review* 1 (January 1894): 34-38.

Edwin Kirkpatrick, "An Experimental Study of Memory," *Psychological Review* 1 (1894): 603-09, as reported in "A Study of Visual and Auditory Memory Processes," *Psychological Review* 3 (May 1896): 258-69, by L. G. Whitehead. L. G. Whitehead experimented with visual and oral presentations and concluded that visual exposure produced more initial absorption but that auditory exposure produced increased retention. Similar conclusions were reached by Robert MacDougal in "Recognition and Recall," *Journal of Philosophy and Scientific Method* 1 (April 1904): 229-33, when he obtained data verifying that a visual approach to teaching was more effective than a verbal one. This conclusion was also supported in "The Mnemonic Span for Visual and Auditory Digest," *Journal of Experimental Psychology* 1 (October 1916): 393-403; and by Helen Koch, "Some Factors Affecting the Relative Efficiency of Certain Modes of Presenting Material for Memorizing," *American Journal of Psychology* 42 (July, 1930): 370-88.

Koch indicated the superiority of a visual approach but concluded that ". . . the simultaneous combination of the visual and auditory presentation was . . . rather uniformly superior, and the simple auditory presentation was uniformly inferior.''

Conflicting studies revealed data that supported an aural rather than a visual presentation for producing acquisition and/or retention. J. O. Quantz, ''Problems in the Psychology of Reading,'' *Psychology Review Monographs* 2 (December 1897): 1–51, describes comparisons made of visual and auditory learners and concluded that only small differences existed that appeared to favor the use of the aural method. Clifford Woody supported Quant's study in ''The Effectiveness of Oral versus Silent Reading in the Initial Memorization of Poems,'' *Journal of Educational Psychology* 13 (November 1922): 477–83.

Robert Larsen and D. D. Feder, ''Common and Differential Factors in Reading and Hearing Comprehension,'' *Journal of Educational Psychology* 31 (1940): 241–52, found that low scholastic aptitude groups were fairly even in listening and visual comprehension, the middle group demonstrated a statistically insignificant superiority in favor of the visual, and the top group had a definite superiority in learning through a visual (reading) approach.

T. S. Krawiec, ''A Comparison of Learning and Retention of Materials Presented Visually and Auditorially,'' *Journal of General Psychology* 34 (April 1946): 193–94, indicated that the visual mode appeared to be superior for the learning of simple materials but that for retention neither the visual nor the auditory presentations appeared to verify better results.

Henry DeWick, ''The Relative Effectiveness of Visual and Auditory Presentation of Advertising Material,'' *Journal of Applied Psychology* 19 (June 1935): 245–64, stated that the auditory method seemed to be a superior teaching method, but this was refuted by Harry Goldstein, ''Reading and Listening Comprehension at Various Controlled Rates,'' *Contribution to Education,* vol. 821 (New York: Bureau of Publications, Teachers College, Columbia University, 1940), pp. 57–59, who concluded that (1) listening comprehension is, in general, superior to reading comprehension; (2) the superiority of listening comprehension is decidedly more marked for the easy than for the difficult materials; (3) the relative superiority of listening comprehension is in inverse proportion to the intelligence and reading speed of the group (supporting D. D. Feder); (4) the relative superiority of listening comprehension declines with increased rate of presentation; and (5) reading comprehension is more of a variable than listening comprehension. Goldstein's study was relatively more inclusive than many former ones, for, for the first time, he implied that the teacher must carefully analyze the physical, emotional, intellectual, and social makeup of the class (not the individual) in order to teach on a comprehension level for all. (He did not suggest the methodology appropriate for such instruction.)

Robert M. Friedman noted the conflicting reports in ''The Relationship between the Retention Level of Orally and Visually Presented Science Material to Selected Fifth Grade Students'' (unpublished Ph.D. dissertation, New York University, 1967), in which he concluded that neither a visual nor an auditory presentation produced significant recall differences among a small selected population (p. 76).

Sam Ducker, ''Listening and Reading,'' *Elementary School Journal* 65 (March 1965): 321–29, stated ''Certainly the research on the relative learning value of auditory and visual presentation reveals sharply conflicting findings. This disagreement . . . can be explained on the basis of the differences in learning materials presented, the diverse characteristics of the populations . . . and the varying means of testing employed.'' More recently, the focus on perceptual differences has shifted toward other accents such as the perceptual differences between middle-class and disadvantaged children—(see Meryl Silver, ''A Comparison between Visual Association and Auditory Association in Disadvantaged and Middle-Class Children,'' *Graduate Research in Education and Related Disciplines* 6 (Fall 1970): 229; and the unreliability of learning and testing for children with low visual perceptual ability when these occur solely through their weakest perception).

See Howard M. Coleman, ''The West Warwick Visual Perceptual Study,'' *Journal of the American Optometric Association* 434 (April 1972): 452–62; and the differences between the sexes as they relate to auditory-visual integration skills and reading success.

See Clifford J. Drew, ''Research on the Psychological-Behavioral Effects of the Physical Environment,'' Review of Educational Research, vol. 41, Dec., 1971, pp. 447–65.

William Gingold, ''The Effects of Physical Environment on Children's Behavior in the Classroom'' (Ph.D. dissertation, University of Wisconsin, 1971).

Curtis Banion Kilbrough, ''An Investigation of the Effects of Abrupt Change in Educational Environment upon the Reported Self-Concept of Third-Grade Pupils'' (Ed.D. dissertation, University of Southern Mississippi, 1969).

David H. Reilly, ''Auditory-Visual Integration, Sex, and Reading Achievement,'' *Journal of Educational Psychology,* vol. 62, no. 6, 1971, pp. 482–86.

Paul Edward Sumpter, ''Learning Experiment: Effectiveness of Controlling Environmental Distractions'' (Ph.D. dissertation, Iowa State University, 1969).

26. Harry Reinert, ''One Picture Is Worth a Thousand Words? Not Necessarily!'' *The Modern Language Journal* 60 (April 1976): 160–68.

27. Rita Dunn and Kenneth Dunn. *How to Raise Independent and Professionally Successful Daughters* (Englewood Cliffs, N.J.: Prentice-Hall, 1977), pp. 110–11.

28. Bliz, *The Open Classroom,* p. 61.

D. Braddeley, J. E. Hatter, D. Schoot, and A. Snashall, ''Memory and Time of Day,'' *Quarterly Journal of Experimental Psychology* 22 (November 1970): 605–609.

Sidney Trubowitz, ''The Tyranny of Time,'' *Elementary School Journal* 73 (October 1972): 1–6.

Jerome Kagan, Howard A. Moss, and Irving A. Siegel, ''Psychological Significance of Styles of Conceptualization,'' Society for Research in Child Development, Monographs, no. 86 (1963) pp. 927–40.

For time adaptations in industry, see ''Germans Setting Own Office Hours,'' *The New York Times,* July 12, 1971, sec. 1, p. 10; ''Flextime Seems to Lessen Tension,'' *The San Juan Star* (Puerto Rico: February 19, 1973), p. 36; Robert Stuart Nathan, ''The Scheme That's Killing the Rate-Race Blues,'' *New York,* July 18, 1977, pp. 36–38.

29. Rita Dunn and Kenneth Dunn, *Educator's Self-Teaching Guide,* p. 92.

30. Blitz, *The Open Classroom,* pp. 74, 194.

Chapter 2

1. Rita Dunn and Kenneth Dunn, *Educator's Self-Teaching Guide to Individualizing Instructional Programs* (West Nyack, N.Y.: Parker Publishing Company, 1975), chap. 4.

   Dunn and Dunn, "How to Redesign Your Classroom in Approximately One Hour" in *Instructor,* October 1977.

2. The illustrations of various room redesigns were created by John Macellari.

3. Rita Dunn and Kenneth Dunn, "How to Include Game Tables, Magic Carpet Areas, Media Corners, and Other Areas in Your Classroom" reprinted from *Instructor,* January 1978, pp. 72–77.

4. We propose that students receive prior training in the use of techniques like circle of knowledge, team learning, brainstorming, group analysis, role-playing, simulations, etc., so that they may move into a new type of learning situation (the instructional areas) using familiar methods. Thus they will feel secure and be able to function independently and successfully in the beginning stages of individualized instruction.

   For detailed explanations and examples of these small-group techniques, see Rita Dunn and Kenneth Dunn, *Practical Approaches to Individualizing Instruction: Contracts and Other Effective Teaching Strategies* (West Nyack, N.Y.: Parker Publishing, 1972), chaps. 5–7.

Chapter 3

1. George C. Homans, *The Human Group* (New York: Harcourt, Brace, 1950).

2. Chris Argyris, *Personality and Organization* (New York: Harper, 1957).

3. I. Lorge, D. Fox, J. Davitz, and M. Brenner, "A Survey of Studies Contrasting the Quality of Group Performance and Individual Performance, 1920–1957," *Psychological Bulletin* 55 (1958): 337–72.

4. Norman E. Hankins, *Psychology for Contemporary Education* (Columbus, Ohio: Charles E. Merrill, 1973), chap. 7.

5. Gerard A. Poirier, *Students as Partners in Team Learning* (Berkeley, Calif.: Center of Team Learning, 1970).

6. Bernard M. Bass, *Organization Psychology* (Boston: Allyn and Bacon, 1965), p. 13.

7. This team learning was designed by Laurie Borok, St. John's University, New York, for her Contract Activity Package, "How Tall Are You in Metric Terms?"

8. This team learning was designed by Irene K. Flatley, Rosedale, New York, for her Contract Activity Package, "Learning about Our Eyes."

9. This team learning was designed by Patti Reilly, St. John's University, New York, for her Contract Activity Package, "Contemporary Music and Its Relation to Society."

10. This illustration was designed by Dr. Edward J. Manetta, Chairman, Department of Fine Arts, St. John's University, New York.

11. For another description and series of examples of small-group techniques at different school levels see Dunn and Dunn, *Practical Approaches to Individualizing Instruction: Contracts and Other Effective Teaching Strategies,* chaps. 5–7. In addition to many samples of circles of knowledge, team learning, brainstorming, and case studies, you will also find explanations and examples of role-playing and simulations.

Chapter 4

1. Rita Dunn and Kenneth Dunn, *Practical Approaches to Individualizing Instruction: Contracts and Other Effective Teaching Strategies* (West Nyack, N.Y.: Parker Publishing, 1972), chaps. 3 and 4.

2. Robert F. Mager and J. McCann, *Learner-Controlled Instruction* (Palo Alto, Calif.: Varian, 1963). Research conducted by these two authors demonstrated the superiority of students who were permitted to control the instructional sequence of certain training tasks. It was also reported that the learners' motivation increased with the amount that they exercised over their own studies.

3. The National Commission on the Reform of Secondary Education, B. Frank Brown, Chairman, *The Reform of Secondary Education: A Report to the Public and the Profession* (New York: McGraw-Hill, 1973); *The Rise Report: Report of the California Commission for Reform of Intermediate and Secondary Education* (Sacramento, Calif.: California State Department of Education, 1975).

4. *The Rise Report,* p. xiii.

5. Rita Dunn, Kenneth Dunn, and Gary E. Price, "Learning as a Matter of Style," *The Journal* (New York: School Administrator's Association of New York State) 6 (Fall 1976): 11–12.

6. Beatrice J. Farr, "Individual Differences in Learning: Predicting One's More Effective Learning Modality" (Ph.D. dissertation, Catholic University of America, 1971), (Ann Arbor, Mich.: University Microfilms, July 1971), p. 1332A. An experiment with 72 college students confirmed that individuals could accurately predict the modality in which they would demonstrate superior learning performance. The data also revealed that it is advantageous to learn and be tested in the same modality and that such an advantage is reduced when learning and testing are both conducted in an individual's nonpreferred modality. The most desirable conditions existed when learning and testing were both in the student's preferred modality.

Also see George Domino, "Interactive Effects of Achievement Orientation and Teaching Style on Academic Achievement," *ACT Research Report* 39 (1970): 1–9. One-hundred students were grouped in accordance with their perceptions of how they learned. Some of the groups were then taught in a manner consonant with their perceived learning style (achievement orientation), while others were taught in a manner dissonant with their orientation. The testing data revealed that the students who had been exposed to a teaching style consonant with the ways they believed they learned scored higher on tests, fact knowledge, teacher attitude, and efficiency of work than those who had been taught in a manner dissonant with their orientation.

7. Mager and McCann, *Learner-Controlled Instruction.*

8. Dunn and Dunn, *Practical Approaches to Individualizing Instruction,* chaps. 3 and 4.

9. Mager and McCann, *Learner-Controlled Instruction.*

10. Gerard A. Poirier, *Students as Partners in Team Learning* (Berkeley, Calif.: Center of Team Learning, 1970), chap. 2.

11. Robert F. Mager, *Preparing Instructional Objectives* (Palo Alto, Calif.: Fearon, 1962), pp. 1–2, 53.

12. The examples cited in this section of Chapter 4 were taken from a Contract Activity Package designed by Vivian Recupero, Public School 32, Flushing, New York.

13. Rita Dunn and Kenneth Dunn, "60 Activities that Develop Student Independence," *Learning,* February 1974, pp. 73–77. A more extensive list of 152 activities and reporting alternatives is found in Dunn and Dunn, *Educator's Self-Teaching Guide to Individualizing Instructional Programs* (West Nyack, N.Y.: Parker Publishing, 1975), pp. 176–201.

14. *Educator's Self-Teaching Guide,* pp. 214.

15. *Educator's Self-Teaching Guide,* p. 215.

16. This Contract Activity Package was designed by Helen Latsys Bruder, St. John's University, New York.

17. *Educator's Self-Teaching Guide,* pp. 208–11.

18. This Contract Activity Package was designed by Fran Ryan, Freeport, New York.

19. This Contract Activity Package was designed by Helen Pozdniakoff, Astoria, New York.

Chapter 5

1. Don Mack, "Privacy: A Child's Need to be Alone in the Classroom," *Teacher,* February 1976, pp. 52–53.

   James Victor Griesen, "Independent Study versus Group Interaction in Medical Education: A Study of Non-Cognitive Factors Relating to Curricular Preferences and Academic Achievement" (Ph.D. dissertation, Ohio State University, 1971).

2. Gerard A. Poirier, *Students as Partners in Team Learning* (Berkeley, Calif.: Center of Team Learning, 1970).

3. Rita Dunn and Kenneth Dunn, *Practical Approaches to Individualizing Instruction: Contracts and Other Effective Teaching Strategies* (West Nyack, N.Y.: Parker Publishing, 1972), chaps. 5–7.

4. M. Roderick and R. C. Anderson, "Programmed Instruction in Psychology versus Textbook Style Summary of the Same Lesson," *Journal of Educational Psychology* 59 (1968): 381–87.

5. G. C. Kress, Jr., *The Effects of Pacing on Programmed Learning under Several Administrative Conditions* (Pittsburgh: American Institute for Research, 1966).

6. L. Gotkin, "Individual Differences, Boredom, and Styles of Programming," *Programmed Instruction,* December 1963/January 1964).

7. S. B. Parry, "What the West Africans Taught Us about PI," *Programmed Instruction* 4 (1965): 10–11; see also G. C. Kress, Jr., "A Study of the Effects

of Administering Programmed Learning to Interacting Groups,'' *Journal of Educational Psychology* 60 (1960): 333–38.

8. L. B. Kornreich, ''Discovery versus Programmed Instruction in Teaching a Strategy for Solving Concept-Identification Problems,'' *Journal of Educational Psychology* 60 (1969): 384–88.

9. R. C. Anderson, G. W. Faust, and M. C. Roderick, ''Overprompting in Programmed Instruction,'' *Journal of Educational Psychology* 50 (1968): 88–93.

10. B. F. Skinner, ''Reflections on Teaching Machines,'' *Problems and Issues on Contemporary Education* (Glenview, Ill.: Scott, Foresman: Teachers College Record, 1968).

11. This programmed sequence on ''Shapes'' was designed by Antonina Bruccoleri, Floral Park, New York.

12. This programmed sequence on the ''Life Cycle of Freddy Frog'' was designed and illustrated by Sydell Kane, Public School 220, Queens, New York.

13. This programmed sequence on ''Uni- Bi- Tri- Made as Simple as 1, 2, 3'' was designed by Maria Gill, St. John's University, New York.

14. This programmed sequence on ''Exponents'' was designed by Mary Brewer, Half Hollow Hills, New York.

Chapter 6

1. Rita Dunn and Kenneth Dunn, ''How to Construct Multisensory Learning Packages,'' reprinted from *Instructor,* April 1978, pp. 90–99. Used by permission from Instructor Publications, Inc.

2. Rita Dunn and Kenneth Dunn, ''Seeing, Hearing, Moving, Touching: Learning Packages,'' *Teacher Magazine,* May/June 1977, p. 49.

3. ''Seeing, Hearing, Moving, Touching . . .,'' p. 52.

4. This instructional package on ''Transportation'' was designed by Janet Perrin, Malverne, New York.

5. This instructional package on ''Subtraction'' was designed by Denise D'Acunto Johnert, St. John's University, New York.

6. This instructional package on ''Alexander the Great'' was designed by John Papanikolaou, Principal, The Greek Afternoon School of St. Demetrios, Jamaica, New York.

Chapter 7

1. Rita Dunn, ''Individualizing Instruction through Contracts—Does It Work with Very Young Children?'' *Audiovisual Instruction,* March 1971, pp. 78–80.

Rita Dunn and Kenneth Dunn, ''How to Create Hands-On Materials,'' reprinted from *Instructor,* March, 1978, pp. 134–141, used by permission from Instructor Publications, Inc.

Rita Dunn, Kenneth Dunn, and Gary E. Price, ''Learning as a Matter of Style,'' *The Journal* (New York: School Administrators Association of New York State) 6 (Fall 1976): 11–12.

Dunn, Dunn, and Price, "Diagnosing Learning Styles: A Prescription for Avoiding Malpractice Suits against School Systems," *Kappan,* January 1977, pp. 418–420.

2. Rita Dunn and Kenneth Dunn, *How to Raise Independent and Professionally Successful Daughters* (Englewood Cliffs, N.J.: Prentice-Hall, 1977), pp. 115–117.

3. Directions for designing a learning circle were made by Sydell Kane, Public School 220, Forest Hills, Queens, New York.

4. The task cards designed to supplement the Contract Activity Package on "Ants" were created by Fran Ryan, Freeport, New York.

5. The task cards on "States" and "Famous Buildings" were designed by Jeanne Pizzo, New Hyde Park, New York.

6. This task card on the "Parts of the Eye" was designed by Irene K. Flatley, Rosedale, New York.

7. This touch-compute can was devised by Barbara Gardiner, Public School 100, Richmond Hill, New York.

8. The activity card samples in Exhibits 7–17 through 7–25 are from the "Happy to Be Me" Easy Primary Series, Creative Teacher Publications, P.O. Box 41, Williston Park, New York 11596.

9. The activity card samples in Exhibits 7–26 through 7–30 are from the "Happy to Be Me" Primary Series.

10. The activity card samples in Exhibits 7–31 through 7–34 are from the "Happy to Be Me" Intermediate Series.

11. "The Mystery Animal," *Manual of Educational Materials: Creative Ideas for Teachers* (Millersville, Pa.: Educational Development Center, Millersville State College, 1977), p. 82.

12. This sample of a scrambled word game was designed by Roberta Wheeler, Kew Gardens, New York.

13. "Learning Center Blueprints for Real-Life Skills," *Instructor,* August-September 1976, pp. 64–66.

14. The body-action game on "Perimeters" was designed by Miriam K. Landau, Flushing, New York.

15. The body-action game on "The Battle of Manila Bay: May 1, 1898" was designed by Robert Shea, Island Park, New York.

16. The body-action game on "Westward Expansion" was designed by Lee Marcus, Elmont Memorial High School, Nassau County, New York.

Chapter 8

1. Rita Dunn and Kenneth Dunn, *How to Raise Independent and Professionally Successful Daughters* (Englewood Cliffs, N.J.: Prentice-Hall, 1977), pp. 134–137.

2. Rita Dunn and Kenneth Dunn, *Administrator's Guide to New Programs for Faculty Management and Evaluation* (West Nyack, N.Y.: Parker Publishing, 1977), p. 93.

3. *How to Raise Independent and Professionally Successful Daughters,* p. 93.

4. Wayne W. Dyer, *Your Erroneous Zones* (New York: Funk & Wagnalls, 1976).

5. Robert W. Cole and Rita Dunn, "A New Lease on Life for Education of the Handicapped: Ohio Copes with 94–142," *Kappan,* September, 1977, p. 4. See also "Policies for the Development of Written Individualized Education Programs," *Exceptional Children,* May 1977.

6. Rita Dunn, "Teacher—As Change Agent," *Administration of Catholic Schools: Current Issues,* October 1975, pp. 48–55; Rita Dunn, "Looking into Education's Crystal Ball," *Instructor,* August 1977, p. 39.

Research Supplement

1. Beatrice J. Farr, "Individual Differences in Learning: Predicting One's More Effective Learning Modality" (Ph.D. dissertation, Catholic University of America, 1971) (Ann Arbor, Mich.: University Microfilms, July 1971), 1332A.

2. R. J. Rummel, *Applied Factor Analysis* (Evanston, Ill.: Northwestern University Press, 1970).

3. Gary Price, Rita Dunn, and Kenneth Dunn, "A Summary of Research on Learning Style" (Paper presented at the American Educational Research Association, New York, N.Y., March 1977).

4. C. E. Hoyt, "Test Reliability Estimated by Analysis of Variance," *Psychometrika* 6 (1941): 153–60.

5. G. F. Kuder and M. W. Richardson, "The Theory of the Estimation of Test Reliability," *Psychometrika* 2 (1937): 151–50.

6. Stephen Isaac and William B. Michael, *Handbook in Research and Evaluation* (San Diego, Calif.: Edits Publishers, 1975).

Bibliography

Books

Bell, Helen Davis. *Individualizing Instruction.* Chicago: Science Research Associates, 1972, pp. 126–37.

Bloom, Benjamin S. *Human Characteristics and School Learning.* New York: Mc-Graw-Hill, 1976.

Breyfogle, Ethel, Nelson, Sue, Pitts, Carol, and Santich, Pamela. *Creating a Learning Environment.* Santa Monica, Calif.: Goodyear Publishing, 1976.

Brophy, Jere E., and Everston, Carolyn M. *Learning from Teaching: A Developmental Perspective.* Boston: Allyn and Bacon, 1976.

Brophy, Jere E., Good, Thomas L., and Nedler, Shari E. *Teaching in the Preschool.* New York: Harper and Row, 1975, pp. 133–50.

Bruno, Angela and Jessie, Karen. *Hands On Approach to Grammar, Spelling, and Handwriting.* Dubuque, Iowa: Kendall/Hunt Publishing, 1976.

Dunn, Rita, and Dunn, Kenneth. *Practical Approaches to Individualizing Instruction: Contracts and Other Effective Teaching Strategies.* West Nyack, N.Y.: Parker Publishing, 1972.

_____*Educator's Self-Teaching Guide to Individualizing Instructional Programs.* West Nyack, N.Y.: Parker Publishing, 1975.

_____*Administrator's Guide to New Programs for Faculty Management and Evaluation.* West Nyack, N.Y.: Parker Publishing, 1977.

_____*How to Raise Independent and Professionally Successful Daughters.* Englewood Cliffs, N.J.: Prentice-Hall, 1977.

Fisk, Lori, and Lindgren, Henry Clay. *Learning Centers.* Glen Ridge, N.J.: Exceptional Press, 1974.

Scribner, Harvey B. *Make Your Schools Work.* New York: Simon and Shuster, 1975.

Stephens, Lilian S. *The Teacher's Guide to Open Education.* New York: Holt, Rinehart, and Winston, 1974, pp. 60–73.

Thomas, John L. *Learning Centers: Opening up the Classroom.* Boston: Holbrook Press, 1975, chaps. 1, 2, and 7.

Special Reports

Dunn, Rita, Dunn, Kenneth, and Price, Gary E. *Identifying Individual Learning Styles and the Instructional Methods and/or Resources to Which They Respond.* Paper presented at the Annual Meeting of the American Educational Research Association, New York, N.Y., March 1977.

Dunn, Rita, and Shockley, Alonzo H. *That a Child May Reach: Expanded Education in Freeport, New York.* Freeport Public Schools, pursuant to a U.S. Office of Health, Education and Welfare grant, under the supervision of the New York State Education Department, 1971.

Price, Gary E., Dunn, Rita, and Dunn, Kenneth. *Summary of Research on Learning Style Based on the Learning Style Inventory.* Paper presented at the Annual Conference of the American Educational Research Association, New York, N.Y., March 1977.

The Reform of Secondary Education: A Report of the National Commission on the Reform of Secondary Education. B. Frank Brown, chairman. New York: McGraw-Hill, 1973.

The Rise Report, Report of the California Commission for Reform of Intermediate and Secondary Education. Sacramento, Calif.: California State Department of Education, 1975.

Articles

Button, Christine Bennett. "Teaching for Individual and Cultural Differences: A Necessary Interaction." *Educational Leadership* 34 (March 1977): 435–38.

Dunn, Rita. "Individualizing Instruction through Contracts—Does It Work With Very Young Children?" *Audiovisual Instruction* 16 (March 1971): 78–80.

_____"Individualizing Instruction—Teaming Teachers and Media Specialists to Meet Individual Students' Needs." *Audiovisual Instruction* 16 (May 1971): 76–79.

_____"A Position Paper for Further Individualization of Instruction in the Schools." *Audiovisual Instruction* 17 (November 1972): 49–55.

_____"Practical Questions Administrators Ask about Individualizing Instruction—and Some of the Answers." *NASSP Bulletin* 59 (April 1975): 30–36.

_____"Teacher—As Change Agent." *Administration of Catholic Schools: Current Issues,* October 1975, pp. 48–55.

———"Looking into Education's Crystal Ball." *Instructor,* August 1977, p. 39.

———"Teachers and Kids Beat the System." *Learning,* August/September 1977, p. 31.

———"Another Look at Individualized Instruction." *Kappan,* February 1978, pp. 400–02.

Dunn, Rita, and Cole, Robert W. "A New Lease on Life for Education of the Handicapped: Ohio Copes with 94–142." *Kappan,* September 1977, pp. 3–6, 10, 22.

Dunn, Rita, and Dunn, Kenneth. "Practical Questions Teachers Ask about Individualizing Instruction—and Some of the Answers." *Audiovisual Instruction* 17 (January 1972): 47–51.

———"Kids Must Learn How to Learn Alone." *Learning* 1 (April 1973): 17–18.

———"60 Activities That Develop Student Independence." *Learning* 2 (February 1974): 73–77.

———"Learning Style as a Criterion for Placement in Alternative Programs." *Kappan,* December 1974, pp. 275–79.

———"A Regional Approach to Individualization: Rationale and Performance Criteria." *The Journal* (New York: School Administrators' Association of New York State) 4 (January 1975): 37–41.

———"Finding the Best Fit: Learning Styles, Teaching Styles." *NASSP Bulletin* 59 (October 1975): 37–49.

———"Seeing, Hearing, Moving, Touching: Learning Packages." *Teacher Magazine,* May/June 1977, pp. 48–51.

———"How to Diagnose Learning Styles." *Instructor,* September 1977, pp. 122–144.

———"How to Redesign Your Classroom in Approximately One Hour." *Instructor,* October 1977, pp. 124–30.

———"How to Develop Individualized Contract Activity Packages." *Instructor,* November, 1977, pp. 74–84.

———"How to Include Game Tables, Magic Carpet Areas, Media Corners, and Other Areas in Your Classroom." *Instructor,* January 1978, pp. 72–77.

———How to Design Programmed Learning Sequences." *Instructor,* February 1978, pp. 124–128.

———"How to Create Hands-On Materials." *Instructor,* March 1978, pp. 134–141.

———"How to Construct Multisensory Instructional Packages." *Instructor,* April 1978, pp. 80–99.

———"Identifying Individual Learning Styles and the Instructional Methods and/or Resources to Which Handicapped Early Childhood Youngsters Respond." *Early Childhood Education.* Wayne, N.J.: Avery Publishing, 1977, pp. 221–27.

Dunn, Rita, Dunn, Kenneth, and Price, Gary E. "Learning as a Matter of Style." *The Journal* (New York: School Administrators' Association of New York State) 6 (Fall 1976): 11–12.

———"Diagnosing Learning Styles: A Prescription for Avoiding Malpractice Suits against School Systems." *Kappan,* January 1977, pp. 418–20.

Gregorc, Anthony F., and Ward, Helen B. "A New Definition for Individual." *NASSP Bulletin* 61 (February 1977): 20–26.

Hudes, Sonia, Saladino, Antionette, and Meibach, Donna Siegler. "Learning Style Sub-Scales and Self-Concept among Third Graders." *The Journal* (New York: School Administrators' Association of New York State) 7 (Fall 1977): 7–10.

Marcus, Lee. "A Comparison of Selected 9th Grade Male and Female Students' Learning Styles." *The Journal* (New York: School Administrators' Association of New York State) 6 (January 1977): 27–28.

_____"How Teachers View Student Learning Styles." *NASSP Bulletin* (National Association of Secondary School Principals) 61 (April 1977): pp. 112–114.

Raywid, Mary Anne. "Models of the Teaching-Learning Situation." *Kappan,* April 1977, pp. 631–35.

Reinert, Harry. "One Picture Is Worth a Thousand Words? Not Necessarily!" *The Modern Language Journal* 60 (April 1976): 160–68.

Index

A

B

C

D

E

F

G

I

O

P

R

S

T

ABOUT THE AUTHORS

Dr. Rita Dunn is a Professor in the Department of Curriculum and Teaching, St. John's University, New York. She earned her Ed.D. at New York University where she received the N.Y.U. Research Scholarship Award.

Dr. Kenneth Dunn is Superintendent of Schools, Hewlett-Woodmere, New York, and an Adjunct Professor at Hunter College. He is the former Executive Director of The Education Council for School Research and Development.